Formerly a victim of vicious laws that were brutally applied, Bulelani Ngcuka, the first National Director of Public Prosecutions in a democratic South Africa, had to find the wisdom and moral strength to enforce good laws in a good way. To do so he had to discover who were the honest, open-minded, highly trained prosecutors from the apartheid era and link them up with sharp, inexperienced but thoughtful and idealistic recruits drawn from the struggle who were more practised in defying the law than enforcing it.

Before long, Bulelani was faced with the challenge that if evidence showed that comrades he had been in the struggle with appeared to have committed crimes, he would have to be willing to prosecute them – without fear or favour. In the period that preceded and led up to state capture, he supported prosecutions that sent major public figures to jail. The decisions he took and the price he paid are compellingly related in this powerful legal and moral tale. Bulelani's courage and principled perspicacity are highly relevant today as prosecutors are tasked with dealing with the aftermath of state capture.

I was fascinated from the first page to the last.

Albie Sachs
Former Justice
Constitutional Court

Also by Marion Sparg

Comrade Jack. The Political Lectures and Diary of Jack Simons, Novo Catengue
with Jenny Schreiner and Gwen Ansell (Eds)
2001.

THE STING IN THE TALE
BULELANI NGCUKA

Marion Sparg

JONATHAN BALL PUBLISHERS
Johannesburg • Cape Town • London

All rights reserved.

No part of this publication may be reproduced or transmitted, in any form or by any means, without prior permission from the publisher or copyright holder.

© Text 2022 Marion Sparg
© Published edition 2022 Jonathan Ball Publishers

Originally published in South Africa in 2022 by
JONATHAN BALL PUBLISHERS
PO Box 33977
Jeppestown 2043

ISBN 978-1-77619-197-0
eISBN 978-1-77619-198-7

Every effort has been made to trace the copyright holders and to obtain their permission for the use of copyright material. The publishers apologise for any errors or omissions and would be grateful to be notified of any corrections that should be incorporated in future editions of this book.

Twitter: www.twitter.com/JonathanBallPub
Facebook: www.facebook.com/JonathanBallPublishers
Blog: http://jonathanball.bookslive.co.za/

Cover design by Sean Robertson
Design and typesetting by Martine Barker
Set in Athelas/Bilo

Contents

Preface		vii
Author's note		xiii

PART I: The Decision

1	Without fear or favour	1
2	The thunder mutters	8
3	The nightmare begins	15

PART II: The Beginning

4	Back to the roots	37
5	The Bulwark	46
6	Prison	71
7	Exile	94
8	Homecoming	109

PART III: A New South Africa

9	A year of hope	125
10	Rebirth of a country	150
11	The 'poisoned chalice' job	166
12	Lawyers for the people	171
13	A balancing act	190
14	Bombs, arms caches and carjackings	211

PART IV: Fighting Organised Crime
- 15 Taking the profit out of crime — 231
- 16 The Scorpions — 241

PART V: The Final Straw
- 17 A whispering campaign — 265
- 18 Spies, lies and more lies — 273
- 19 The Hefer Commission — 286
- 20 Time to go — 302
- 21 Hoax emails and 'spy tapes' — 316
- 22 Moving forward — 328

Abbreviations — 338
References — 340
Acknowledgements — 353
Notes — 354
Index — 383

Preface

From the moment I first met Bulelani Ngcuka in Geneva in the mid-1980s he struck me as a go-getter: passionate about South Africa, he was an intelligent conversationalist, knowledgeable and strategic about law, and inseparable from his wife Phumzile.

At the time I was serving as a parish priest in the Church of England, and was a member of the Programme to Combat Racism of the World Council of Churches.[1] It had, in fact, been Bulelani who'd called and persuaded me to apply for the vacant position of director of the Programme.

When we met, it was as if Bulelani and I had known each other all along. He'd served his articles as a candidate attorney at the practice of GM Mxenge in Durban, and I'd got to know the Mxenges during the time I'd lived in Durban working for the South African Students' Organisation.[2] Bulelani was also friends with a former colleague and good friend of mine, Ntobeko Patrick Maqubela. Ntobeko and I had been articled clerks at D Kondile & Somyalo attorneys[3] in what was then Port Elizabeth.[4] At the time I was serving restrictions under banning orders, but I was allowed to undertake articles.

I spent many months with Ntobeko, among others, detained under Section 10 of the Terrorism Act in Grahamstown prison. I was released on 12 August 1978 after a year of detention without

THE STING IN THE TALE: BULELANI NGCUKA

trial, and Ntobeko was released shortly thereafter. When I went into exile later that year, I donated my law library to him.

Ntobeko Maqubela left Port Elizabeth and continued his articles with GM Mxenge in Durban, and it was in that cauldron of law and politics that he and Bulelani bonded. Sadly, in June 2009, Ntobeko, who was an acting judge in the Cape High Court at the time, was murdered in his apartment in Bantry Bay.

Bulelani's biography by colleague and comrade Marion Sparg is full of profound insights about the life of activism, the risks we took and the abiding idealism that drove us as professionals of the anti-apartheid era. It was a life lived in the present, with the imagination of the reality and certainty of a time when apartheid would inevitably be no more. It was a moment when we all recognised the imperative of agency, a kind of self-surrender to a cause whose ultimate end was not always known or obvious. To that extent, the struggle was a venture of faith and hope. Bulelani's conduct was always that of a freedom fighter.

With the participation of Bulelani, Marion dissects his life. She is methodical but selective in wielding her scalpel. For example, she is very brief about Bulelani's rural childhood and about the family that bore him, and we learn very little about the ethos and ethical teachings of the home. But we understand the importance of education and close family relations, and we get to know that he was a good student and also a hard worker.

That combination of love of education, the influence of religion and hard work soon became the seal that marked Bulelani's character. In other words, Mxenge may have imbued Bulelani with courage and resourcefulness, and defiance of the oppressive system, but what shaped him most were those early times at home and at school.

Having spent time as a political prisoner, Bulelani survived interrogation and the torture of solitary confinement, defied the system that lured friends and comrades to betray each other, and remained steadfast and upheld his human dignity. Indeed, as Steve Biko said, the greatest weapon in the hands of the oppressor is the mind of the oppressed,[5] and to be a self-avowed enemy of the state is to be adept at a game of cat and mouse, to seek to outwit the enemy and win in a tug-of-war.

Bulelani's residence in Geneva from the end of 1985 to 1987 was a time for the widening of horizons. It was also a time to get closer to Phumzile, his fiancée, and it was the place where they began family life together and where their son was born. It is not far-fetched to say that Geneva was the place of marital bonding for the Ngcukas.

While life outside South Africa may have served as a respite for Ngcuka from harassment by the security police, it was also the theatre for an even more determined, defiant and life-affirming identification with the African National Congress in exile. Bulelani, while not officially in exile, had to take many risks, and he knew it. He had, of course, the cover of being an official of the International Labour Organization (ILO),[6] but that is small comfort at the hands of a brutal regime. Still, in Geneva he had a taste of being truly free and fell in love with that freedom.

It was with this sense of freedom that he formed friendships at the ILO with Baldwin Sjollema, a former director of the Programme to Combat Racism, and with many staff in the United Nations system who felt passionately about the scandal of apartheid. There is a sense that what could have been interpreted as recklessness was as much cunning and strategy, in that Bulelani's international connections in the anti-apartheid solidarity movement were a protection against the evil machinations of the apartheid system at home.

THE STING IN THE TALE: BULELANI NGCUKA

The freedom he experienced in Geneva liberated him to make friends with many ANC comrades, and it was a freedom that enabled him and Phumzile to make the decision to return to South Africa in 1987.

Above all else, Bulelani was a pioneer. His affinity with the workings of the ANC stood him in good stead when negotiations with the apartheid government began in earnest in 1990. He had insight into the strategic thinking of the ANC, and at home he was connected to all the forces of resistance.

In Cape Town he found his way back into private legal practice, but politics and activism had a magnetic pull. Thus it was that he could be part of the people at the heart of the negotiations and get to grips with the inner workings of parliament as well as the judiciary and the legal professions. In 1994 he was among the first cohort of parliamentarians as a member of the senate.[7] It is fair to mention that it was as a member of the ad hoc committee tasked with the appointment of the South African Human Rights Commission and other bodies that he approached me for a nomination to that commission.

After his groundbreaking elevation to become the inaugural National Director of Public Prosecutions, it could not have come as a surprise to him when the poisoned arrows were pointed at him by comrades and foes alike. He would have known that it was a position in which integrity mattered, and his professional ethics were what stood between success in his job and abject failure. It meant that he had to be wary of political manipulations, and he had to know enough of the ANC to make grave judgements about what was for the public good. At critical moments, though, he was lucky that he had in the leadership of the ANC comrades who had confidence in him and who trusted him implicitly.

PREFACE

Nonetheless, to know the politics of the dominant forces in the country did not mean that he was spared making mistakes or being found to be at fault from time to time, or being subjected to political favouritism. All these were to visit Bulelani during his tenure at the National Prosecuting Authority but none of it destroyed him.

In this book Bulelani's authentic voice can be heard loud and clear. His vision of a democratic society founded on the values set out in the constitution was what he articulated to the Hefer Commission in 2003 when he was accused of being an apartheid spy. It later transpired that the baseless accusation of a comrade as a spy was made by Jacob Zuma, who would be Bulelani's nemesis at the Zondo Commission in 2020. Zuma had mastered the art of weaponising rumour, gossip and downright lies. What we get to realise in this work is the truth that our freedom did not come on a platter. It was hard fought at all levels, within and outside of the liberation movement.

The second thing that strikes me is that, notwithstanding the care with which the National Prosecuting Authority and its agencies were established to address the concerns of citizens about rising crime, I have often thought that nothing could be more daunting and debilitating in heart and thought than to be a crime fighter and realise that it is a neverending war. Viewed from the effort that went into it, Bulelani would be excused if he were to conclude that his energies were an exercise in futility. But this was not the case. Instead, what society needs to come to terms with is not just the ethical nuances of human living, and the confidence that all societies are never ready-made, but that they are purposively constructed, often from below. This is the responsibility that we take on when we undertake public service.

As I noted in 2015, 'What I fear most about our society today is a culture of compromise with evil, a failure to challenge wrongdoing because we have become too comfortable in it and cannot imagine a future without it, and we fear to let our voices be heard and the truth is blunted.'[8]

N Barney Pityana, GCOB
Professor Emeritus of Law: University of South Africa
Former Principal and Vice Chancellor: University of South Africa
Addo, Eastern Cape, 8 November 2021

Author's note

'So, where do we begin?'

This is the question Bulelani put to me six years ago, as we sat down for the first interview.

'Wherever you like,' I responded. 'It doesn't really matter.'

When it came to writing the book, it did matter, of course; and I have chosen to start with the decision he took back in 2003 that changed the course of political history in South Africa and continues to haunt him, and our country, 17 years later.

It's a decision Bulelani stands by to this day.

Bulelani Ngcuka, South Africa's first National Director of Public Prosecutions, announced in August 2003 that a prima facie[1] case of corruption existed against Jacob Zuma, who was then the deputy president of the country, but that he had decided not to prosecute him because the case was unwinnable. This set in motion a process that saw a deputy president dismissed, a president resign, and the same deputy president elected president, all within the space of a few years.

The story after that is a very sorry one, a period many have referred to as 'the lost years', as corruption swept through the corridors of power and almost brought our country to its knees.

Bulelani has a story to tell, and he has given generously of his time in the writing of this book, which is based on over 150 hours of interviews, mainly with Bulelani himself. (In the text that follows, the extracts from these interviews appear in blocked type and a different font.) He and I share the same political home, the African National Congress. I first met and worked with him in parliament, and then at the National Prosecuting Authority, where I held the position of chief executive officer of the National Prosecuting Authority and the Scorpions for seven years, from 2000 to 2007. I write this account therefore not as an impartial observer but I've hopefully avoided what some view as hagiography.

Still, this is not a detached account. There is not much middle ground when it comes to how people feel about Bulelani. He's either the villain or the hero, depending on which side of the law you stand. He himself would never choose to describe himself as a hero: his personality is simply too big to need that kind of recognition. He's no saint either: he's too honest and forthright to be described as such.

There has been so much written and said about him, and I wanted to write a book in which he would tell his own story. It's a complex story, and an important one, so it was with a sense of responsibility and excitement that I sat down to begin the first interviews in September 2015 at Bulelani's offices in Sandton, Johannesburg.

Since he took that fateful decision in 2003, and as the Zuma corruption case goes on and on, Bulelani's name has been repeatedly dragged into courtroom battles and political-party infighting. But he is so much more than that. I have attempted to tell a story of his humble beginnings in the rural Eastern Cape, his time as a struggle lawyer and political prisoner, his life

AUTHOR'S NOTE

outside of South Africa, his experience as an ANC activist and his career as a politician up to his appointment in 1998 to one of the most powerful positions in the new South Africa. He was our first National Director of Public Prosecutions, so this story also attempts to give some account of the institutions he built: the National Prosecuting Authority, the Asset Forfeiture Unit and the Scorpions.

Throughout this journey, Bulelani has displayed the kind of courage that our country needs so desperately now – the courage to stand your ground, to be your own person and to remain true to your conscience and duty.

Asoze ndijike. No turning back.

Marion Sparg
Johannesburg, January 2022

PART I

The Decision

PART 1

1.
Without fear or favour

'I knew that if I did my job well, without fear or favour, there would be some in our society who would come to bay for my blood. I knew that they would try and bribe, intimidate and blackmail me, and even try to kill me.'[1]

When Bulelani Ngcuka, National Director of Public Prosecutions (NDPP), walked into the small, crowded press room at the headquarters of the National Prosecuting Authority (NPA) on 23 August 2003, he was about to make an announcement that would possibly not only determine the fate of the second-most-powerful individual in government, but also unleash a political tsunami.

The Scorpions – the nickname given to the NPA's Directorate of Special Operations (DSO), an independent multidisciplinary agency that investigated and prosecuted organised crime and corruption – had been scrutinising the country's then deputy president, Jacob Zuma, and Schabir Shaik, a businessman and one of Zuma's close associates, for nearly two years. This had been followed by weeks of Bulelani agonising over a decision, weighing up all the evidence, the possibilities and consequences.

Pens were poised and cameras ready as he spoke.[2]

'Today, after a long and difficult investigation, I have come to pronounce the decision of the National Prosecuting Authority on whether to prosecute the Deputy President of the Republic of South Africa, Mr Jacob Zuma. This decision has been reached after what I consider to be one of the most difficult investigations that the National Prosecuting Authority and indeed our young democracy [has] had to witness ...

'The investigating team recommended that we institute a criminal prosecution against Deputy President Zuma. [However,] after careful consideration in which we looked at the evidence and the facts dispassionately, we have concluded that, while there is a prima facie case of corruption against the Deputy President, our prospects of success are not strong enough. That means that we are not sure if we have a winnable case.

'Accordingly, we have decided not to prosecute the Deputy President.'[3]

Two days later, Schabir Shaik was charged for corruption – including soliciting a bribe on behalf of the deputy president – fraud, theft of company assets, tax evasion and reckless trading.

❑

> It was a very difficult decision. There was no way we could just say that we were not charging Zuma, and not mention that a prima facie case existed. We had to be transparent.[4]

Bulelani later explained this in an affidavit, pointing out that the decision to charge Schabir Shaik had already been taken, and that the same evidence pointed to Zuma. 'At the time I prepared my announcement, I was in possession of a draft indictment against ... Schabir Shaik. In it reference was of necessity made to his relationship with "Accused No 1" [Zuma] and the bribe agreement with [Alain] Thétard [then head of Thales South Africa].'[5]

Zuma was accused of agreeing to accept R500 000 annually from Thales from 1999, in exchange for protecting the company from an investigation into a deal to supply military hardware to South Africa. (Thales, one of the largest arms companies in the world, was known as Thomson-CSF in 1999.) This Strategic Defence Package, or 'arms deal', was a multibillion-rand military acquisition by the South African government, and the first major foray of the African National Congress (ANC) into the world of multimillion-rand tenders. Depending on who you believe, it ended up costing the state over R140 billion.[6]

Bulelani's affidavit continued, 'The Shaik draft indictment spelled out, far more eloquently than my statement, what was clearly a prima facie case of corruption against Accused No 1 [and] ... what I felt obliged to explain to the public was the reason why, despite the prima facie case disclosed by the indictment, I had come to the conclusion that I was not able to prosecute Accused No 1.'[7]

Bulelani had to balance the prospects of success against the interests of the country. 'Although a thrust of strong circumstantial evidence ran throughout our case, I had to be mindful of the danger of building a case on mistaken inferential reasoning. Mr Zuma was referred to in a lot of letters, correspondence and diaries that had been seized and were part of the evidence, but in very few instances could criminal knowledge be implied to him, and his direct involvement be proven.'[8]

> When considering whether to prosecute a deputy president for corruption, you cannot approach it as though it is just any other case. My decision could have had serious implications for the country, for our political stability and the economy. The public interest had to be taken into account.

THE STING IN THE TALE: BULELANI NGCUKA

And Zuma wasn't just the deputy president; he was a popular political figure with a support base in KwaZulu-Natal, a province that had experienced political instability and violence before and after 1994. It was not inconceivable, therefore, Bulelani noted, that a decision to prosecute at the time, when the prospects of success were so slim, could lead to political violence.[9]

He emphasises that this does not mean that senior political figures are above the law. Far from it. What it means is that when you charge someone at the level of a deputy president, you'd better be damned sure you have a watertight case. Or, as Leonard McCarthy, head of the Scorpions from 2002 to 2008, once told his investigators, 'If you shoot at the king, make sure you don't miss.'[10]

❑

Claims about who did or did not support Bulelani's decision, some 20 years later, may well be subject to dispute. What remains clear is that Bulelani's decision not to press charges against Zuma did not find favour with all members of the prosecuting team. This included lead prosecutor Billy Downer and prosecutor Gerda Ferreira, who, Bulelani says, told him afterwards that had he not mentioned there being a prima facie case against Zuma and that the investigating team had recommended that he be charged, she would have resigned.

> It wasn't the entire team that disagreed with my decision. People like Leonard McCarthy, [special Director of Public Prosecutions (DPP)] Silas Ramaite, [deputy DPP and Gauteng regional head of the Scorpions] Gerrie Nel and [senior state advocate and Bulelani's legal advisor] Lungisa Dyosi agreed with me.

But the fracas extended beyond the NPA, and many people asked why, if there was a prima facie case of corruption, charges hadn't been brought against the deputy president.

> Overnight the entire country was talking about this phrase 'prima facie'. Chief [Mangosuthu] Buthelezi [then leader of the Inkatha Freedom Party (IFP)] told me that to say that there was a prima facie case but not enough evidence for a conviction, was 'talking from both sides of your mouth'.

Member of parliament (MP) Gavin Woods of the IFP was, surprisingly, not as hostile as his party president, noting that the IFP appreciated that charges of a criminal nature needed to be supported by substantial evidence, and that 'at this stage' the party accepted the assessment by the NDPP that 'existing evidence was insufficiently conclusive to proceed against Zuma'.[11]

But Bantu Holomisa of the United Democratic Movement was of the view that Bulelani had given way to political pressure from the ANC, President Mbeki and the government. He said Bulelani was 'confusing' the public: 'In a nutshell, he says to the public we will not prosecute Zuma; on the other hand, he is telling us that the deputy president is corrupt.'[12]

Patricia de Lille, then leader of the Independent Democrats,[13] accused Bulelani of 'selective justice' for not prosecuting Zuma,[14] while the leader of the Pan Africanist Congress (PAC), Motsoko Pheko, said Zuma should be given the opportunity to clear his name and noted that 'there is too much interference with the work of the judiciary by sections of the justice system in our country. This is endangering democracy.'[15]

The Congress of South African Trade Unions (Cosatu) under the leadership of Zwelinzima Vavi was vociferous in its support of Zuma at the time. Cosatu would later describe the charges against Zuma as 'a political trial', and delegates at the federation's congress in September 2003 gave Zuma a hero's welcome and sang songs telling Bulelani he was 'calling for war'.[16]

Some of the strongest criticism came from the ANC Youth League. 'While the Scorpions agree that they don't have a case against the deputy president, they still insist that he is guilty and that they will continue to bid for his blood,' Youth League president Malusi Gigaba said, adding that the league was 'flabbergasted' at this 'desperate endeavour' by the Scorpions to besmirch the image of Zuma, thus creating doubts about the credibility of the ANC leadership.[17]

From the mother body itself, ANC spokesperson Smuts Ngonyama said the party accepted and supported the decision not to prosecute Zuma, and that it was a victory for South Africa's democracy and the justice system.

Zuma himself accused Bulelani of abusing his powers and said he had been found guilty with no evidence. 'No matter what the NDPP says, there can only be one reason I am not being charged: there is no case against me. I know this, and so does the NDPP,' Zuma told reporters. 'The purpose of the latest public announcement is to leave a cloud hanging over my integrity. The hallowed principle of presumption of innocence until proven guilty has been completely ignored ... I am forced to continue to question the real motives of the investigation and the manner of its conclusion by the NDPP.'[18,19]

❏

As far as Bulelani was concerned, he had acted without interference and was confident he had support from the highest office in the land to fulfil his duties without fear, favour or prejudice. In fact, the case had demonstrated the 'maturity' of the country's democracy, as the NPA had conducted the investigation without any undue influence from the executive or any arm of the government.[20]

> I knew I was going to be attacked but I was naïve. I thought the attack would come from the opposition and from some quarters of the media who would say that I had abused my office, that I should have charged Zuma, that by not charging him I had in effect given him a get-out-of-jail-free card. In fact, the attack came from a different quarter, from a direction I was not expecting.

2.

The thunder mutters[1]

'They somehow wanted to find fault.'

The clouds had first started to gather when the new ANC government approved the Strategic Defence Package, or so-called arms deal, in the late 1990s. The deal included contracts for a range of sophisticated military hardware, such as corvette warships, submarines, helicopters and fighter aircraft. Cabinet approved the deal in November 1998.

Almost immediately, the auditor-general, Shauket Fakie, identified the deal as high risk and asked the department of defence for permission to conduct an investigation. This permission was only forthcoming in September 1999, by which time President Mandela had stepped down and President Mbeki was head of state.

In that same month, on 9 September 1999, the then leader of the PAC, Patricia de Lille, told parliament that she had in her possession a dossier with information on corruption in the arms deal which she said she'd received from 'concerned ANC MPs'.[2]

De Lille handed the dossier directly to Judge Willem Heath, then head of the Special Investigating Unit (SIU), the job of which was (and is) to investigate serious issues in the administration of the state.

The auditor-general's first report was tabled in parliament in September 2000 and concluded that there were 'a number of deviations from generally accepted procurement practice'. He recommended that an audit or an investigation should be undertaken.[3]

The following month, the national assembly's standing committee on public accounts (Scopa), which acts as parliament's watchdog over the way taxpayers' money is spent by the executive, started its investigation. It held meetings with the auditor-general, the public protector, the NPA and the SIU to discuss how the different agencies could combine their skills, resources and legal mandates.[4]

In order to formalise the Scorpions' participation, Leonard McCarthy authorised a preparatory investigation in November 2000 into corruption and/or fraud in connection with the arms deal.

❏

While Willem Heath was part of the early discussions to form a joint investigating team to look into the arms deal, President Mbeki decided in January 2001 that the SIU should not be involved. The Constitutional Court had ruled in November 2000, in an unrelated case, that for a judge to head up a unit responsible for spearheading criminal prosecutions was a violation of the separation of powers required by the constitution and compromised the independence of the judiciary. It was different from a judge heading a commission of inquiry. Heath offered to resign as a judge but this was not accepted by Mbeki, and Heath then had no choice but to resign as head of the SIU. Willie Hofmeyr, then head of the Asset Forfeiture Unit (AFU) at the NPA, was appointed to the position and filled both roles for the next decade.

Heath's exclusion from the investigation was seen as a political ploy in some quarters, and from the time he was excluded, Heath appeared to adopt an antagonistic position towards the joint investigating team, and Bulelani in particular. (This antagonism surfaced later in 2011, when Heath attacked both Bulelani and former president Mbeki, and finally ended with Heath resigning as head of the SIU, a position he had been re-appointed to by president Zuma.)[5,6]

The continued suspicion about the alleged political bias in the investigation came into the open again when Bulelani and Selby Baqwa, then serving as the country's public protector, were accused of having attended a meeting at the house of Tony Yengeni, the ANC chief whip, in Cape Town in December 2000 to discuss 'what to do' about the investigation.[7]

The story was carried in *Noseweek* magazine, and this time Bulelani – who had not even been in Cape Town at the time, but at his family home in the Eastern Cape – had had enough. He and Baqwa decided to press criminal charges for defamation against *Noseweek* editor Martin Welz. Bulelani referred the case to Frank Kahn, DPP in the Western Cape.

Kahn did his own investigation and confirmed that Bulelani had in fact not been in Cape Town at the time the meeting was alleged to have taken place, and Welz conceded that his sources and information were wrong and said he was prepared to apologise. Bulelani accepted the apology, which received widespread publicity. Baqwa was less inclined to accept the apology but was persuaded by Bulelani, who said the point had been made that journalists needed to be more careful before making spurious allegations against figures in senior public office.

The joint investigating team were aware that their credibility was being questioned, and decided to tackle the issue head-on. A joint press conference was convened at the NPA head office in Pretoria.

> So I told the media, 'I know that I am the elephant in the room. I'm told I sleep with cabinet and that I will therefore sweep this whole matter under the carpet. Do I sleep with cabinet? Yes, I do.' [He smiles.] 'My wife [Phumzile Mlambo-Ngcuka] is in cabinet. [At the time, she was minister of minerals and energy.] Let's deal with that matter now. It does not compromise my integrity.'
>
> The fact that I dealt with it upfront, there in front of them, I think helped to clear the air.

❑

The team divided the work as follows: the public protector would hold public hearings; the auditor-general would look at the actual process followed, and roles played by various committees and individuals; and the Scorpions (led by prosecutors Billy Downer and Gerda Ferreira) would focus on the criminal aspects.

'The joint investigation was unique in that the three organs of state, for the first time, conducted an investigation into alleged irregularities and criminal conduct simultaneously. The holding of a public phase as part of the investigation can equally be described as unique. This was by no means an easy assignment as all three agencies had to pioneer their way through uncharted and, at times, difficult territory.'[8]

THE STING IN THE TALE: BULELANI NGCUKA

It was a mammoth task. The team received over 700 000 pages of documents from the department of defence. There was enormous public interest and the media had to be kept informed as far as possible. The Scorpions received many complaints and all sorts of allegations were made; a number were investigated and found to have no merit and were therefore dismissed.

Before finalising their report, the team presented a draft report to the president and cabinet ministers involved in the arms deal, including then finance minister Trevor Manuel, minister of public enterprises Jeff Radebe, trade and industry minister Alec Erwin and defence minister Mosiuoa 'Terror' Lekota. This was normal procedure – parties connected with an audit would be approached for comment to ensure there were no factual inaccuracies.

> We met with the cabinet subcommittee responsible for the arms deal in Cape Town. They were very hostile, to say the least. The impression had been created that they were corrupt. They thought we had already decided they were corrupt. President Mbeki chaired the meeting. He was visibly angry.

This wasn't surprising – these and other cabinet members involved with the arms deal had been contemptuous in their earlier comments on Scopa's 14th report, which had been tabled on 14 November 2000 in the national assembly. Erwin, Manuel, Lekota and Radebe had addressed a press conference in January 2001 in which they'd said that Scopa was incompetent and irresponsible, and did not understand how arms deals worked.[9]

> We stood our ground and said, these are the questions we need you to answer. And they did.
> We gave them a copy of the draft report and asked

them to respond. Things were changed in the draft report as a result of their intervention. We didn't have the background that they had.

The team, led by Shauket Fakie, Bulelani and Selby Baqwa, reported to parliament in November 2001 after a nine-month investigation.

So, in the end, we came to the conclusion that in fact there was nothing wrong with the procurement; there was no corruption involved.

The issue of confirmation bias was addressed upfront in the Joint Investigation Report into the Strategic Defence Procurement Packages, which stated, 'Because of human nature, news that an investigation is under way tends to create the expectation that something bad will be found. Any investigation is expected to either implicate or exculpate. Often that is not the case.'[10]

That didn't mean everyone was off the hook, though. The report made the point that 'there may have been individuals and institutions who used or attempted to use their positions improperly, within government departments, parastatal bodies and in private capacity, to obtain undue benefits in relation to these packages'.[11]

When we delivered the report to parliament, Patricia [de Lille] immediately called it a whitewash.

At a press conference immediately afterwards I said I was amazed at how fast she could read – in 30 minutes she finished reading a 350-page report! Obviously, she had just read the conclusion and didn't like it.

We were later invited to appear before Scopa and spent days with them answering questions. People like

Raenette Taljaard (Democratic Party MP and spokesperson on finance) had studied the report very carefully and we answered all her questions. They couldn't find fault, but people didn't like the outcome. They somehow wanted to find fault.

The report was referred to seven committees in parliament, including Scopa, which could not reach consensus on their position on the report, and for the first time in parliament's history, took a vote. The Democratic Party, the New National Party and the United Democratic Movement did not vote; the Inkatha Freedom Party noted an objection. The findings and recommendations of the report were accepted, and the national assembly adopted the Joint Investigation Report into the Strategic Defence Procurement Packages in August 2002.

The Scorpions were, however, continuing with criminal investigations.

3.
The nightmare begins

'You have no understanding of what is about to happen.'

In July 2001, a few months before the Joint Investigation Report into the Strategic Defence Procurement Packages was handed to parliament, Bulelani was enjoying a few days' break at the National Arts Festival in Grahamstown.[1] He received a call from prosecutor Gerda Ferreira.

> Gerda was so excited. 'We've made a breakthrough, sir. We've got evidence that links Zuma to corruption in the arms deal.'
>
> My heart sank. I asked what this evidence was. She told me about the famous encrypted fax.

Ferreira was referring to a fax that Judge Hilary Squires, who later presided over the Schabir Shaik fraud and corruption trial in 2004, concluded was the bribe agreement between Shaik, Zuma and Alain Thétard, head of Thales South Africa. This communication had taken the form first of a handwritten note by Thétard, which his personal assistant had typed up and sent by encrypted fax to Thales' offices in Paris and Mauritius.

> That was the beginning of my nightmare. I sat there for

an hour or so. So many questions ran through my mind. At first I thought, *No, it can't be true. No, no, no. There must be a mistake.*

But what if it is true? What do I do? Who do I tell? How do I handle this?

What is it going to do to the ANC? What will this do to the government? What will this do to South Africa? What will this do to the Scorpions?

All these thoughts were running through my head.

That essentially was the end of my holiday. I can't remember much of the rest of the weekend. I can't even remember what shows I attended that day. I was like a zombie. My friend Saki [Macozoma] was there, and he kept on asking me what was wrong, and I told him I wasn't feeling well.

On Monday morning Bulelani was back in his office at NPA headquarters in Pretoria with a team of Scorpions investigators and prosecutors.

The investigation had cleared government, but the Scorpions were following up on possible criminal conduct by individuals like Schabir Shaik. In some Thomson-CSF audit working papers, they had come across a reference to a report of bribery relating to the corvettes in the arms deal. According to Leonard McCarthy, 'The auditors added that they had been told that the possible bribery also involved a senior government official, namely Zuma.'[2]

The Scorpions now wanted Bulelani's authorisation to extend the investigation to include the deputy president – but they didn't have the handwritten note from which the encrypted fax had been typed.

THE NIGHTMARE BEGINS

I told them I couldn't authorise further investigation without the note. If they had the note, I said, I would not hesitate to authorise the investigation.

Was I relieved there was no note? To be perfectly honest, I was very relieved. At the same time, it would be better if there had been a note because then there would have been no doubt and we would not just be relying on the word of Thétard's secretary versus the word of the deputy president.

A few days later the team came back and said they had the note.

I had a feeling they were setting me up. I had this nasty, nagging feeling that the first time they came, they wanted me to commit, and now they came back, looked me in the eye, and asked for authorisation to extend the investigation to include Jacob Zuma, deputy president of the country.

I told them to leave the matter with me and I would get back to them.

He told the investigators he needed time to think it through.

They said, 'Okay sir, we understand.'

No, I thought to myself, *you don't understand. You don't understand the implications of this thing. You have no understanding of what is about to happen.*

I knew at that point there was no way I could stop the investigation. It was not whether I would authorise the investigation – that was clear in my head. The issue for me was how to manage the fallout, the political fallout. That was number one.

The second issue was how I was going to protect my

investigators. When you're investigating a deputy president, it's just a matter of time before information leaks. People start taking positions. This is what was uppermost in my mind.

Up to that point I had not told Phumzile anything, but she is my wife and my confidante. I now had to talk to her. She was out of town. I called her and asked her to return home immediately.

She flew home, and we spoke that evening. She shared my concerns about the political ramifications and how these should be managed.

I was also concerned for her. She was a member of cabinet and sat in cabinet with the deputy president. This could be extremely difficult for her.

'Of course,' I said, 'nothing has been proven and there may well be an explanation for this fax. Schabir may well have been trying to extort money using Zuma's name.'

Then I called [minister of justice Penuell] Maduna and went to see him. He was as shocked as I was. He had enjoyed a very close working relationship with Zuma until then. They were part of the first group that the ANC sent into the country ahead of everybody else from exile in the 1990s to meet with the regime to prepare for talks.

We sat talking and agreed we had to inform the president. I met the president a few days later at his official residence in Pretoria.

I was also dealing with the Tony Yengeni [chair of the joint standing committee on defence in parliament and accused of fraud] case at the time, so I briefed him first on that matter. I explained that Tony's case didn't amount to much in the bigger scheme of things but that

THE NIGHTMARE BEGINS

I had no choice. We had to proceed with the matter.[3]

And then I told him about Zuma. He was shocked, very shocked. He was silent for a while and then he told me a story.

The leader of the PAC, Clarence Makwetu, lost his position as president of the organisation in 1996 and the party told him to vacate his seat in parliament. Makwetu took parliament to court in an attempt to keep his seat but lost the case. He was ordered by the court to pay his costs and those of parliament. He had no income and could not pay the costs.

He went to see the president and asked if he could appeal to Frene [Ginwala, speaker of the national assembly] on the matter of costs. So the president called Frene but she refused. She said she had to account to the auditor-general. So the president arranged for a few business-people to help Makwetu.

After telling me this story, the president turned to me. 'Zuma is my brother. If I can do these things for Makwetu, nothing would have stopped me from helping Zuma. All he had to do was ask. Why would he ask Schabir Shaik for assistance and not come to me?'

He was visibly pained as he spoke to me.

He asked what I was going to do. I told him I was going to authorise the investigation.

The Scorpions investigators had by this stage recommended to McCarthy that the preparatory investigation he had authorised in November 2000 be converted into a formal investigation. McCarthy duly authorised the investigation in August 2001.[4]

The Scorpions' investigation of Shaik, Zuma and Thint ((the South African subsidiary of Thales, the French arms company which was formerly known as Thomson-CSF)) was complicated, and involved over 50 000 pages, typed and handwritten, and documentation from various entities, including 118 bank accounts. Witnesses from across the private and business spectrum were interviewed, consulted and questioned over a two-year period. Evidence was found in searches and seizures conducted in Durban, France and Mauritius.[5] A number of parties were involved, including South African and international companies, politicians and businessmen.

Part of the challenge was to investigate the matter speedily and focus the scope so that it remained within the ambit of the authorisation. Two teams were involved. One team, which included investigators and a forensic accountant, gathered and analysed evidence; the other, which included a DPP and four deputy DPPs, provided strategic oversight, gave legal advice, and directed the investigation.

> During the joint investigation, an issue that had arisen was the question of [Schabir Shaik's younger brother] Chippy Shaik, [head of the government's arms procurement committee], and conflict of interests, but, in the bigger scheme of things, his involvement was small. Cabinet had made the decision and approved the arms deal.
>
> The other person's name that had arisen was Joe Modise.

The allegation was that Modise, who was minister of defence, had paid for shares in a company that benefited from the arms deal, with a bribe received from a successful contractor.

> Early in the investigation I learned that Modise had cancer and was dying [he died in November 2001]. I felt it was a waste of time to make him the focus of the investigation,

but I was aware of the suspicions many of the members of my team had of me, and my role as national director.

These are some of the difficulties I faced that some people will never appreciate. I was working with prosecutors and investigators who had come from the previous regime. We were deeply suspicious of each other. Deep down, I believe they wanted to prove at any cost that we were dealing with a corrupt black government and that I was there to protect this government.

I had handpicked each of them because of their skills as investigators and prosecutors but I had no illusions about their political loyalties. It would come as no surprise to me to learn that some of them celebrated each time they found a piece of evidence against Zuma or a government official. They probably will say I am unfair when they read what I am saying today. I have no reason to doubt their integrity or professionalism in doing their work. But I need people to be aware of the kind of tensions that were at play in the team. I was aware that members of my team were constantly watching over my shoulder, waiting for me to make a mistake.

I didn't want to be the first black National Director of Public Prosecutions to be found to be undermining the rule of law in the country. Everything we were doing in the office at the time was creating precedents and we were very conscious of that.

It's also important to understand the psychological makeup of an investigator. Investigators are like bulldogs. Once they have a piece of evidence, they smell blood and they don't let go. It doesn't matter what colour you are. In the South African context, this enthusiasm might be perceived as being unnatural but this is what investigators are like. Once they are in there, they want that smoking gun.

The 'smoking gun' in this case was Thétard's handwritten note, which his secretary, Sue Delique, said he had given her to type up and fax in encrypted form to Yann de Jomaron of a Thomson-CSF company, Thales International Africa Ltd, in Mauritius, and to Jean-Paul Perrier of Thomson-CSF (International) in Paris.[6]

At the time the Scorpions first made contact with Delique in 2001, she could not find the note. However, she unearthed it a week later and handed it to the Scorpions. It finally surfaced in court in 2004. It made clear reference to a meeting that Thétard had held with Zuma during which, he wrote, he had received 'a clear confirmation or at least an encoded declaration' to 'validate' the request he said Shaik[7] had made for funds for Zuma. He received this confirmation, he wrote, and then 'reminded' one of the recipients of the fax, De Jomaron, of the 'two main objectives' of the 'effort' requested of Thomson-CSF: Thomson-CSF's protection during the investigations, and Jacob Zuma's permanent support for the future projects.[8]

He ended off by saying that the amount agreed on was R500 000 a year. These payments were to continue until Shaik's company started paying dividends as a result of the arms deal.

The story, which came out once this fax was uncovered, and which was confirmed at Shaik's trial in 2005,[9] was that several meetings had taken place between Shaik and Thétard, during which a proposal to pay Zuma R500 000 a year was discussed. In return, he would protect Thales from any arms deal investigation and promote Thomson-CSF's further business interests in future government bids. Thétard had then discussed this with his superior, Jean-Paul Perrier, CEO of Thales International, who had agreed to the proposal.

This had led to the all-important meeting between Zuma, Thétard and Shaik in Durban in March 2000, during which Zuma allegedly indicated his agreement with the proposal by way of a coded gesture, after which Thétard had written to the Thales head office advising them that the proposal had been confirmed and accepted. (At the time, the Scorpions did not know what the code was, as none of the witnesses knew it. Bulelani later found out from his sources that the code consisted of the question 'Is the Eiffel Tower visible on a cloudy morning?')

❏

A month after the note had been found, the investigating team approached Bulelani and said they needed to apply for a warrant to search the premises of Schabir Shaik, Thales and the deputy president. The searches would take place simultaneously in South Africa, Mauritius and France.

> They had prepared papers which they presented to me. I went through them. They seemed to be in order, but I baulked when it came to Zuma. I said I would not authorise the search of the deputy president's offices or his house. I asked why they wanted to search the deputy president's house. 'What is it that you think you will find in his house?'
>
> Billy said they wanted to find a diary or something that had a note about meeting Thétard.
>
> 'I know the deputy president,' I told them. 'He doesn't write down anything. You can find that information at Thétard's place.'

> We argued. I said there was no need to search the deputy president's house or offices. 'I'm convinced, Billy,' I told him, 'that the damage that will be done to the country is far greater than what you are likely to get out of any search. I know the deputy president. He writes nothing. Whatever you think you will find there, you will find somewhere else.'

Bulelani was proved right when the team found Thétard's 2000 diary among the documents seized in Mauritius. The diary contained an entry relating to the meeting with Zuma on 11 March 2000.

> More importantly, my point was that this was not just about the individual but the Office of the Deputy President. A search would be an indictment not just against the person but against the country. Once you do a search, people will believe that you already have a conclusive case against him.
>
> We cannot be naïve. It doesn't matter what we say about equality before the law. We have to consider the implications for the *country*.
>
> I also said we could not reveal Zuma's name in the affidavit and had to refer to him as Mr X. I said I would tell the judge who Mr X was if he asked when we applied for the warrant. 'I will go to court with you,' I said, 'so if you are under pressure to disclose the identity of Mr X in the affidavit, the judge will see that I am present and realise this is a very serious matter and that we have not taken this decision lightly. Because if this thing is leaked, that Mr X is in fact the deputy president of the country, the implications are huge.'

THE NIGHTMARE BEGINS

The team were not happy but I was adamant. I accompanied them to court, and we went to the judge's chambers. When the judge saw me, he smiled and said, 'Hm, if you are here, Mr Ngcuka, then it means there is something big coming. Should I watch TV tonight?'

After he read the affidavit, the judge immediately asked about Mr X and Gerda explained that it was Zuma. He said he understood the reason for anonymity. I felt vindicated and we got the warrants we needed.'

[The searches] were quite successful but the search in France was an interesting one. We found what we wanted [which was documents relating to the arms deal], but then the French sealed up everything and said we should make an application for mutual legal assistance,[10] which we did.

Up until the point I left the office in August 2004, we had still not received the evidence. I don't know if it was ever received.

❏

Zuma's identity was first revealed by Schabir Shaik himself, in September 2002, when he challenged a subpoena from the Scorpions to question him and made 'certain allegations to the effect that Zuma might be one of the persons under investigation'.[11]

Up until this point nobody knew who Mr X was. Schabir Shaik dragged him into it. They got it from the court papers.

Madiba called Maduna and me. He said we should meet him in Stellenbosch [where the ANC's 51st national conference was taking place, in December 2002].

Now, Madiba was very conscious about security. When

you visited Madiba and discussed certain things, he would write them down on a piece of paper and show it to you, you would read it, then he would take it and burn it and destroy it, there and then in his office.

On this occasion he said we must sit in his car. We sat and spoke in his car for two hours. He wanted all the details about the case so I told him everything. There was talk that he had given Zuma R2 million to help him with his debt. I told him about this and he said I should leave it with him.

He called me [about a month later], and we met at his offices in Houghton. He confirmed that he had given Zuma R2 million some time in 2000 to help with his debts. 'I gave Zuma money, and I am surprised that the money I gave him now reflects as having gone to Schabir Shaik,' is what Madiba told me.

Madiba said he had met [with] Zuma. 'I was helping him, but he became very angry and told me to stay out of this thing. He said this was just a conspiracy by Mbeki against him. He refuses to see clearly what is happening, so you must continue with your investigation.'

The first media report of the Zuma investigation appeared in November 2002 when the *Mail & Guardi*an published an article headlined 'Scorpions probe Jacob Zuma',[12] and after this his name was in the media every day.

Bulelani felt it was important to talk to the deputy president face to face, and a meeting was arranged at OR Tambo House, his official residence in Pretoria.

'You may have heard many things in the news, Deputy President,' I told him. 'This is what we have, and this is what I want you to know. I have no power to stop an investigation, but I know you and I am convinced that Schabir is abusing your name. It is important that we do this investigation, and that this investigation is not hindered. I would like you to urge Schabir to cooperate so that we can finish this thing. I'm clear as I'm sitting here that you will be vindicated. It's important that your name is cleared. I am convinced that your name will be cleared. I don't want this investigation to drag on forever. It's important for you, for the ANC, and it's important for the country. We can't allow an allegation like this against the deputy president not to be finalised.'

He thanked me and said he appreciated my visit. 'Thank you, *mfana kithi* [my boy],' he said. 'Anything you want from me, I'm ready to cooperate. We must clear this thing.'

We parted ways, and I thought I had the support of the deputy president to finish the investigation as soon as possible. I told the team to move with all possible speed.

❑

The investigation had been widened in October 2002 and now included issues that were not directly connected to the arms deal.

McCarthy explained in his affidavit, 'By 2002 the picture that had emerged from the various sources of information and types of investigation was of a financial relationship between Shaik and Zuma that was far more extensive than the investigators initially thought, based on the terms of the encrypted fax and the documents obtained from the Nkobi group's auditors.'[13] Furthermore, it now appeared that Zuma was connected to some of Shaik's private business dealings, not all related to the arms deal. The [Scorpions] investigators inferred from the wider financial relationship between Shaik and Zuma, and from Zuma's suspected involvement in some of Shaik's private business dealings, that Shaik's payments to Zuma might constitute corruption unrelated to the arms deal. As a result, the [Scorpions] investigators decided to recommend that the terms of reference for the investigation be expanded to cover this new aspect.

'On 22 October 2002 I accepted this recommendation and formally extended the investigation to encompass the suspected general corruption between Shaik and Zuma that was not connected in any way to the arms deal. ... [T]he extended scope of the investigation included: the suspected commission of offences of fraud and/or corruption, or the attempted commission of those offences, arising out of payments to or on behalf of or for the benefit of Zuma by Shaik, the Nkobi group of companies and/or the Thomson/Thales group of companies; and Zuma's protection of, wielding of influence for and/or using public office unduly to benefit Shaik, the Nkobi group of companies and/or the Thomson/Thales group of companies.'[14]

This part of the investigation involved, among other things, a number of business deals in which Schabir Shaik had either used or attempted to use Zuma's name for his own benefit, and various payments Shaik had made to Zuma over a number of years, from 1996 to 2002, when Zuma had held office as a member of the KwaZulu-Natal legislature, and a member of the executive council (MEC)[15] of economic affairs and tourism, from 1994 until his appointment as deputy president in June 1999.

The next major step in the investigation came in 2003 when the team decided they wanted to question the deputy president.

They wanted this to be a face-to-face meeting but Bulelani suggested they send him a list of questions.

> I felt that if we insisted on questioning him [in person], it could be perceived as if we were humiliating him. Billy, of course, didn't like it – he thought I was protecting the deputy president – but I insisted.

The team drafted a set of questions and gave these to Bulelani and McCarthy. Both men felt that many of the questions were not directly relevant to the investigation.

> Leonard and I were a bit puzzled about the relevance of some of the questions [but] when we were satisfied that the questions were proper and directly relevant to the investigation, Leonard hand-delivered the final questions to Zuma's lawyers. Leonard locked the only copy of the final questions in his safe.

Despite these security measures, the 35 questions were leaked to the *Sunday Times* and Zuma immediately went on the radio and blamed the Scorpions for the leak.[16]

> It was absolute rubbish. I knew the investigators could not have leaked the questions because the only people who had the final set of questions were Leonard and myself.

What emerged later was that it was, in fact, Zuma's lawyers who had leaked the questions and then blamed Bulelani for doing so.

Mzilikazi wa Afrika, then a *Sunday Times* journalist, later gave a detailed account in his book *Nothing Left to Steal*[17] of exactly how the questions had arrived at the newspaper. He had heard that the Scorpions had sent the questions to Zuma's lawyer but could not lay his hands on them, so he'd contacted a colleague, Ranjeni Munusamy, also on the *Sunday Times*, who told him that Zuma had agreed to give the questions to the *Sunday Times* if the paper would agree to publish a story the following week about Ngcuka being an apartheid spy.

'After a lot of discussion with my colleagues and our editor at the time, Mathatha Tsedu, it was agreed that if it were true that Bulelani was a spy, as Munusamy claimed the documents could prove, the *Sunday Times* would publish the story,' he wrote in his book. 'A few minutes after I called Munusamy to explain our position, a fax was rolling out the questions, which were being sent from the offices of one of Zuma's lawyers.'[18]

The next day, 27 July 2003, the *Sunday Times*'s front page screamed 'Scorpions grill deputy president', and detailed how Zuma had been sent a list of questions by the Scorpions about his financial interests as part of a probe into the arms deal. The story ended with a quote from Lakela Kaunda, Zuma's spokesperson: 'We ... question the motives of people who keep leaking information to the media.'[19]

Immediately after the *Sunday Times* hit the streets, Zuma gave radio interviews in which he accused Ngcuka of leaking the questions to the newspaper.[20] Wa Afrika said this made him angry. 'I felt that he had used me and my colleagues to fuel his political agenda and conspiracy.'[21]

Wa Afrika said that for the purposes of his book, he'd interviewed his former boss, Tsedu, who'd told him that Ranjeni had got the questions on the basis that the source would not be identified. 'Without naming anybody, he said, "We all know that they [a reference, no doubt, to Zuma's office] woke up with a prepared press statement to accuse Bulelani for something they know he didn't do."'[22]

THE NIGHTMARE BEGINS

Wa Afrika wasn't the only one who was angry – the extent of Zuma's rage became evident a few weeks before the NPA's announcement in August 2003, when he launched an unprecedented attack on justice minister Penuell Maduna during a cabinet meeting that he, Zuma, was chairing in President Mbeki's absence. He berated Maduna for 'allowing' the investigation to continue.

Maduna wrote a note to Zuma during the meeting but Zuma put the note aside when he received it and continued with his attack on Maduna. When Zuma was done, Maduna stood up and told Zuma that he had worked with him for a long time, that he respected him, and that if this was the view that the deputy president had of him, he had no choice but to tender his resignation from cabinet.

He wrote a letter of resignation there and then, handed it to Zuma and left the meeting.

When Bulelani heard about the day's events, he was devastated – if there were ever a time he needed the support of a minister like Maduna, it was now.

> Without him I knew I would be mincemeat. I needed his support, so I went to see him and pleaded with him to withdraw his resignation. I told him we were about to make a major decision. The vultures were circling. I needed his support.

Following an apology from Thabo Mbeki, and some persuasion, and a visit from Bulelani and then minister of social development Zola Skweyiya, Maduna finally withdrew his resignation, but announced that he would not be available to serve in government after the 2004 elections.

THE STING IN THE TALE: BULELANI NGCUKA

❏

The pressure was on, and Bulelani smiles when he recalls a conversation with Kgalema Motlanthe [ANC secretary general] around this time.

> He said to me, 'I can see the Philistines are unsettling you and I've been asking myself how long you will survive.' I will survive, I told him. My wife is not Delilah. He laughed and we ended the conversation.

Once the investigating team had completed their work, they recommended that Zuma face two charges – one of having enjoyed in broad terms a 'generally corrupt relationship' with Shaik and others, and a specific one in relation to the 'famous fax'.

They then handed over the matter to a team whose task it was to sift through all the evidence and take the final decision whether to prosecute or not. The team consisted of Bulelani, Leonard McCarthy, deputy NDPP Silas Ramaite, and advocates Lynette Davids, Sibongile Mzinyathi, Siyabulela 'Saks' Mapoma, Rudolf Mastenbroek and Lungisa Dyosi.[23]

Lungisa, who was 32 years old at the time, was Bulelani's legal advisor. 'That first meeting [of the team] was one of the strangest I have attended in my life. Everyone was quiet. If any of us were not yet aware of the magnitude and importance of the task that confronted us, Bulelani made it clear when he spoke. "If you decide we should prosecute, and we lose, you must know that I will have to resign and will probably have to leave the country." Those words sat us with. We knew we had to be certain about our case.'[24]

As Lungisa recalls, when it came to the issue of charging

THE NIGHTMARE BEGINS

Zuma for a 'generally corrupt relationship', they were split down the middle. The evidence was largely circumstantial, he explains, and this would be the first time someone would face such a charge under the Prevention of Organised Crime Act, No 121 of 1998, which, among other things, was intended to prohibit certain activities relating to racketeering. 'We had to very sure of our case.'[25]

In the end, Bulelani decided not to prosecute Zuma.

❑

In May 2005, nine months after Bulelani had quit as NDPP, Schabir Shaik was found guilty of corruption and fraud, and sentenced to two terms of fifteen years for corruption and one of three years for fraud, all to be served concurrently.

Zuma was not on trial in the Shaik matter but this did not mean he escaped unscathed. President Mbeki told parliament in June 2005 that he had studied Judge Hilary Squires' judgment in the Shaik matter, not to determine whether it was right or wrong but because the issue of the relationship between Schabir Shaik and the deputy president had been raised during the trial. Mbeki was careful to say that while the court had been 'unambiguous' about an 'assumed unsavoury relationship' between the deputy president and Shaik, Zuma was yet to have his day in court. Nevertheless, he said, he had decided it was in the best interests of the country and the deputy president to relieve him of his duties.[26]

Zuma resigned as an MP and two weeks later, on 29 June 2005, he was formally charged with corruption by Bulelani's successor, Vusi Pikoli. Thint Holdings and Thint (Pty) Ltd, two South African subsidiaries of Thomson/Thales, were also charged.

PART II
The Beginning

Part II

4.

Back to the roots

'For as long as I can remember, I wanted to be a lawyer.'

Bulelani Thandabantu Ngcuka was born on 2 May 1954 in Annshaw, a small mission village in the Eastern Cape.

The Ngcukas belong to amaGqunukhwebe, an offshoot of amaXhosa, who came into being in the late 16th century, during the time of King Tshiwo. Tshiwo is said to have rewarded one of his trusted counsellors, Khwane, with a chieftainship.

Chief Kama kaChungwa, a great-grandson of Khwane, first encountered William Shaw, the Methodist minister to whom Annshaw owes its name, in 1823. Shaw proved useful as a go-between with the British in talks that saw amaGqunukhwebe being 'permitted' to occupy the land between the Fish and Keiskamma rivers.

Kama, who converted to Christianity in 1829 at the age of about 30, established his chiefdom in Middledrift at Annshaw in 1853.[1]

One of the most important developments at Annshaw was the establishment of a school, which gave the place its distinct character as a community. What started as a missionary settlement became the home of great African intellectuals such as Dr Roseberry Bokwe, who qualified as a doctor in 1928 in Scotland. On his return, he set up a practice in Middledrift and would become the first African to be appointed a district surgeon in South Africa. Bulelani was born in the hospital established by Dr Bokwe.

> My elder brother was named Vuyani [Rejoice]. When I was born, [my parents] were grateful for receiving another son, so they called me Bulelani [Thank You].

Professor Davidson Jabavu was another famous resident of Annshaw. Like his father, Dr John Tengo Jabavu, who had founded *Imvo Zabantsundu*, the first black newspaper in South Africa, Professor Jabavu was an activist and passionate educationist, and the first black professor at the University of Fort Hare, the first university for Africans in Southern Africa, established in 1916. Bulelani's home was not far from the railway line connecting Annshaw and Alice, and he remembers watching Professor Jabavu walk to the railway station each morning to take the train to Fort Hare.

❏

Bulelani grew up in a large family, the second of five children, with two brothers (the eldest, Vuyani, born in 1951, and the youngest, Phelelani, in 1966) and two sisters (Phumla Feziwe, born in 1956, and Phindiwe, in 1962). His close friend Dumisani Tabata notes, 'He's the second born but has always behaved like he's the eldest.'[2]

Their father, Douglas, worked as a senior superintendent for the department of public works in King William's Town. He would only come home on weekends.

Their mother, Kholosa, was a Xhosa princess from the royal house of Mgudlwa. She was a schoolteacher who gave up her career to look after the family. She had to subsidise her husband's earnings to keep the family going, and she raised goats, sheep and cattle and cultivated a range of vegetables. This meant daily chores for the Ngcuka children, such as milking and herding cows.

> Before school, we had to go and milk the cows, then drive the cattle into the fields, and then go to school. After school we had to go and fetch the cattle and the goats and milk them again.
>
> During school holidays and on weekends we had to plough the fields. We planted maize, pumpkin, peas, beans and wheat in winter. We also had a family garden where we would plant cabbages and carrots. This is what we lived on.
>
> Once a month, on a Thursday, we had to take the cows to the dipping tank. The whole village would take their cows, so you had to get there very early in the mornings. Dipping was supposed to start at six, but invariably it was late and you had to wait and only finish at nine. Then you still had to go to school.

In the 1960s, the young Bulelani attended Annshaw Primary School, along with about 200 other children. As soon as school was done for the day, the children would spend a few hours playing sports like rugby, tennis and cricket, which was played with tennis balls.

On weekends, Bulelani and his siblings sometimes travelled to King William's Town, where their father worked.

> That was a real treat. We would take a train in the morning and come back again by train in the evening.

THE STING IN THE TALE: BULELANI NGCUKA

When he was in standard 6 (today's grade 8), Douglas and Kholosa decided that the quality of education in the then homeland of Transkei[3] was better, and sent him to stay with his aunt and uncle, Feziwe and Govin Ngcukana, in Centane.

Govin, a teacher at Macibe Primary School who also owned a small shop, was a tough taskmaster. At first the 13-year-old Bulelani was unhappy and wanted to return home to Middledrift. In time, however, he won his uncle's respect, both for his performance at school and for his diligence in completing his chores at home.

One of his cousins, Bonisiwa,[4] had been expelled from school and was working in her father's shop at the time; she would go on to be a prominent activist in the PAC. And both of Govin's sons, Moyisi and Monde, were imprisoned on Robben Island. So it was at his uncle's home that Bulelani first became exposed to political activity.

> Politics was the daily bread at home.
> The area we lived in, Centane, was a PAC stronghold at the time. We learned a lot from discussions; we learned about what was happening on the rest of the continent. These were discussions we held every day, day in and day out.

After an eventful year in Centane, in 1969 Bulelani went on to board at Freemantle Boys High School in Lady Frere. There, the students were given one study choice: agriculture or Latin, and Bulelani was clear, even at that young age, that his future did not lie in farming.

> One of the people who inspired me and many others was Louis Mtshizana, a famous African lawyer in the Eastern Cape. He was based in East London and had spent time on

Robben Island. He was very popular and all of us wanted to be like Mtshizana.

His teachers also made quite an impression. He speaks of his Latin teacher, a Mr Hermanus.

We called him 'Bosh' because if you gave him an answer and it was nonsense, he would tell you it was 'bosh'.

Bosh was the teacher who asked Bulelani about his future plans, spoke about Fort Hare University and told him never to give up on his dreams.

He would ask each one of us what were our dreams, and then we would tell him and he would comment on each one of us. If only I had the opportunity to do law, I told him, and he would tell me about people who had done law. 'Go on and do law!' he would say. He inspired us.

Another lesson Bulelani learned at Freemantle was setting high standards for himself, and being aware that his behaviour reflected on those around him.

It was not whether you were going to pass, it was whether it was a first-class pass or a distinction. That school had a reputation. When you arrived, you knew straight away that they would not entertain anybody who failed. If you failed at Freemantle, you would leave the school. Nobody repeated.

After Bulelani matriculated in 1973, it was time for his initiation ceremony into manhood, which would take place over some months, away from prying eyes.

Like all Xhosa boys, I had to go to the mountain. I played a lot of cricket in those days and when I went to the mountain, the cricket tournament was being played in our village. My team members went to my father and said they must bring me back. 'He must come and play. You can't keep him there!' Of course, my father refused, and I didn't play in the tournament that year.

❑

With a bursary in hand from Standard Bank, Bulelani proceeded to Fort Hare to study law and political science. The university, which had fought incorporation into the apartheid system in the 1950s and the bantustan system in the 1970s and 1980s, became the 'seedbed of African nationalism'[5] and produced leaders of the calibre of Nelson Mandela, Oliver Tambo, Govan Mbeki, Robert Sobukwe, Chris Hani, Stanley Mabizela and many others.

> My dream had always been to go to Fort Hare. Fort Hare was the place to be. So I went to Fort Hare and stayed at Wesley House.
>
> The bursary was important. My mother had opened a small shop, which made a huge difference to our family situation, but with the bursary, all [my parents] had to do was pay for books and give me a little bit of pocket money. I would also get book prizes every year and this supplemented my income.

Bulelani arrived at Fort Hare in 1974, not long after a major student strike had taken place there, and the campus was relatively quiet after the turbulence of the previous years.

Despite its relative isolation in the Eastern Cape, Fort Hare was not immune to the student protests at universities of the early 1970s, led by the South African Students' Organisation (SASO), during which student leaders were harassed and many expelled or suspended, while others chose to abandon their studies. In 1972, over 300 students were expelled from Fort Hare for political activities.

Classes were not easy for these young African law students. In some instances, lecturers were more interested in their private practices than in fulfilling their responsibilities to students.

In 1976, the lecturer who was teaching the law of evidence left midyear, and his replacement lasted only two weeks after finding out how far behind the students were in the syllabus.

Professor Labuschagne, who was responsible for constitutional law, stepped in to help, and, when the students asked for extra lessons in the afternoons so that they could catch up on the syllabus, he also arranged for a Professor Smit from the University of South Africa (Unisa) to lend a hand.

> Professor Smit was a good lecturer. We really enjoyed his company. He made the law of evidence exciting for us and he said he missed being in front of a class. Everything at Unisa was done from a distance.

Bulelani remembers the day Fort Hare closed down in 1976.

> Professor Labuschagne was lecturing us one afternoon in 1976. His lecture was the last lecture of the day. We saw that outside everyone was walking around with their suitcases. The university was shutting down. He knew this but he was determined to finish the class so he carried on with the lecture.

This shutdown was the result of an incident during a debate among students about what to do in reaction to the violence in

Soweto following the uprising on 16 June 1976.[6] One of the students, Peter Paul Ngwenya, became impatient and set fire to a curtain at the entrance to the Great Hall. Very little damage was done but the university was closed and students were expelled because of the protests, Bulelani among them.

Bulelani arrived home in Middledrift in the late afternoon and spent time talking to his father. He was woken in the early hours of the next morning by his mother, who told him his father had passed away during the night.

This tragic loss placed extra pressure on Bulelani to support his mother and his younger siblings, and he was reluctant to return to his studies. He was still busy with his B Proc at the time. He decided not to proceed with his LLB but did return to Fort Hare when the university reopened in October 1976, coming home as often as he could to help his mother in the general-dealer shop she had set up to help make ends meet.

❑

In September 1977, Steve Biko, one of the most prominent leaders in the anti-apartheid struggle, was murdered while in police detention. The students at Fort Hare wanted to hold a memorial service at the university Great Hall but were refused permission by the administration. They were therefore forced to go to the Davidson rugby stadium. They called on black university lecturers to join them, which they did.

The university administration tried to persuade the students not to proceed with the service but the students went ahead. The police were called in and over a thousand students were arrested, including Bulelani. This was his first experience of prison.

The father of one of the students who was imprisoned with

Bulelani and about 300 others, Mpumelelo Canca, was a lawyer in Idutywa and he wanted to bail out his son. Mpumelelo refused, saying that if his father bailed him out, he had to do the same for all 300 students. And so Mr Canca proceeded to pay bail for all the students, who by then had spent a week in jail.

Bulelani met Mr Canca later in life and thanked him, saying that he owed him a debt of gratitude. Mr Canca said that it had been a good investment, considering what Bulelani had gone on to achieve.

5.

The Bulwark

'This is not just my story. It's Griffiths' story also.'

It came as no surprise to those who knew Bulelani when the NPA headquarters in Silverton, Pretoria, was named the Victoria and Griffiths Mxenge Building.

Mlungisi Griffiths Mxenge played many roles in Bulelani's life – father, big brother, commissar and, above all, teacher and mentor when it came to the practice of law. As Silas Ramaite once remarked, 'I always wondered where Bulelani got his courage from, then I found out about Griffiths and their relationship, and I knew that's where he found the steel.'[1]

If ever there was a man of steel, it was Mxenge. A human-rights lawyer with a thriving practice in Durban, Natal (later KwaZulu-Natal), he was also one of the most senior ANC leaders in the country. Most people called him 'GM'. Another, lesser-known nickname for him was 'The Bulwark'[2].

The lessons Bulelani learned from Griffiths and the experiences he recounts not only explain the influence Griffiths had on Bulelani; they are also a valuable contribution to piecing together the role Griffiths played in law and politics in South Africa.

THE BULWARK

❑

When he was done with his university exams, Bulelani had gone to work at the Mdantsane Magistrate's Court as a prosecutor.³ So he had some experience as a prosecutor but now needed to find a position as an articled clerk, and he applied to various firms in East London. He was not accepted by any.

Then, on Thursday 27 March 1978 at 8.10 am – he remembers the exact date and time – his life changed.

> I was preparing to go to court and the phone rings. I pick it up.
>
> 'My name is Mlungisi Mxenge.'
>
> 'Yes, sir?'
>
> 'How are you?'
>
> 'I am fine.'
>
> 'I hear you want articles. I have a firm in Durban. When can you start?'

Bulelani was reluctant: He wanted to be a lawyer in the Eastern Cape, where he was known, and where he felt that his parents' reputation would assist in his getting clients; and, after the passing of his father the year before, he didn't want to be away from home.

> 'Well, I don't know ... I need to think about it. Can I call you back?'
>
> 'Please do. Because I need somebody.'
>
> I was supposed to go to court but I called my brother, Vuyani, who was working as a clerk at the department of agriculture in Zwelitsha in King William's Town. He told me to go for it.
>
> My mother [also] said I must go. She didn't bat an

eyelid. 'This is the time for you. You must go,' she said.

I asked her who would look after her. 'This is your opportunity. You must go for it,' she said.

Now, this is something very important: at every critical moment in my life, my mother has been there for me.

Bulelani submitted his resignation at the Magistrate's Court the next morning, a Friday; he was to start his new job on the Monday almost 700 kilometres away at GM Mxenge & Associates in Victoria Street in downtown Durban.

Vuyani said he would drive Bulelani to Durban and hired a car. They left that same evening for Durban and arrived on the Saturday morning. First on the agenda was to find Sizinzo Skweyiya ['Mgadini'], who came from Bulelani's village, and secure accommodation.

> This is very important because this is how we were brought up. I did not phone this fellow. I went to his home in Middledrift and asked them to give me his address. They gave me his address in KwaMashu. I said, 'Okay, I'm going to Durban and I'm going to stay with him.' His family was happy to give me his address. We are not related. He's just an elder brother who grew up in the same area and is in Durban. He comes from my village and so is part of my family.

In KwaMashu, the brothers found Sizinzo's house but he was not around. They were told his wife was a nurse, working at Clairwood hospital.

> We went to the hospital and met her. She told us her husband was away for a month[4] but said I was welcome to stay in the meantime.

THE BULWARK

Bulelani stayed at Sizinzo's house for a month before getting an offer to live with Jack and Sibongile Mabaso, who stayed close by. They were also from Eastern Cape. He stayed there for a year.

❏

This was the first time that Bulelani had been in a big city; he was used to the smaller streets of King William's Town and East London. The newness of his surroundings became more intense as he travelled on a packed train to Griffiths' offices. Those around him were all speaking isiZulu, a language he was not used to hearing.

He arrived at the offices to be told that Griffiths was not there – he was away, handling a case that would become known as the 'Bethal 18', in which 86 members of the PAC had been arrested on various charges related to 'fomenting revolution'.

> GM was in Bethal, handling the [PAC leader] Zeph Mothopeng case. He would be back on the Friday, so I spent the week with Mrs Mxenge. We would meet new clients and take statements from them. She taught me the rules.
>
> That first week I was at sea, didn't know whether I was coming or going. The clients would talk to me, and I didn't understand most of what they were saying to me. I would ask, '*Ntoni lokuza? Ntoni ntazinga?*' [What is this thing?] I would pretend to understand Zulu and the client would just catch me out.
>
> Then, on Friday, the place was abuzz. I could see that Victoria, uSisi, was agitated, checking everything, making sure the office was spotless and everything was all right. 'GM is coming, and he mustn't find anything wrong.'
>
> I thought, *Oh, God! This fellow is a terror.*

> He arrived on Saturday morning. I heard this big booming voice. He greeted me as I walked into the office: 'Yes!'
> I must admit I was afraid of him at first. I had heard so much about him during that week, lots of stories.

Bulelani was one of Griffiths' very first articled clerks. Towards the end of that year Patrick Maqubela, or Ntobeko, as he was known to close friends, joined the practice to complete his articles. Patrick, who hailed from Port Elizabeth[5], had started his articles with his uncle's law firm, D Kondile & Somyalo, but his repeated detention by the security police had made it impossible for him to complete them, and Griffiths' firm had taken him in. He and Bulelani not only worked together but became close friends, living and travelling together.

❏

During his articles with Griffiths, Bulelani dealt with a variety of cases. They were very different from those he'd handled in his days as a prosecutor in East London.

> In Mdantsane, it was always common assault, assault with intent to do grievous bodily harm, possession of dagga, selling of liquor at a shebeen, and theft now and again. But in Griffiths' practice we were dealing with political trials and civil cases against the state, cases like the Steve Biko matter and Nohle Mohapi.
> We sued the police in the case of Joseph Mdluli [and] we won that case for Lydia Mdluli. We were not so lucky with Nohle Mohapi.

Joseph Mdluli's death in detention in 1976 at the hands of the security police was one of the most notorious in apartheid history. Mdluli was a commander in the armed wing of the ANC, Umkhonto we Sizwe (MK), at the time of his death. Four policemen were charged with Mdluli's death but were acquitted. The judge who acquitted the policemen said it was not possible to say which of the policemen had assaulted Mdluli. Lydia Mdluli sued the apartheid state with Griffiths' help, and received a R15 000 out-of-court settlement.

Mapetla Mohapi was a Black Consciousness activist who, like Mduli, died at the hands of the apartheid police, in a police cell in Kei Road outside King William's Town on 5 August 1976. The police produced a 'suicide note', claiming that Mohapi, who was then 28 years old, had committed suicide. Magistrate AJ Swart found that Mohapi had died from 'an application of force to the neck' and that nobody was to blame.[6]

Griffiths represented Mapetla's wife, Nohle, in the civil proceedings against the apartheid state. Thenjiwe Mtintso, a journalist at the *Daily Dispatch* and a Black Consciousness activist[7] who had been detained at the same time as Mapetla, gave evidence from Lesotho, where she had gone into exile. Thenjiwe testified that the security police had demonstrated to her how they'd killed Mapetla, torturing her with a wet towel over her head[8] in a similar manner to how they had killed him.

Despite this, they lost the case and Nohle was ordered to pay R250 000 in court costs.

Steve Biko died 13 months after Mapetla, and once again Griffiths was involved in assisting the family. Biko's wife, Ntsiki, sued the state and was awarded R30 000 but refused to accept it, regarding it as 'blood money', and instead donated it to a community project.

❑

THE STING IN THE TALE: BULELANI NGCUKA

When Bulelani graduated later in April – no small feat, as only seven of the sixty students he started with graduated in the prescribed four years – GM said he wanted to attend the celebrations.

> At that time, GM was banned. He was not confined to any geographical space, but he couldn't attend or address gatherings. His banning order was going to expire in July, so he insisted that the celebration be postponed so that he could attend.

Bulelani's family agreed to postpone the celebrations, but Bulelani still had to attend his graduation. He flew to East London, his first time on a plane; he remembers that the ticket cost R30.

His mother had a surprise for him when it was time to return to Natal: she gave him a car, a Chevair with the number plate CDX181.

> I'm mentioning this CDX because it made it stand out. The cars in Durban were ND and here is this young Xhosa lawyer driving a Chevair with CDX plates!

That wasn't the only reason the 'young Xhosa lawyer' stood out. Apartheid legislation like the pass laws and 'influx control' meant that Bulelani was not supposed to live in Durban – this 'right' was afforded only to black people who were born in a town and had lived there continuously for not less than 15 years, or who had been employed there continuously for at least 15 years, or who had worked continuously for the same employer for at least 10 years.

Griffiths took Bulelani to an old ANC contact in the government offices in KwaMashu who used his influence and got the necessary papers for Bulelani, legalising his stay in Durban.

That done, he registered his articles at the end of May 1978.

When Griffiths' banning order lapsed, he was able to travel with Bulelani back to the Eastern Cape to attend the graduation celebrations.

> Graduation parties were a big thing in those days. People would travel a great distance. It was important to celebrate progress in education.
>
> We had a wonderful party. GM was guest speaker. It was the talk of the town for GM to be there. He had been banned and had not addressed people for a long time. Many years thereafter, people would still talk about GM and say they were inspired to find out that he came from King William's Town.

During the journey, Bulelani took the opportunity to ask GM about his cases.

> What made you famous, I asked. GM said that the case that put him on the map was that of Delase Chiliza vs. the Minister of Police, the so-called 'K... Case'. Chiliza was a banned member of the ANC who had been called a 'k...' by a member of the security police. He approached Griffiths and they decided to sue the state. Griffiths found a witness who corroborated Chiliza's story, but this did not convince the magistrate. The magistrate found that the policeman had called Chiliza a 'k...' but said this was not an insult.
>
> Griffiths was very angry and he became very emotional when the state attorney approached him in court at the end of the case and asked if GM was going to appeal. 'Yes, I'm going to appeal', GM said. 'And just you dare try and call me a k... and see what will happen to you.' The poor

fellow told GM not to be emotional and tried to apologise but GM was having none of it. 'Of course I'm emotional. I'm very angry. I'm going to appeal and I'm going to win.'

Griffiths went on to lodge an appeal but decided he needed to mobilise public opinion as well. By the time the matter came back to court, he had the support he needed and organisations like the Black Sash and various churches gave him their backing. Griffiths won the appeal. This was the first time that a court ruled that the 'k' word was indeed an insult.

❑

Bulelani learned the story of Griffiths' life in stages. His father was a quiet, unassuming man who had worked as a labourer for Checkers. His mother hadn't worked; she'd stayed at home and raised the children.

> GM took after his mother. She didn't take nonsense from anyone. GM didn't drink or smoke. He never had a girlfriend other than his wife.
>
> His father could never afford university fees [for GM]. His father's employer helped him. He went to school at Forbes [Grant] High School just outside King William's Town, and then went to Fort Hare. He met his wife, Victoria, while he was at Fort Hare.
>
> Victoria was a nurse at Victoria Hospital in Alice. She was very clever. In those days, clever girls would be nurses and less clever girls were invariably sent to do teaching.
>
> From Fort Hare, Griffiths went to Natal to study for his LLB.
>
> Victoria and Griffiths were married in 1964. When they

moved to Durban, Victoria first did her midwifery training at King Edward Hospital and studied for a public health diploma at Edendale Technical College. However, she also registered for a B Proc with Unisa in 1974. She graduated in 1981, did her articles at Griffiths' firm, and was admitted as an attorney in the same year.

Griffiths was very active in the ANC. He was arrested in his final year of LLB in 1965. He spent six months in solitary confinement in detention before he went to trial. At the time, Victoria was expecting their first child, Mbasa, who was born in 1966. The police told GM his wife had had a miscarriage, so he mourned the death of his baby. Then, when he went to trial, his wife approached him with a baby.

'Who is this?'

'It's your son.'

Griffiths was imprisoned on Robben Island in 1967 for two years. He completed his articles when he was released in 1969. However, he couldn't be admitted as an attorney because he was listed under the Suppression of Communism Act.

> GM was not a communist. He was a member of the ANC and a real nationalist. He was listed under the Act because he had been convicted for furthering the aims of a banned organisation, and if you were listed, you needed the permission of the minister of justice before you could practise law.

Griffiths tried everything, without success, but then finally, through a contact, was able to engineer a meeting with the deputy minister of Bantu administration, Punt Janson.

Janson told Griffiths that he had no problem with him practising. 'We Nationalists', he told Griffiths, 'are not as bad as you people think. In fact, we are a lot better than the communists.'

This put Griffiths in an invidious position: he wanted to practise but not at the expense of his principles, so he began to argue.

Janson backed down: 'I don't want to discuss politics with you. I'll allow you to practise.'

And, finally, Griffiths was admitted as an attorney. 'That's the mistake they made,' he told Bulelani: 'they allowed me to practise law.'

❑

Bulelani learned his first lesson from Griffiths on the first day he accompanied his new boss to court. The case they were supposed to handle was postponed. Lillian Baqwa, the second African woman to be admitted as a lawyer in South Africa, and the first in Natal, was dealing with another case, and Griffiths said they should go and observe her case.

> This was a very interesting case. Her client was accused of stealing 365 pairs of Italian shoes. The court benches were packed full of shoes. Some were old, with holes in their soles. The police had had to go and collect these shoes from whoever this guy had sold them to. Some were wearing the shoes at the time and the police had to tell them to take them off so they could be used as evidence.
>
> Lillian had decided to plead guilty on behalf of her client but GM said no. You cannot plead guilty! You must fight the case.'
>
> 'Yes, GM, but the evidence against us is overwhelming.'

'Fight it out!'

The evidence was indeed overwhelming and Lillian had nothing to put across. We realised this guy was going to be found guilty, so after an hour we said goodbye and good luck to Lillian and left.

It was a measure of the confidence that Griffiths had in Bulelani that he assigned the young law graduate to the Bethal Treason Trial – one of the first political cases he dealt with. The trial was held in the small rural town of Bethal, several hours' drive from Johannesburg, a deliberate move by the apartheid authorities to avoid media attention.

It was the biggest political trial since the Rivonia Trial of Nelson Mandela and other senior ANC leaders in 1964. The legal team was led by Andrew Wilson, who later became a judge, and included Lewis Skweyiya, who went on to become a judge in the Constitutional Court. Because, under apartheid legislation, the hotels could not accommodate blacks, there was nowhere for Bulelani and the other black lawyers to stay, so, overnight, hotels were upgraded to 'international status' and Bulelani and Lewis ended up staying at the Bethal Motel.

The Bethal case presented its own share of experiences for Bulelani and Lewis, and Bulelani recalls one incident with amusement. He and Lewis returned to the motel late one evening, and Bulelani dropped his colleague at his room then went to collect his keys at the main reception. When he came out, he was confronted by a white man, a stranger, pointing a gun at him.

I think he wanted to shoot me, but he was drunk. I screamed and Lewis came running out of his room. He jumped on him and bundled him into the car and drove him to the police station and had him arrested. I only realised when we got to the police station that Lewis was in his pyjamas.

This was one of the speediest cases of justice I have ever seen. The security police did not want this thing to be in the newspapers. They also didn't want us to use this incident to argue that we were under threat and that the case should be moved back to Johannesburg. So, by 10 o'clock in the morning he had been tried, found guilty and sentenced.

Bulelani recounts also the tactics Griffiths used in the Bethal trial to gain access to detained people.

One of the people the defence needed to lead evidence for the accused in the Bethal case, Lawrence Tlokwa, was detained in Modderbee prison in Johannesburg. The defence needed to consult with him, so they submitted a subpoena on a Friday and on the Sunday received a call from him saying he had been released and was available to give evidence.

This immediately gave Griffiths an idea. One of the people who had not been seen for some time was Peter Jones.

Jones was a close colleague of Steve Biko and had been arrested in August 1977 with him. They had been separated in Port Elizabeth and no-one had had access to Jones since.

Using our experience now with Lawrence Tlokwa, Griffiths said we must subpoena Peter. He was not implicated in the Bethal case – there was no connection – but we thought that if we subpoenaed him, he might be released. I submitted a subpoena and a few days later he was released and sent straight to Bethal.

It was all over the newspapers. Everyone now wanted access to Peter and wanted to know what he knew about Steve Biko. Remember, no-one had been able to speak to him since he was arrested with Steve.

Peter came to Bethal. The judge wanted to know what Peter was going to say. He said he didn't want to pre-empt us, but he had been reading in the newspaper about Peter Jones. He said that at no stage had Peter been implicated in the trial and he was curious therefore to know what Peter was going to say.

In the end, Peter did not give evidence. He came to Bethal, spent some time with us, and then we sent him home to Cape Town.

After 18 months, the Bethal trial finally drew to a close in 1979. The transcripts of the trial are 7 000 pages long. All but two of the accused were convicted and sentenced to various terms of imprisonment – but, says Bulelani, the state really had nothing.

> I really felt an injustice had been done. We all hated apartheid. They would talk about things and would want to do things, but nothing ever came to fruition. All those guys were accused of was talking.

It was a baptism of fire but it was also a vital learning curve for Bulelani.

> I learned a lot of politics and I learned a lot of law. For me they went together.

There was one bright spot that came out of the brutal Bethal experience. It was during the Bethal trial that Bulelani met his wife, in 1978.

THE STING IN THE TALE: BULELANI NGCUKA

Phumzile was on the same plane as Bulelani, travelling to Durban. 'During those days there were very few black people who travelled on planes, so we greeted one another,' she recalls. 'I had a lot of hand luggage and he helped me.'[9]

❑

On 2 June 1980 Bulelani was admitted as an attorney of the Natal provincial division of the Supreme Court. He and Patrick Ntobeko Maqubela were admitted on the same day.

His admission was moved by Lewis Skweyiya. Bulelani was admitted by Judge Ramon Leon (Tony Leon's father) and Pieter Thirion in 1978. (This becomes important because it was Judge Leon who later refused to remove Bulelani from the roll when he was imprisoned. When Bulelani was sworn in as a member of parliament in later years he was introduced to Judge Leon by Sydney Kentridge, who said, 'This is the young man whose career we saved all those years ago and look where he is now.' Sydney Kentridge argued Bulelani's case at the hearing.)

That same year, Bulelani worked on a case with George Bizos in which five teenagers from KwaMashu, all under the age of 18, were charged under the Terrorism Act with attempting to undergo military training.

The group had been listening to Radio Freedom, the ANC's station broadcast from exile, and heard that Mozambique was a free country. They were all excited and wanted to visit this 'liberated zone'. One of the teens said that his grandmother lived in Maputo and he would take them there. They got on a train and unwittingly made their way to Maputa, a tiny settlement in northern Natal close to the Mozambique border. There, they asked a black policeman where they could find the ANC offices.

Instead of just putting the confused youngsters right, he arrested them and called in the security police. They were taken back to Durban and during interrogation were said to have confessed to wanting to travel to Maputo to join the ANC to undergo military training.

> The case was heard in the regional court where an over-confident prosecutor approached George Bizos on the first day and declared, 'I've got an open-and-shut case, Mr Bizos. Your boys are going to jail.'
>
> George responded by telling the prosecutor a story about Metternich, the famous Austrian diplomat of the 1800s, who, when asked by his son, 'What must I do to be as famous as you?' replied, 'Don't be too ambitious.'
>
> And, of course, George destroyed the prosecutor's case.

Bulelani was also involved in the case of Penuell Maduna, then an ANC activist from his university days who had been arrested and detained several times over the years. In 1979 he was on trial, charged – along with a group of co-accused – with attempting to recruit people for military training and attempting to leave the country to join the ANC.

The Maduna case went on for nearly two years.

> There were about eight of them. The first time they appeared in court in Pietermaritzburg they were wild. And I mean wild. They were spitting mad. When Maduna talks about it, he calls it 'the battle of the sputum'. On one occasion they got into a physical fight with the security police in court. It was a free-for-all. I thought they would get beaten up with batons and everything else. But they didn't care. They just didn't care. So the next time they appeared in court, they were in a cage.

THE STING IN THE TALE: BULELANI NGCUKA

Bulelani smiles as he recalls an incident that took place after the trial.

> One of the security policemen involved in the case was the notorious Seketsheketshe Ntombela, who seemed to go out of his way to be mean and cruel, earning himself a reputation as a vicious person. A week after they were acquitted, Maduna was walking in Durban when he bumped into Seketsheketshe. Maduna chased him and Seketsheketshe ran for his dear life.

Bulelani takes up the story of Sabelo Ngobese. Sabelo was charged with Penuell Maduna, but no-one was aware that he had been detained until they were approached by a cleaner, an elderly woman and ANC activist, who worked at Addington Hospital.

> She went up to Griffiths and said: 'Mxenge, there's an ANC child that's been hurt by the police. He's been badly assaulted and he's in Addington Hospital. Do something about it.'
>
> She had been asked to clean up his blood. She also told him that there was a white nurse at the hospital who was very disturbed by what had happened and would talk to us about it.
>
> 'Who is she?'
>
> 'Hayi Mxenge, be careful now. Don't expose me.'
>
> 'Who is this boy?'
>
> 'I don't know.'
>
> At first, we were not sure where to start but then we started asking about who in the ANC in Durban had been detained. We found the white nurse who had attended to Sabelo at the hospital; and she confirmed what had happened and gave us an affidavit.

She was a brave woman. She was apolitical but hated what she had seen. So, we went to court and demanded that the security police bring Sabelo to court. We were challenged of course. The security police brought in their big legal guns and argued about the Terrorism Act and so on.

We were lucky to get a liberal judge like John Didcott. He also raised questions and asked the security police why he as a judge could not see someone who had been assaulted. This was what was important for us, to see Sabelo brought to court.

This case was important for two reasons. We had used the courts to force their hand. This was something that GM drummed into me. He said that even though this is their law, we must use their law to expose them. We must at every given moment advance the frontiers of freedom. We must use whatever instruments are at our disposal. Let them know we are monitoring them, and we hold them accountable. We should expose the state. Either use the media to expose the atrocities they were committing or use the courts.

Bulelani goes on to explain another lesson he learned in the case of Muntu Timothy Nxumalo, who was charged with undergoing military training, possession of a pistol and ammunition and attempting to kill a Chesterville town councillor.[10]

The first person the state called to give evidence against Muntu was his father. It was a painful thing and we were all disgusted that a father could give evidence against his own son. We brought his wife to court to sit in the front seats so that he could see that she could see what he was doing to his son. Of course, he was not deterred and he went ahead and gave evidence.

Muntu was convicted, sentenced to 22 years, and sent to Robben Island in 1978. He was 22 years old. The state had called for the death penalty.

> There were many lessons for me from that case. When Muntu's father was released from detention, he went back to his wife, and they reconciled. Muntu was the first one to forgive his father. All of us were bearing a grudge against the man for what he had done to his son. But the family bond was strong and Muntu understood the pressure he was under and was more forgiving than we were. I felt bad. I had not experienced the kind of pain that the man must have gone through for him to have to take such a decision.
>
> He had probably worked out that they could not both go to jail and that somebody had to stay behind to protect the family. But that was of no consequence to me at the time. I just thought he was just a collaborator. And that prepared me for later in life, that we don't co-operate with the system.

The first case Bulelani handled in the Eastern Cape is one that went on to set a precedent and is one he still speaks of with pride.

> This was the case of Mrs Thembisa Mbilini from King Williams Town, who was banned along with her husband. She had been travelling in a car with Mrs Nontsikelelo Biko and was stopped by security police.
>
> When the police approached the vehicle, they told her in isiXhosa, *'Uza kunya wena.'* [You are going to shit.]

> We sued the minister of police. During the trial, a Sergeant Fouche, said he was talking to a colleague and that what he had in fact said was *'Uza kuya wena?'* ['Are you going there?']
>
> Charles Nqakula [who went on to become minister of defence] was covering the case for the *Daily Dispatch* and wrote an article about 'the case that hinges on an N'. It was great doing the case with Griffiths sitting next to me, especially when I cross-examined the security police. He was very proud of me. We lost the case. The magistrate said the police had lied but they were not acting in their official duties and the government was therefore not responsible for their actions. We won it later on appeal but by this time I was already in prison. It has gone on to become one of the leading cases in the course and scope of employment.

Two other cases Bulelani recalls working on with Griffiths demonstrate the impact apartheid had on every aspect of the lives of those disenfranchised by the system – and some of the inbuilt ironies.

David Sponono Gasa was head of the Umlazi Residents' Association. He had been banned and restricted by the apartheid regime and had to be home by 6 pm every evening; his comings and goings were closely monitored and recorded by the security police.

> David was self-employed. He did all sorts of things to make ends meet – making bricks, selling stuff. The first charge they brought against him was failing to render tax returns. I managed to get him off on a technicality.
>
> A month later, they charged him for contravening his

banning order, about 24 charges in all. This time we were not so lucky. He was sentenced to one month in prison for each violation – even if he had been five minutes late [getting home in the evening], he got a month in prison. He ended up serving about 16 months.

Bulelani and Griffiths also worked on the case of King Sabata Dalindyebo of the abaThembu, who was arrested in July 1980 for insulting Kaizer Matanzima, a senior chief and president of the Transkei 'homeland'. The Transkei government had passed a law criminalising any criticism of Transkei's 'independence' and President Matanzima.[11] In an attempt to put pressure on Matanzima to get the charges withdrawn, Griffiths decided to call Nelson Mandela as a witness, to explain the difference in status between Sabata and Matanzima, and how it wasn't possible for a king to insult a subject.

> Madiba was keen but after we consulted, we decided he couldn't appear before a homeland court. In the meantime, Griffiths and Winnie Mandela went to Matanzima to ask him to withdraw the case, but Matanzima refused. He told GM that Sabata had insulted him for the past 40 years.
> Sabata was found guilty and sentenced. We knew they would send him to jail. He was ill and we couldn't allow him to spend a day in jail. So we noted an appeal and he left the country.

Sabata died in exile in April 1986.

❑

Bulelani learned more than law from Griffiths; he recalls the time he learned a valuable lesson in humility.

They had travelled to the countryside to consult clients about a motor-vehicle accident case. When they arrived, they were offered tea and amadumbe, a root vegetable popular in Natal. Bulelani turned down both. He doesn't drink tea or coffee, and amadumbe, he says, is an acquired taste.

> GM was disgusted and told me I was a snob. 'Poor people have nothing. This is a social thing. You can't come here as a big lawyer from Durban and not take the tea you are offered. This is all they can afford. To add salt to the wound they brought amadumbe and you refused that too!'
>
> All the way back to Durban, he lectured me and told me I must live with the people and drink tea. I felt so hurt.
>
> When we got back to the office, he was still angry and told Victoria what had happened. 'This son of yours, he thinks he's better than the people. He doesn't want to drink their tea.'
>
> That was an important lesson for me. But I still don't drink tea and I still don't eat amadumbe!

One of the people Bulelani met at this time was Chris Hani, who was then living in Lesotho, from where he was organising guerrilla operations of MK in South Africa.

> I had to go to Lesotho and brief Chris about a case and other matters. There was a dispute that needed to be solved. We needed Chris's help and he said, 'Just tell *Bhuti* [GM] he must set up a meeting and we will be there.'
>
> I couldn't believe it. I thought to myself, *How can this man come to South Africa?* He was one of the most wanted men and he just said he would come to wherever he was needed, just like that.
>
> Chris arrived for the meeting, just like he said.

THE STING IN THE TALE: BULELANI NGCUKA

❏

On 20 November 1981, a Friday morning, Bulelani received a call from Victoria Mxenge.

GM had not come home on the Thursday evening. It was unheard of.

'Have you checked with the police?' I asked her.

'Yes. They say they don't know where he is.'

'Did you check the hospitals?'

'Yes. There've been no accidents reported.'

I told her I was certain he had been detained, that the police were lying, but we agreed that we should go and check at the mortuary in Gale Street.

I had to go to court first and postpone a case, then I collected Victoria and we went to the mortuary. On our way there, we said to each other that when GM came back, he was going to laugh at us for going to look for him at the mortuary. We were still convinced that the security police had him and that they were lying to us.

We arrived and asked the policeman on duty. No, he said, he knew Mr Mxenge and he wasn't there, but we were welcome to check. So we entered the mortuary. All those bodies.

Victoria was walking on my right-hand side. I saw GM first and tried to shield uSisi. I didn't want her to see him. It was such a terrible thing. He had been stabbed so many times.

I was thinking how to tell her that she couldn't see him in this state but then she just stopped. 'Wait. That's Mlungisi.'

'No, that's not him. Let's go.'

'No, this is him. So many stab wounds.' She just looked at him. She didn't scream. She didn't cry. 'What did you do for them to hate you so much?' That's all she said.

Among the many brutal killings in South Africa's apartheid past, the murder of Griffiths Mxenge stands out as one of the most violent.

His killers were apartheid government policemen and agents Dirk Coetzee, Almond Nofomela, Joe Mamasela, Brian Ngqulunga and David 'Spyker' Tshikalanga. Coetzee was the head of Vlakplaas, the notorious South African Police (SAP) hit-squad headquarters. They had been ordered not to use a gun and therefore used three Okapi knives, a hunting knife and a wheel spanner. They stabbed Griffiths 45 times, the wounds piercing his body, lungs, liver and heart. They slit his throat, cut off his ears and ripped open his stomach.

Coetzee told the Truth and Reconciliation Commission (TRC) in 1996 that he had been given the instruction to kill Griffiths by Johannes van der Hoven, the regional security commander at CR Swart police station in Durban. He was given background information on a certain Griffiths Mxenge and told to *'maak 'n plan met hom'* (make a plan with him). 'To make a plan in our language means one thing only: take him out, kill him, murder him, assassinate him; get rid of him.'[12]

'When I agreed to make a plan with Mxenge, Van der Hoven said that we should not shoot or abduct him, but that we should rather make it look like a robbery.'[13]

Coetzee said he left the details of the murder to be worked out by Nofomela and Mamasela, and also assigned Spyker and Ngqulungwa to do the job.

'I cautioned them to wear old clothes and old shoes that I could destroy if necessary. They were also to see that their pockets were empty so that nothing could be lost at the site of the crime – no cigarettes, no ID documents, no watches with names or serial numbers, etc. I arranged to meet them [afterwards] at a bar.'

At the prearranged meeting place, 'I called them out [of the bar] and they gave me a brief account in the street,' Coetzee said. The unarmed Mxenge had reportedly put up a fight right to the end, at one stage even pulling a knife out of his own chest and chasing his attackers with it, after which he was bludgeoned with a wheel spanner and then killed in a stabbing frenzy.

Coetzee told the TRC that Mamasela, Tshikalanga and Nofomela were given R1 000 each by the police as *'kopgeld'* (a bounty) after the killing. Ngqulunga, who was later (in 1990) killed by his own colleagues, did not receive a 'reward', according to Coetzee, because he had played a 'passive' role in the whole sordid affair.[14]

Coetzee, Nofemela and Tshikalanga eventually got amnesty from the TRC. Nofomela served 22 years in prison on unrelated murder charges.

Mamasela confessed to the Mxenge killing and others but refused to apply for amnesty. He has never been prosecuted for crimes he committed as an apartheid 'askari' (a member of the ANC who turned on his comrades and joined the ranks of the security police). He was charged and acquitted on murder charges in 2010 in an unrelated matter.

6.
Prison

*'We looked after each other. That's how we are in the
ANC. These principles and values were instilled in us in
prison. We were taught to take care of one another.'*

Griffiths was no ordinary man – he was the most senior ANC leader to fall inside South Africa since Chief Albert Luthuli's death in 1967. The message had already come from Chris Hani in exile that the funeral had to be fitting for someone of his stature.

> GM was a very important political figure. Chris was constantly checking on arrangements to ensure a proper funeral was organised. 'The regime must know that the ANC is alive, that GM was an ANC leader. Tell me what you need. We will help you.'

Griffiths' offices were closed, and evening prayers were arranged at his home in Umlazi. Rev Mcebisi Xundu conducted the prayers.[1]

> His prayers had a calming effect. His message was simple yet very powerful. He told people it was alright to be angry but that our anger must be channelled in the right direction and that anger must be directed at oppression, not God.
>
> The message was that God will avenge us, but that does

not mean we must sit back and do nothing. God helps those who help themselves.

In the decisions about funeral arrangements, Bulelani represented Griffiths' family.

I was Mrs Mxenge's mouth, as it were. Fumbatha [GM's brother] was in Ireland doing medicine. He flew back in time for the funeral but before he arrived, the weight of the funeral was on my shoulders. It was not a burden. This was something I had to do.

On the Tuesday after Griffiths' death, Patrick Ntobeko Maqubela, who shared a house with Bulelani, and was also an MK commander at the time, was arrested.

I heard about Ntobeko's arrest from another close friend and comrade, Mbulelo Hongo. I said I would deal with it later. I had to continue with arrangements for the funeral.

The next day the security police came looking for me at the office. My secretary saw them, and she took me to the women's toilet and hid me there. The security police searched the place and left.

After they left, I had to think hard. I had to sort out GM's funeral. This was my priority.

We gave GM a wonderful sendoff. One of our clients was the South African Municipal Workers' Union [and] they came out in full force. Bishop [Desmond] Tutu did the sermon at the funeral. Ma [Albertina] Sisulu and Dullah Omar also spoke.

I will never forget Dullah's words. 'How are we going to remember Griffiths Mxenge? What are we going to do?

Are we going to build a cenotaph like they did for the 1820 settlers? Will we put up a concrete slab and say, "Here lies a hero of the people?" Never! What we must build for Griffiths is for us to attain our freedom.'

The sense was that we must rededicate ourselves and use his blood to ensure that we attain our liberation. Freedom songs were sung about Mandela and Sisulu, who both sent messages of support that were read out at the funeral. The ANC flag was flying high.

The level of anger at Griffiths' murder became evident, however, when a man was discovered in the crowd with a tape recorder. The crowd pounced on him, suspecting that he was a policeman, and beat him to death despite attempts by Bishop Tutu to intervene and save his life. It later turned out that the man was indeed a detective in the security police.

❑

After the funeral, Bulelani had issues of his own to deal with. The security police had visited Phumzile's apartment in Durban and were looking for him.

> It was clear I was going to be arrested. We had to think about what I was going to do. Do I run or stay? I had been to Botswana, Lesotho and Swaziland, and had seen how our comrades lived there and I was not keen on exile. I was also certain that they [the apartheid authorities] did not have enough on me to sentence me for long.
>
> I thought I would confront them.
>
> I didn't think they had enough to charge me. Most of the information was about me helping people to leave

the country and those guys were outside the country.

Phumzile didn't agree. But she also didn't want me to go into exile.

What I didn't think about was what actually happened. I didn't think they would ask me to give evidence against Patrick. I slept at a friend's place on that Sunday and on Monday 30 November, just two days after GM's funeral, I went to court.

Later in the day, Luyanda [Mpahlwa, another of Bulelani's close friends] picked me up at court and took me to the offices. As we got there, I saw the security police and they had Phumzile in their car. I told Luyanda I was going to them.

'No,' he said, 'you can't. You will be arrested too.'

'They have Phumzile. I'm going to them.'

I went up to the car. 'Okay,' I said, 'you are looking for me. I'm here now. Let her go.'

'Get into the car,' they said.

'Let her go first.'

So they let her go and that's how I was detained. This was on 30 November 1981, around five in the afternoon.'

Bulelani was detained in terms of Section 6 of the Terrorism Act. This allowed for the detention of anybody suspected of terrorism for 60 days, which could be renewed indefinitely.

I was taken to CR Swart police station, to the security police offices on the top floor. There I was confronted by a Captain [David] Van Zyl and Lieutenant [Andy] Taylor, who had been involved in Joseph Mdluli's death.'[2]

You sit there, looking at these men. I mean, we had been involved in suing the minister of police for Mdluli's murder.

PRISON

I had faced Taylor in court. You know these men are murderers and now they are in front of you.

They started asking questions. My answers were very short. No. Yes. No. I don't know. No.

They went on and on and on, and then they came to the real issue and [unconsciously] I took my hands out of my pockets and they noticed. They told me later this was a signal to them that I was about to lie.

I had learned as a lawyer that when you deal with cases of this nature, you had to give a version so close to their version that it becomes plausible. They asked about the guys I had helped to leave the country. I admitted that I had helped them all. However, I said they were not fugitives from justice in South Africa. They were fugitives from justice in Transkei, which was an independent state, so I had committed no offence in South Africa.

Of course, they wanted to know what they were going to do in exile. I said I didn't know. All I did was help them leave the country. What happened after they left was not my business.

It was now late in the evening. I was taken down to my cell that first day. It was a Monday. I was very, very tired. I was in a state of shock. I was so tired. I slept the whole night and the whole of the next day. Nobody came for me that Tuesday. I looked around my cell. It hit me now. I was alone and I was in detention.

On Wednesday, the Transkei police came and asked me questions about the guys we had helped escape from Transkei, and I gave them the same story. But this time I told them I was a South African citizen and I told them that for the purposes of that day I recognised that Transkei was

> an independent state and that as a South African citizen I had committed no crime against Transkei. They interrogated me for some time, but I stuck to my story.

One of the tactics many detainees used was to befriend the uniformed police, and Bulelani was quick to identify a likely candidate: a white policeman who guarded the cells and brought detainees their meals.

> These guys were also bored. They sat outside our cells with nothing to do and no-one to talk to. I would start talking to them about cricket and rugby, and as soon as they realised you knew about cricket and rugby, they opened up. They would open the cell door and chat to you, give you a cigarette and books to read. The one chap loved Wilbur Smith books and he shared his books with me. He would give me a book during the day and say, 'Don't tell the *laanies*' [smart people, referring to the security police], and then take it back when he left in the evening.

Bulelani also befriended an Indian policeman who gave him a pen and paper to write a note to Phumzile. He soon received a reply and was relieved to have established a channel of communication with the outside world.

He was soon communicating with fellow detainees too, who he discovered included not only Patrick and his MK comrades but also Pravin Gordhan, a prominent United Democratic Front (UDF) and underground ANC activist at the time, who occupied the cell next to him.

> On my first Christmas in detention, this Indian policeman brought me food from home and a bottle of rum. I didn't drink rum, but I decided to drink it that Christmas.

He poured it into a tin mug. After he left, I thought about it for a bit, about whether I should drink it not, and then thought, *Why not?* and just downed it. It turned out I was not the only one who got rum. The other guys also got some rum that day.

And so December passed.

We went on a hunger strike for five or six days. Our demand was to be charged or released.

In February '82 we got the news that Neil Aggett had died in detention. We had smuggled in a copy of the *Sunday Times*.

Aggett, an anti-apartheid activist, had been detained a few days before Bulelani, in Johannesburg. He'd been severely tortured and allegedly committed suicide in detention on 5 February 1982 in John Vorster Square police station, the only white person to die in detention in the history of the struggle against apartheid.

In the same month as Aggett's death, Patrick and two others were charged with treason and moved from CR Swart police station.

Before this, Litha [Jolobe, Bulelani's co-accused and close friend] agreed to be a state witness against Patrick and came back and told us. He had such a good time from that day on. They would take him out all the time and he ate good food.

They asked me too and I refused. I knew then there was no way out. The maximum sentence [for refusing to give evidence] was five years.

I was a lawyer with legal training and experience. But still, one's thinking can get muddled. This one policeman, Van Dyk, would tell me that they would make sure I got a hanging judge, and I would be sentenced to death. It's ridiculous. You don't think about it at the time – how can you be sentenced to death for refusing to give evidence? – but I would panic. Of course I realised later he was talking nonsense but I knew that I would go to prison.

Pravin was released at about this time and a new person now moved into the cell next to Bulelani's. This young man had also been asked to give evidence against a comrade and had refused. Bulelani told him he had made the right decision.

The young man wanted to communicate with his family so Bulelani put him in touch with one of the uniformed policemen who was helping the detainees. The youngster, however, told the security police, and the policeman was arrested with a letter he was carrying from Phumzile for Bulelani that had not yet been delivered. Phumzile was arrested and detained overnight.

The policeman who'd been carrying the letter was now placed in the cell next to Bulelani and wanted to discuss the letter. Bulelani was aware the cells were being monitored and told the policeman he didn't know what he was talking about. The policeman was eventually charged and fired.

❏

Phumzile had applied repeatedly to visit Bulelani, and the security police finally relented and gave permission for Bulelani's mother and Phumzile to visit.

Phumzile then applied for permission for Bulelani to study for his LLB and they agreed. By then he had been in detention for six months.

Most of those detained with Bulelani also started studying.

You know, we were all smoking at that time. The only way you could get cigarettes was to ask a black policeman to buy you some when you went to see the doctor in town. So you had to find something wrong with you to see the doctor.

I said I had a fungal infection on my foot. I went to the doctor in handcuffs. One of my clients was in the lift. He was so excited to see me and greeted me but when he saw the handcuffs, he got the fright of his life and ran as soon as the lift doors opened.

The black policemen would always tell us that they were good guys. One of them told me a story about visiting a farmer with a white colleague. 'We went to a farm and the farmer served the white guys tea in cups and saucers and he gave me [mine] in a jam tin. Of course, my white man told him I'm not that kind of a black. He must give me a cup. So, you see, I also drink tea from a cup and saucer, not from *itoti ka jam* [jam tin].'

When they sat in the interrogation room, one of them, this same man who told me he drank from a cup, would plead with me. 'Hey, Ngcuka, the white man is angry. Please, Ngcuka, *tshela mina. Mina ndiza kutshela abelungu.* [Tell me. I will tell the white man.] Hey, *wena*, man, cooperate.'

'*Hai, suka wena.* [No, go away.] Nonsense. I'm not going to do any such thing. Don't you realise we are fighting to liberate you too?'

'No, me, I'm okay. I drink from a cup.'

On 3 August 1982, after spending nearly a year in detention, Bulelani and his co-accused were taken to court.

Litha was the first to be called. Although he had told the security police he was prepared to testify against Patrick Ntobeko, who faced charges of treason and 'terrorism', he went into court and refused. The security police, shocked by this turn of events, asked the court to be given a chance to talk to him. Litha objected, saying he had been assaulted, but to no avail.

As they left the court, Bulelani says, Taylor turned to Litha and said, 'You say we have assaulted you. Wait until you see what is going to happen tonight.'

Litha stuck to his story when he was brought back to court the following day, and was sentenced to four years' imprisonment for refusing to turn state witness against Ntobeko and his comrades.

> We had very good lawyers. One of the lawyers defending me was Boyce [Marumo] Moerane. They said they didn't want us to go to prison for refusing to give evidence. They recommended that we go into court and say that we had been in detention for a long time and could not remember anything.
>
> I said no, I could not use such a defence. I wanted the system to know that they were illegitimate. Ntobeko was my brother. They wanted me to testify against him, but I believed in what he was doing. I would not be the one who signed his death warrant.
>
> So I was going to defy the system and refuse to give evidence, but if some of my comrades wanted to use the defence they suggested, I was okay with that. And some of the guys did try that. One of the guys who drove for us, Gabula Ndamase, Ntobeko's cousin, agreed to give evidence but said he couldn't remember anything, and he was released. I was fine with that. His role was minimal.

Almost a year after they were arrested, on 4 August 1982,

Bulelani and Mbulelo Hongo were sentenced to three years in prison for refusing to testify against Ntobeko. Luyanda Mpahlwa and Litha Jolobe got four years on the same charge and Mpilo Taho was sentenced to five years.

Their sentencing was closely followed by that of Patrick and his two comrades, Richard Maqhutyana and Mpumelelo Gaba, who were convicted of treason and sentenced to 20 years each.³

Immediately after their sentencing, Bulelani and his comrades were moved to Pietermaritzburg prison. As with most political prisoners after sentencing, prison was a relief from the isolation of detention and solitary confinement.

Bulelani arrived first, with Litha and Mbulelo, and they spent the whole first night talking. The companionship more than made up for the rougher physical side of prison. There were no beds, just sisal mats on the floor, dirty blankets, old prison clothes, and a bucket for a toilet which was emptied once a day.

They were joined the following Monday by Luyanda. Bulelani remembers seeing Luyanda walk into the prison with beautiful, long hair. He complimented him on his hair and Luyanda responded proudly, 'Ah, touch of silk, bru, touch of silk,' referring to jazz musician Eric Gale's hit song. 'But you, you look like a *bandiet* [prisoner]!' he teased Bulelani.

> 'Don't worry,' I told him 'You will be like this very soon.'
>
> I had my revenge when I saw him in prison clothes. Luyanda is a very tall guy. They couldn't find prison trousers to fit him, so the trousers he wore looked like three-quarter pants on him. When he walked into our cell, he was a sight to behold.
>
> We were given prison food, real rubbish. That first night Luyanda was horrified and asked how we could eat such

junk. Litha just looked at him and said, 'Please give it to me if you are not going to eat it.' By the end of the week, of course, Luyanda was eating the junk food and also asking for more.

They were moved to Leeuwkop prison in September 1982. Serving as a halfway house of sorts for the prison service at the time, Leeuwkop was where an assessment took place, after which the apartheid authorities would decide where prisoners would serve their time.

Bulelani met many other sentenced prisoners at Leeuwkop, including Thabo Ndabeni, a leading figure in the 1976 uprising; journalist and activist Thami Mazwai; and Naphthali Manana, an MK cadre who had just been moved from death row and whose sentence had been commuted to life.

The first reaction from warders to Bulelani and his colleagues being lawyers at Leeuwkop was notable.

> They couldn't understand how lawyers like Ntobeko, Mbulelo and myself could land up in jail. When I filled in the forms, in one section you had to state what your highest standard of education was. I wrote down 'B Proc'. They didn't believe me.
> '*Nee, man,*' the warder said. 'Do you have Standard 10?'
> 'Yes,' I said.
> 'Okay,' he said. 'Write Standard 10.'

Bulelani and his colleagues were later moved to Victor Verster prison near Paarl in the Western Cape. Patrick went to Pollsmoor in Cape Town, where he joined Nelson Mandela, and his two colleagues went to Robben Island.

Bulelani was pleased with the move to Victor Verster, which was a much better prison with good facilities and, he says, prison staff who were more enlightened than those at Leeuwkop. Prisoners were allowed to sit outside during the day, although the prison authorities decided they would be locked up during lunchtime. Much of their time during the day was taken up with playing draughts and chess, and reading.

> The food at Victor Verster was much better, much better prepared. We received biscuits at Christmas. On Christmas Day we got a carrot cake, which prisoners had baked. It's the best carrot cake I have ever tasted in my life; even after I left prison, I have travelled everywhere and have never tasted carrot cake as good as that cake.
>
> For one of my birthdays [after the advent of democracy], Phumzile ordered a huge carrot cake, and she was certain that this time the cake would match up to the cake I ate in prison. Of course, it did not. When I look back, I'm sure that that cake in Victor Verster did not taste as good as I imagined it. It tasted wonderful because I had been so deprived.

In January 1984 they were joined by a small group of prisoners from Robben Island, among them Billy Nair, a veteran activist and MK commander who had been sentenced in 1963 to 20 years on Robben Island. He was now about to be released, and Bulelani spent a few months getting to know him. They were not in the same section but were able to communicate, albeit not easily.

Phumzile had applied to see Bulelani and been refused permission; now she tried again, and was refused again. Phumzile was politically active, and this was no doubt the reason her applications were turned down; the excuse the prison authorities used, however, was that she and Bulelani were not married. The two hadn't seen each other since Bulelani had been sentenced in August 1982.

At the time, Wilton Mkwayi, an ANC and MK leader who had been sentenced to life imprisonment in the 1964 treason trial, had made an application to get married and it was granted in 1984. Bulelani immediately put in his own application but it was refused.

The family decided to proceed with an engagement outside of prison anyway. Bulelani's family sent a delegation that included Pius Langa, Steve Tshwete, Victoria Mxenge and Bulelani's brother, Vuyani, to Phumzile's family to ask for her hand in marriage. A big engagement party was then held at Phumzile's family home in Clermont, a township outside Durban, and Vuyani represented Bulelani, placing the ring on Phumzile's finger.

The engagement sent an important message to the apartheid regime: that the couple would not allow themselves to be frustrated – that they were going to win in the end.

❏

In Victor Verster prison, Bulelani found himself in great demand, being consulted by prisoners and warders about legal problems. The warders invariably owed money and received summonses, and he assisted them in drafting responses to summonses, and in turn would ask for their help in a range of matters.

He recalls the incident that led to his group being transferred from Victor Verster. Prisoners who belonged to the Azanian People's Organisation (Azapo) had fought with authorities and embarked on a hunger strike. The strike was not supported by ANC prisoners.

PRISON

Prison was the only place in South Africa at the time where you could openly be a member of the ANC or PAC, and so we would classify ourselves according to which movement we supported – ANC, PAC, Azapo and so on. We differed politically, but there was cooperation.

Most of the prisoners were ANC prisoners. If the ANC prisoners were not on hunger strike, we knew the authorities would not take it seriously. We knew also that if we didn't join the hunger strike, the Azapo guys wouldn't listen to us. So we joined the hunger strike.

We knew their demands could never be met so we put in our own demands, which were more reasonable. After three or four days, the authorities conceded to these demands, and we called off the strike.

That weekend, however, they moved all the political prisoners to Helderstroom prison in Caledon. Others were sent back to Leeuwkop.

In Helderstroom, they joined a much bigger group of political prisoners with lots of guys from Robben Island, and Bulelani recalls how special it was to meet real veterans of the struggle in prison and to learn about the ANC from them. 'Oom Tom' Charlemagne was one of these.[4]

> Charlemagne was first arrested in the Defiance Campaign in 1952 and had been in and out of prison since then. He liked to speak about a friend of his who was the chairperson of the ANC branch in Uitenhage who had agreed to join him in the Defiance Campaign. The two had decided to sit on 'whites only' benches at the train station in Uitenhage in the Eastern Cape.
>
> When he arrived at his friend's home on the day to

collect him, his friend's wife was breastfeeding their child. She stood up, handed the baby to his friend and walked out.

'You can see that I cannot join you now,' his friend told him.

Charlemagne said he was never sure if this was a strategy the couple had jointly worked on or whether the wife was just fed up and had walked out in the heat of the moment.

Charlemagne told me, 'My friend drifted away from the struggle from that day on. Look at me, still here in jail today 27 years later, and my friend is well established outside.'

I learned a lot about the lessons of life in prison from those people.

In Helderberg, politics was the order of the day.

I learned a lot of politics and I became a better man. Prison made me a better person. It strengthened my resolve and my commitment to the struggle. Prison educated me, not just through the books we read. Of course, I got my LLB[5], but still I place greater value on what I was able to learn from my comrades and colleagues in prison.

Prisoners organised political classes. I remember one lecture about man and his country; it was about the history of South Africa from a very different perspective from what we had learned in school. We had always learned history from the perspective of the coloniser. Now, for the first time, we were learning it from the side of the colonised. And we were being taught by people who did not even have matric. And there were classes about dialectical materialism and Marxism being taught in Zulu.

I was studying, and I would be asked to order books [on loan] from Unisa. The guys would sit overnight and transcribe the book, and by the time the book had to be returned, we would have our own copy. This is how we built our own library in prison.

I also learned how to relate to people. I was trusted with leadership positions. We formed a kolkhoz, a cooperative, to share resources. There was also another structure, an ANC committee that worked with other parties and the authorities. I was a member of this committee and would help with negotiations and discussions. Each cell had its own representatives and after discussions we would report back to the comrades.

Some of the comrades in prison were serving 20-year sentences and had lost contact with their families after 10 years. They had no financial support. Those of us who had some support would put our resources together and share. Whatever money we had would be put together and we would buy cigarettes and other things for everyone. Whatever we had, we would share.

When Bulelani arrived in Helderstroom, he was still a Group D prisoner, which meant he was allowed to receive one letter and one visit a month. At the end of his first year in prison, he received several Christmas cards (anti-apartheid movements abroad would regularly arrange for political prisoners to receive cards), and prison authorities told him he had finished his quota for the new year. Naturally, he objected and, after lengthly negotiations, Bulelani was allowed to receive the usual quota of letters for the following year. This was one of the prison tactics used to isolate political prisoners from their families and friends. Tactics also included heavy censoring of letters. Bulelani says many of the letters were cut mid-sentence.

> They literally cut up our letters with scissors. By the time we received them, the letters would no longer make any kind of sense.

Bulelani only became a Category C prisoner a year before his release and could then receive 18 letters and 18 visits a year.

He managed to organise jobs as a cleaner and in the prison library.

> This was important because as a cleaner you spent a lot of time outside your cell, and as a librarian I could spend a lot of time reading. We spent a lot of time in prison reading.

There were other small privileges that helped make prison life more bearable.

> I don't drink tea or coffee so I asked the prison authorities to give me milk instead. They said they could only do so if the prison doctor agreed. The doctor refused, saying he could only recommend it if I suffered from a particular condition which required that I drink milk. But the warder in charge of our section, who we used to call Oom Sy, told the doctor to give me the milk, and the same doctor who had earlier refused now prescribed milk for me. I used to keep the milk in my cell to make sour milk.
>
> I experienced the same thing with rations. We would be locked up early, at about 3 in the afternoon, until 8 the next morning. This was a long time to go without food. I knew the doctor would refuse to give me double rations but again Oom Sy told him I needed double rations.
>
> Later, when I was studying, it would be so cold, so I would order hot water. I would keep it in bed to warm the

bed and wash myself in the morning with it.

All of these privileges could, of course, be rescinded at the whim of the prison authorities.

> We would inevitably find something to fight about, and they would take all those privileges away. My sour milk, double rations, warm water would all be gone. A week later, we would sort out the issues and it would all be back again.

While Bulelani was in prison, the Law Society of South Africa applied for him to be struck off the roll as an attorney as a result of his conviction. Although he had assumed that he would never be allowed to practise again, he decided to oppose the application on principle.

The case was argued on his behalf by Sydney Kentridge, and the application was eventually dismissed. Bulelani later received a letter from Selby Baqwa, who explained what had happened in court. Judge Ramon Leon felt that there was no merit in the application and dismissed it. His fellow judge however, disagreed and because of the stalemate the matter had to go to a full bench. Selby also told Bulelani that nearly every black lawyer in Durban had attended the hearing, making it clear to the Law Society that they did not represent the interests of the legal profession.

In January 1985, Priscilla Jana, who had represented many prisoners, including Nelson Mandela, arrived to consult with inmates following President PW Botha's conditional offer to release political prisoners if they rejected violence. She told them the leadership had rejected the offer. Bulelani and his colleagues also rejected the offer and opted to stay in prison rather than compromise their principles.

THE STING IN THE TALE: BULELANI NGCUKA

Two weeks later Botha released a statement to say that his government would hold talks with the ANC if they renounced violence.

Both Mandela and the ANC in exile responded by demanding the unconditional release of prisoners, the unbanning of organisations, free political activity and that Botha's government commit itself to ending apartheid.

◻

At the end of May 1985, Bulelani and Mbulelo were suddenly transferred to Pretoria Central prison. They were not given the chance to say goodbye to anyone, just told to pack their bags and immediately put on a truck for Pretoria.

> It was a shock, very painful, leaving like that without being able to say goodbye. Some of those guys I have not seen since I left.

In mid-July 1985, Bulelani and Mbulelo were moved to Point Prison in Durban to prepare for their release.

Bulelani had much to look forward to, not least getting married, practising law again and being part of the political environment, which had taken new shape with the formation of structures like the UDF, a body that incorporated many anti-apartheid organisations.

Victoria Mxenge was handling the arrangements for Bulelani's release. She visited him on Wednesday 31 July, with Phumzile posing as her legal clerk. It was Bulelani's first physical contact with Phumzile in four years.

Victoria told Bulelani that she needed a rest. 'Griffiths died on 19 November four years ago. You were arrested on the 30th.

I've been alone in the office since then. I'm waiting for your wedding next Thursday, then I'm going on a long holiday,' she said.

On Friday 2 August 1985 Bulelani was awake early, excited about his release the following day. A warder approached his cell and spoke to him through the window. 'Hey Ngcuka *lamfazi ebezo kubona ifile.*' (Hey Ngcuka, that woman who came to see you is dead.)

Bulelani's blood ran cold. Bulelani was still not allowed to receive newspapers, so the warden said he would go and fetch one for him. Bulelani wasn't sure whether the officer was talking about Phumzile or Victoria.

Victoria's picture was on the front page.

> Who would have done this? Why would they want her killed? I had no answers to these questions.
>
> That probably was the longest day of my life. There is a Xhosa term that describes how I felt, "*ngqondo ithatha ibekwa*', which translated literally means 'your brain is wandering about'.

Victoria had been murdered when she returned home after addressing the funeral of the 'Cradock Four', Matthew Goniwe, Fort Calata, Sparrow Mkonto and Sicelo Mhlauli, who had been abducted and murdered by the security police in June 1985.

Victoria had been killed in a similar savage manner to her husband, shot and hacked to death at her front door.

In 1987 a Durban magistrate refused a formal inquest into her killing and ruled that she had died of head injuries inflicted by persons unknown. Ten years later, in May 1997, the ANC told the TRC that they had identified one Marvin Sefako as being responsible for Victoria's murder. Sefako, who had been recruited by the security branch, had allegedly confessed

THE STING IN THE TALE: BULELANI NGCUKA

to the ANC that he had killed at least five people, including Victoria.⁶

❏

Bulelani was released at 7 am on 3 August 1985.

> I had spent three years and eight months locked up, thinking about what I would do the day I got out of prison. Never in my wildest imagination did I think I would go into a committee planning the funeral of one of the people I loved.
>
> I sat in the meeting still in a state of shock. I had no contribution to make. From there, we went to the mortuary to see uSisi [Victoria Mxenge] with GM's brother, Fumbatha. It was terrible.

Victoria's funeral took place on 11 August 1985 in Rayi outside King William's Town. It was attended by over 10 000 people.

Violence broke out when Ciskei soldiers drove into a group of mourners, and the angry crowd pulled a soldier from the van and killed him. His two colleagues managed to drive to safety.

Messages of support from Nelson Mandela and Oliver Tambo were read out but it was Steve Tshwete's speech that captured the mood of the moment. Tshwete, who had been released from Robben Island in 1978 after serving a 14-year sentence, was the regional president of the UDF at the time. 'Now we are going to fight,' he said. 'We are going to use everything we can lay our hands on, even if it is gunpowder. If we have to shoot to get our liberation, then we are going to shoot. If we have to liberate ourselves with the barrel of a gun, then this is the moment.'⁷

Other speakers at the funeral included leading figures in the anti-apartheid movement, such as Zac Yacoob, a lawyer and senior member of the Natal Indian Congress; Sister Bernard Ncube, president of the Federation of Transvaal Women; Helen Joseph, a former 1956 Treason triallist who had been under house arrest for years; and Father Smangaliso Mkhatshwa, secretary of the South African Catholic Bishops Conference. All made it clear that the apartheid regime was responsible for Victoria's death and that, in Tshwete's words, they were going to fight for their liberation using everything they could lay their hands on.

Victoria's death was a tipping point for the anger that had built up in many communities.

7.
Exile

'I was eager to get back into the struggle. I felt I had been deprived of participating and wanted to roll up my sleeves and get on with it.'

South Africa in 1985 was a very different place to the one Bulelani had been living in when he'd been sentenced three years earlier. The country was on fire. The UDF had been launched in 1983 and was now mobilising countrywide. Protest marches were the order of the day.

MK's operations had increased dramatically in the 1980s with attacks such as the bombing of Koeberg nuclear power station and the South African Defence Force (SADF) headquarters at Voortrekkerhoogte, and a car bomb outside the offices of the South African Air Force in Pretoria that killed 19 people. But reprisals followed these attacks, with cross-border raids by the SADF into neighbouring countries like Lesotho, Botswana and Swaziland.

In the Eastern Cape, two savage killings had taken place, increasing the level of anger and resistance. In March 1985, the so-called Uitenhage Massacre took place when apartheid police fired on a crowd attending a political funeral, killing 35 and injuring many more. And two months later, three activists from the Port Elizabeth Black Civic Organisation, who became known as the 'Pebco Three', had been abducted, tortured and systematically beaten to death by security police.

It was into this highly charged and violent atmosphere that Bulelani was released.

> The country was so different. People had been mobilised like never before. The level of political consciousness was so high. As prisoners we thought we knew so much, and then when you come out you find that you have been left behind. That was an eye-opener for us.

Although Bulelani and Phumzile had planned to get married as soon as he left prison, they felt that it would be inappropriate to proceed so soon after Victoria's funeral.

> But we were told a wedding never gets postponed – it must go on. But we would have to trim it down, which suited us because we had never wanted a lavish affair.

Victoria was meant to facilitate the couple's wedding. Instead, as Phumzile recalls, 'Here we were after Bulelani's release, organising a wedding and a funeral. It was crazy.'[1]

So, in the midst of this personal pain, and the rising militancy and violence in the country, Bulelani and Phumzile were married in Durban on Thursday 15 August 1985.

> The wedding took place in Clermont, in Phumzile's church. It all went well until, as we were leaving, police arrived and threw teargas into the hall. So instead of the usual confetti, I had teargas at my wedding, thanks to the security police.

After the ceremony, Phumzile and Bulelani drove straight through to Middledrift the following day, for more wedding celebrations and rituals at Bulelani's home.

> It is traditional that on the first night, *makoti* [the new bride] must wake up very early and make coffee for the relatives. But we didn't. We overslept. We were too tired. When Phumzile eventually woke up, my mother had already made coffee for everybody.
>
> So the following day Phumzile woke up at 3 am and was busy in the kitchen. My mother heard her and asked her what she was doing so early in the morning. She said she was making coffee. My mother laughed and told her to go back to sleep. That has become a joke we tell often in our family.

The next issue was where the newly married couple were to live. By then Phumzile was resident in Geneva, Switzerland, where she had taken up a job as youth coordinator with the Young Women's Christian Association.

> I wanted to remain in Durban. I felt I owed it to GM and uSisi to take over the practice and ensure their legacy lived on. But my family would have none of it.

So it was agreed that Bulelani would move to Geneva. After the wedding, Phumzile left first, but had to travel to New Zealand first, which meant that Bulelani would be travelling separately. It was the first time he was leaving South Africa and he had his doubts about whether he would be allowed to leave the country, despite the fact that he had a valid passport.

Bulelani and Phumzile had initially planned to get married in December 1981 and honeymoon in Mauritius, so he had applied for a passport through Ms Nonceba Tutu, a travel agent, before he went to prison. By the time she received it, Bulelani was in prison so she passed it on to Phumzile for safekeeping. This was the 'much discussed' passport that became the subject of such controversy many years later, at the Hefer Commission, when Bulelani faced false accusations of being an apartheid spy and it was alleged that intelligence agents had arranged for Bulelani to get the passport. Ms Tutu gave evidence to the commission confirming that she had applied for the passport.

Bulelani left South Africa in September 1985 to join his new wife. It was only once the plane was in the air, he said, that he felt he could breathe and knew that he had made it out of the country safely.

❏

Bulelani flew first to London. Among the people he met there was Horst Kleinschmidt, head of the International Defence and Aid Fund (IDAF), which was responsible for, among other things, providing legal assistance to anti-apartheid activists in South Africa. IDAF, which was established in 1956, smuggled over £100 million into South Africa for the defence of thousands of political activists and to provide aid for their families while they were in prison. Horst became a close friend, and Bulelani stayed with him whenever he visited London.[2]

Horst introduced Bulelani to Aziz Pahad, a prominent ANC member in London, who in turn arranged for him to meet ANC leaders like secretary-general Alfred Nzo and Joe Slovo, then chief of staff of MK and general secretary of the South African Communist Party, who had just been elected to the national executive committee (NEC) of the ANC, the first white person to hold such a position.

> Joe asked me how long I thought the regime would last.
> 'Five years,' I told him.
> Joe laughed and told me that in 1948, when the National

Party was returned to power, he was at the city hall in Johannesburg watching the results come in, and he said to his comrades that the Nats would not last more than five years. 'I've been saying "five years" ever since,' he said.

I thought I was being rebuked but then he laughed and said he agreed with me, and this time, he said, 'I think it's really five years.'

Alfred Nzo asked Bulelani what his plans were in exile. He told Nzo that his wife, Phumzile, had applied for internships for him with the International Commission of Jurists and the International Labour Organization (ILO). Nzo immediately said they had someone at the ILO who could help and called Baldwin Sjollema.

The ANC did not have an office in Geneva, but it was a strategic location for the ANC in view of the many South Africans who travelled to Geneva to the ILO and other organisations, so it was agreed that Bulelani would work with Aziz and liaise with him.

Horst had also introduced Bulelani to Zola Skweyiya and he describes a meeting with Zola in a London pub.

> We went to a pub and were joined by many other South African exiles. We were sitting and enjoying a drink. It was a great reunion. I was one of the youngest and most junior.
>
> Suddenly I heard Zola shout, '*Ndakubetha kwedini!*' ['I will beat you, young man!'] He was arguing with someone. I became afraid. This was my first impression of him. He could be fierce.
>
> We exchanged numbers and he said he wanted us to work together. He said I should introduce him to South African lawyers, that there were MK guys who were being

sentenced without legal representation. Money is not the issue, he said; we need to reach out to lawyers and talk to them.

We agreed to work together and organised a meeting with the assistance of the Lutheran World Federation. The group of lawyers we met included Bernard Ngoepe, Pius Langa, Linda Zama and Dumisani Tabata. They later came to Geneva and met with Zola.

After this, Zola became a constant feature in my life.

❏

The newly married couple got a third wedding celebration on their arrival in Geneva, organised by the Young Women's Christian Association, after which they went to Venice for a short honeymoon. They also had the opportunity to visit friends in Germany, Italy and France.

In Geneva, Phumzile and Bulelani were part of a small, close-knit community of exiles from Southern Africa that included Brigalia Bam, Sibusiso Bengu (who went on to become minister of education in Mandela's cabinet), Dr Ishmael Noko from Zimbabwe, Tunkuru Huaraka from Namibia, Nozipho Grootboom from South Africa and Kabelo Makgetha from Lesotho.

> SisHlophe [Brigalia Bam] had been away from home for some time and was staying alone. We became her children. This brought us very close, and we are still very close and regard her as our mother today.

But there were many adjustments to be made. Not only was Bulelani living in a foreign country, he also had to get used to being a free man, and a husband.

THE STING IN THE TALE: BULELANI NGCUKA

Phumzile and I had been apart for a long time and had to learn to live with one another. I also had to begin to get used to the idea that I was no longer a prisoner. In prison, you're rationed. You get one toilet roll a week, one tube of toothpaste a month.

If you leave your toothpaste in one place, you will find it where you left it; if you leave your comb there, you will find it there. Now, I leave the toothpaste here. I look for it. It's not there. It's in the kitchen. I look for the comb. I can't find it. It's in her bag.

These are small things but are very important. For all these years my life had been orderly. Life is highly regimented [in prison]. The first thing you do when you wake up in the morning is to make your bed. Now, people wake up and watch TV before they make their bed.

There were also cultural adjustments to be made. In South Africa we greet one another, whether you know the other person or not. I would say hello to people in the street in Geneva and they would just walk past me. 'Don't worry,' Phumzile said, 'when I first arrived, I was like you too, until I realised that people don't greet here.'

I found it very strange that you can just walk past people without even acknowledging that they exist. Six months down the line, I was just like them.

On one occasion, Phumzile's work colleagues invited us to lunch. Everyone was busy ordering. I was worried about how I was going to pay so I ordered a salad. In South Africa I would have had to pay as the only man present. They were ordering wine and I was drinking water. I didn't enjoy the lunch at all. But before I could ask for the bill, they asked for the bill and were arranging for payment.

> I felt silly then and wished I had ordered something more substantial.
>
> I joined a gym in Geneva, and I thought I was very fit coming out of prison. There was a female instructor there and I thought I would easily cope with whatever she threw at me. I could barely walk afterwards. Hey man, I thought, these women are something else. They pay the bills, *and* they are fitter than I am!

While he was getting used to living in a strange country, starting a new job and married life, Bulelani was also itching to become involved in what was happening at home. If only I had known, he says, all I had to do was wait.

> Geneva was like a train station for South Africans. I was soon to become so busy, working with the team and running the affairs of the ANC without an office or a title.

Bulelani worked with Baldwin Sjollema and Bill Ratteree at the ILO's Division of Equality of Rights, a unit that coordinated assistance to liberation movements and trade unions in South Africa.

Baldwin had worked previously at the World Council of Churches for 11 years and had spearheaded its Programme to Combat Racism. Both Baldwin and Bill, Bulelani says, gave him the space he needed, and this opened doors for him to work directly with the ANC and unions in South Africa. A range of workshops and training sessions were organised, and travel was arranged for people to the ILO in Geneva.

Much of their work focused on communication. One of the local radio stations was popular with the diplomatic community in Geneva and focused largely on South Africa. It was, however, not very favourable towards the ANC and leant towards the Inkatha Freedom Party (IFP). Buthelezi was popularly portrayed as the leader of nine million Zulus, while the ANC was supposedly an organisation of Xhosas, who were fewer in numbers than the Zulus.

On one occasion, Bulelani and his team arranged for Bishop Tutu to be interviewed. The presenter asked him what 'tribe' he belonged to. 'Well, my mother is Sotho and my father is Xhosa, so therefore I am Venda!' he said. The presenter stated that it was the first time she had met a person who supported sanctions who was not Xhosa!

On another occasion, an interview was arranged for Johnny Makathini, the ANC's representative at the UN. The presenter challenged him about Senator Edward Kennedy's 1985 visit to South Africa, to show his anti-apartheid support. The interviewer said that even Azapo had opposed the visit and that Kennedy had used 'poor blacks' to advance his own political career in the USA.

Johnny was not fazed and put her in her place, Bulelani says, telling her that she was being naïve and that there was nothing wrong with Kennedy advancing his own political interests as long as these coincided with the ANC's interests.

> This is politics, he told her. 'Everyone has an agenda. He's bringing attention to the situation in South Africa and that's what's important. When agendas coincide, people work together. You assume he's using us, but we are advancing our cause too.'

In 1986 Baldwin succeeded in arranging for ANC president OR Tambo to address the ILO Conference as a keynote speaker.[3]

EXILE

❏

Phumzile and Bulelani's son, Luyolo, was born in Geneva on 13 December 1986.

> According to our culture, a man is not supposed to go anywhere near the room where the child is born. However, when we arrived at the hospital, the doctor said she only wanted the husband present. Sis'Hlophe [Brigalia Bam] objected and said she was there as Phumzile's mother. I also said that she must go, not me. But the doctor would have none of it. So I was present when my son was born. And it was a wonderful thing.
>
> Luyolo was born on a Saturday. First thing on Monday morning, we got a note from Home Affairs in Switzerland, instructing us to register him at the South Africa embassy because [according to the Swiss laws at the time] he could not become a Swiss citizen.
>
> I was impressed by the efficiency of the system because it meant that people were working on a Sunday for the letter to be delivered on Monday morning. But it also seemed rude and presumptuous. None of us had any desire to become Swiss citizens. We were all proudly South African.

❏

Bulelani recalls the first and only time he returned to South Africa during his time in exile. Early in 1989 he had been contacted by his mother. She was distraught and told him his brother Vuyani and sister Phumla had both been detained. He decided that it was worth the risk and flew back to South Africa to see what he could do to help. He was met at the airport by Dumisani Tabata who, in conversation, reminded him of the time Griffiths Mxenge subpoenaed the detained Peter Jones during the Bethal trial. Bulelani did the same thing. He subpoenaed Vuyani to testify in his sister's trial. Phumla had been charged with possession of banned literature. The apartheid police responded as they did in the Peter Jones case and brought Vuyani to court where he was released. Phumla received a six-month suspended sentence.

> I arrived in South Africa on a Monday and by Friday had succeeded in getting my brother and sister released. Mission accomplished. I was very happy and was able to return to Geneva.

In June 1987 Bulelani was invited to Kingston, Jamaica, to address an anti-apartheid meeting on the occasion of the 32nd anniversary of the adoption of the Freedom Charter. His ticket was sponsored, and he flew to Jamaica via London.

He was in business class, working on his speech, when he noticed a lot of other Africans there too, all having a very jolly time, commandeering the air stewardess's drinks trolley and serving themselves. Bulelani asked her who they were, and she told him they were top soccer players from the UK. One of them was the captain of Liverpool, John Barnes. The players soon called Bulelani over to join them.

> After that I gave up on my speech. Fortunately, I still had time after I arrived in Jamaica.

This was also the first time he met ANC president OR Tambo, who was visiting Jamaica as a guest of Michael Manley's People's National Party, which was in opposition at the time. They had lost to the Jamaica Labour Party in 1980 and again in 1983.

Bulelani asked Manley what had gone wrong. Two things stayed in his mind from his response.

> 'We made a mistake,' Manley said. 'We weren't monitoring the pulse of the nation. We were talking to ourselves, and we believed what we were telling ourselves.
>
> 'Secondly, never make the mistake of underestimating your opposition and the tactics they are prepared to resort to.'
>
> A Russian ship had docked in Kingston harbour shortly before the elections and rumours soon spread that the ship had arrived to take Jamaicans to Russia as slaves. Manley said they didn't think for one minute anyone would believe such nonsense, but Jamaicans are descendants of slaves and the propaganda worked against Manley's party, which was seen as an ally of the Russians.

In September 1987 the International Conference on Children, Repression and the Law in Apartheid South Africa was held in Harare, Zimbabwe. The conference was co-sponsored by Oliver Tambo and Bishop Trevor Huddleston. Bulelani had been introduced to people like Zola Skweyiya, Kader Asmal [founder of the Irish Anti-apartheid Movement] and Abdul Minty [Honorary Secretary of the British Anti-apartheid Movement] and soon found himself co-opted onto the steering committee of the conference. It was attended by over 150 anti-apartheid groups from all over the world, as well as leading anti-apartheid figures such as Lisbet Palme, chair of the United Nations Children's Fund and widow of Swedish prime minister Olaf Palme, who'd been assassinated the previous year; Glenys Kinnock, British politician and wife of Labour Party leader Neil Kinnock; and Angela Davis,

American political activist and member of the Communist Party of the USA.

More importantly, from an internal perspective, the event was one of the biggest platforms for activists from inside South Africa to meet and engage with ANC leadership in exile.

There was some 'talk about talks' between the ANC and the apartheid government at the time, and Tambo used the occasion to dismiss the rumours that the ANC was engaged in secret talks: he said that when the ANC felt the time had come to talk, it would do so openly. He made it clear that the basis for negotiations between the ANC and the apartheid government could not exist as long as obstacles to negotiations such as the release of political prisoners and executions remained unresolved.

Also in 1987, the president of the UDF, Archie Gumede, travelled to Geneva to address the Human Rights Commission of the United Nations. By this time, the situation in South Africa was close to all-out war, with the apartheid state locked into a seemingly unwinnable cycle of resistance, reaction and intensified resistance. The country had been in a state of emergency since 1985, and by June 1987 nearly 30 000 people had been detained.

Gumede's visit was facilitated by the ANC. He arrived unannounced in Geneva. He was accompanied by Moss Ngoasheng, who went on to become President Thabo Mbeki's economic advisor. Gumede had travelled on a Transkei passport to avoid the apartheid authorities.

> People didn't know he was there. When he arrived, he sat quietly at the back and waited his turn to speak.
>
> When Archie stood up at the podium and said, 'I am Archie Gumede, the president of the UDF,' the room went silent. You could have heard a pin drop. There was usually a lot of activity in the room, even when people

were speaking – people would be walking around, passing messages, chatting and so on – but Archie had their full attention.

After his address he was surrounded by government ministers, officials and the media, all wanting to meet with him. We knew we had achieved something. Here was the voice of the people speaking directly from inside the country.

After the UN address, Gumede toured the Scandinavian countries, adding considerable impetus to the campaign for sanctions against the South African government. Bulelani recalls that Gumede was treated with real respect during these visits, with the same deference any senior government official would receive.

❏

In December 1987 Bulelani and Phumzile decided it was time to return home. They were becoming deeply involved in ANC activities, and if they stayed any longer, they reasoned, they would not be allowed to return to South Africa. They were also keen to reinsert themselves in the 'theatre of operations'.

However, Bulelani realised he first had to consult ANC leaders and comrades. He spoke to Zola Skweyiya, who did not approve of their plans; he felt it was too risky. Zola told Bulelani to talk to Thabo Mbeki, who was at the time ANC president Oliver Tambo's political secretary and confidant.

> Thabo supported my decision but told me I should not return if I 'just wanted to throw stones at the police', as he put it. He said I should work with an organisation called Post-Apartheid South Africa that the movement had set

THE STING IN THE TALE: BULELANI NGCUKA

up. It was time to think beyond apartheid, he said, and to start preparing to govern South Africa.

He was not saying I should not be involved in the day-to-day struggles inside the country but that it was important to start focusing on how we would run the country.

8.
Homecoming

*'These were great days. You could feel that
South Africa was another country. We were preparing
to move forward.'*

Bulelani's family had prevailed on him not to return to Durban because of the possible risks. Bulelani says Griffiths' father, Johnson, also told him to avoid Durban 'because I don't want to bury another child'. Bulelani's elder brother, Vuyani, had himself moved to Cape Town to escape continual harassment by the security police in the Eastern Cape, and he told Bulelani it would be best for them to join him in Cape Town. So they lived with Vuyani for a short time, before moving into their own rented accommodation in Malunga Park, Gugulethu.

Only one African law firm existed in the Western Cape in December 1987 when Bulelani returned to South Africa: NJ Yekiso and Associates. Bulelani wasted no time in contacting James Yekiso, and soon he was on board as a fifth partner in the firm. By June 1989 he had established his own practice with Saki Matana, Ngcuka & Matana.

Bulelani was a busy lawyer in a thriving practice but his biggest challenge was his availability: politics was the order of the day. The late 1980s were a turbulent time in South Africa and Bulelani soon found himself in the cut and thrust. The UDF, Cosatu and the Mass Democratic Movement were all piling pressure on the government, and the apartheid state was collapsing.

This did not mean, however, that the liberation movement was not taking strain. Detentions and bannings were common, and hundreds of activists lived life on the run. Two major 'treason trials' – the Pietermaritzburg Treason Trial in 1985–1986, and the Delmas Treason Trial of 1985–1988 – took UDF leadership out of circulation for years. Up to 25 000 people were detained when the second state of emergency was imposed in June 1986, and by August that year, 50 national and regional UDF leaders had been arrested.[1]

One of the few to escape detention at the time was Dullah Omar, then chair of the UDF in the Western Cape, one of the top legal minds in the country and an important political figure. Dullah 'really threw me in at the deep end', Bulelani says. He was soon on the road, travelling the province, addressing meetings, and becoming more and more politically active. He was elected chair of the UDF in the Western Cape when the organisation held its regional conference at the end of 1988.

In 1989 the movement began to regroup and revive its structures, and the Defiance Campaign was launched. This campaign was similar to the Defiance Campaign of the 1950s, aimed at disobeying apartheid laws that demanded segregation of races. There were marches, protests, pickets and other organised efforts to defy laws that required separate facilities for the different races – hospitals, beaches, restaurants and workplace facilities such as canteens, kitchens, changerooms and lavatories.

The Defiance Campaign re-energised the mass democratic struggle inside the country. People were excited. There was a sense of real movement.

HOMECOMING

One of the issues Bulelani was embroiled in was the conflict between migrant workers and more permanent residents of the KTC informal settlement near Crossroads. Those referred to in isiXhosa as *amagoduka* (those who go home) didn't belong to any civic, youth or women's structures, and wanted their own more traditional structures and leadership, and so had set up their own body, the Masincedane Committee.

The conflict in KTC and Crossroads centred around housing and who had the right to remain in the area, with the apartheid government announcing that new arrivals from the so-called independent homelands would have to leave.

Violence had broken out in 1986 when the 'witdoeke' ('white headscarves', so named because of the white head scarves they wore), a vigilante group sponsored by the apartheid government, went on the rampage, and violence flared up again now. In February 1988 over 3 000 homes were burned and people were killed – stoned, hacked and shot. The Masincedane were accused by some of being the new witdoeke. But it was more complex than that.

KTC residents who had resisted forced removals and faced the witdoeke in 1986 had returned two years later and regrouped under the leadership of the Masincedane Committee. They had become increasingly disillusioned by the lack of concern for the issues and struggles affecting informal settlements in the black townships, and the tension had increased when the Western Cape Civic Association bypassed the Masincedane Committee and set up a steering committee in KTC in late 1987. Violence followed and in January 1988 Stormont Madubela, a key leader of the Masincedane Committee, was murdered.[2]

THE STING IN THE TALE: BULELANI NGCUKA

A mediation committee was set up which included Ngconde Balfour, representing Tutu and the Anglican church; Lumko Huna, an ex-Robben Islander from the Roman Catholic Church; Mzwandile Msoki from the South African Council of Churches; and Bulelani's brother, Vuyani, from the Western Province Council of Churches.

> I don't know how but I was dragged in and soon found myself in the middle of it. It became clear to me that we had a problem. This was not just residents fighting the government. Everyone claimed to be ANC. So I spoke to Chris [Hani]. I found out that many of our MK cadres were sheltering in the squatter camps. He said we should bring the leadership of both groups to Lusaka.
>
> We discussed it with Dullah and the mediation committee, and they agreed it was a good idea. However, it was important that neither side should know that the other group was coming.
>
> I spoke to Sibusiso Bengu [by then secretary for research and social action for the Lutheran World Foundation], and the Lutheran Church invited them to a workshop in Lusaka in March. We sent their names to Sibusiso, who sent them on to Josiah Jele [MK veteran and secretary of ANC's political military council in exile] in Lusaka.
>
> We received their letters of invitation and air tickets. They were all very excited. The first group, representing the migrant workers, left, and were followed by the civic group, representing more permanent residents of KTC. OR [Tambo] devoted the whole week to talking to them. They came back united and remain friends to this day.
>
> That was the end of 'black-on-black' violence in that

area. The intervention by OR and Jele was simple but profound. They had convinced both groups to see one another as comrades, not enemies.

Zola was not aware of my involvement. I didn't tell him, but he found out. He was very angry. He said he had told me to stay far away from anything to do with the ANC or MK, and that if I wasn't careful, I would find myself arrested.

Mandela celebrated his 70th birthday in June 1988, during his 25th year in prison. As part of the celebrations, a 'Free Mandela' concert took place at Wembley stadium in London and was broadcast to 67 countries and an audience of 600 million. The line-up included artists like Peter Gabriel, Sting, Tracy Chapman, Whitney Houston and Stevie Wonder.

Inside South Africa, the UDF in the Western Cape decided to organise its own Free Mandela concert in Cape Town and set up an organising committee. Bulelani was the chair of the birthday celebration committee.

> We were busy organising and mobilising from many different formations. Two weeks before the concert, I was detained. A number of us were detained at that time.
>
> I was interrogated. The security police were very interested in the concert we were organising. They wanted to know who had issued the instructions in Lusaka.
>
> 'But we're adults,' I explained. 'We can take a decision to organise a concert on our own. We don't need instructions from anyone.'
>
> I spent a month in detention under the state of emergency before being released. When I was released, I heard from Zola, who said, 'I told you so.'

THE STING IN THE TALE: BULELANI NGCUKA

❏

Before the end of 1988 Bulelani joined the National Association of Democratic Lawyers (Nadel), one of a number of organisations campaigning against the death penalty at the time. He was asked to take the lead on behalf of Nadel.

Between 1980 and 1989 over a thousand people were executed by the apartheid regime, the highest number, 164, in 1987 alone. Political activists, including MK cadres, were among those executed.

Bulelani recalls the case of a trade unionist sentenced to death after taking part in a strike. His sentence was overturned on appeal and he was released the week before a major rally organised by Nadel. He was an important speaker at the rally. He had been on death row for a year and told of his experiences hearing people being taken to the gallows week after week.

Bulelani recalls that Pius Langa, who was president of Nadel at the time, spoke out against the execution of Clement Payi and Lucky Xulu, two MK cadres who were executed in September 1986 for the murder of his younger brother Ben Langa. Payi and Xulu had been misled by their commander, who'd told them that Ben was an informer for the apartheid police. The commander himself later confessed to being an apartheid spy. President Mbeki told the TRC in 2000 that in executing Payi and Xulu, the apartheid state had killed three people without firing a single shot.[3]

Repression was at its height in the late 1980's and Bulelani experienced this first hand. During the early hours one morning in early 1989, an apartheid police task force raided his home. He was held at gunpoint and told to place both hands against the wall as security police searched the house. The police were looking for Ngconde Balfour but had come to the wrong place.

Bulelani's neighbours noticed what was going on and phoned Vuyani, Bulelani's brother, and Balfour. With this early warning, Balfour managed to leave his house and took two MK cadres he was hiding to the residence of the Australian High Commission in Cape Town, where they stayed for two weeks. Balfour was detained so Bulelani took care of the two men, eventually helping them to leave the country.[4]

The last execution in South Africa took place on 4 November 1989, when Solomon Ngobeni was hanged. He had been convicted of shooting and killing a truck driver during a robbery.

In February 1990 FW de Klerk announced a moratorium on executions pending new legislation on the death sentence. Capital punishment was finally abolished in a unanimous decision by the Constitutional Court in July 1995.

❏

The international anti-apartheid sports boycott was an important weapon in the struggle against apartheid.

In August 1989 the names of 16 players who were going to take part in a rebel cricket tour were announced during the fourth Test of the Ashes series in England, in defiance of the boycott. The team would be led by Mike Gatting and sponsored by First National Bank (FNB), which had also supported an international 'rebel' rugby tour that year to participate in the centenary celebrations of the South African Rugby Board.

The UDF was having none of this and organised a protest. It was due to start with a rally at the University of Cape Town and move to a protest inside the premises of the main FNB branch in Adderley Street in Cape Town. The police, however, banned the rally at UCT.

THE STING IN THE TALE: BULELANI NGCUKA

This did not deter the protestors, who moved to a hall in Athlone.

> When I arrived in Athlone, the hall was packed. The police were also there and told the people they had two minutes to disperse.
>
> I asked the police to give me time to speak to them. We didn't want any violence. They said I had one minute.
>
> I took the mic and said, 'Comrades, when we started this campaign, we said it would be non-violent. We said if there is to be any violence, it will come from their side. So I want you to leave. I don't want you to be hurt. You're not hooligans. We must behave. We must move peacefully out of this hall because you know what we're going to do tomorrow. We must have another chance to come back at them.'
>
> At this point the policeman interrupted me and said, '*Maak klaar*' [Finish up].
>
> Of course, the youth were angry and wanted to confront the police but there were elderly comrades there. The crowd left peacefully.
>
> The next day, on Saturday, we were supposed to go into the FNB branch in Adderley Street. We had asked people to go in in numbers, and withdraw and deposit money. In his excitement, one comrade unfurled a UDF banner inside the bank while comrades were still gathering, and [the bank employees] quickly closed the doors and kept them closed the whole day. That was early in the day, before we could get there.

Willie Hofmeyr, a senior UDF leader, was detained on the same day, Bulelani says, and the UDF leadership knew another crackdown was coming and decided they needed to go underground.

They didn't move fast enough.

On the Sunday, the day after the failed FNB protest, Bulelani decided to go home to pack a few things.

> I was so tired. I made the mistake of falling asleep. I woke up at 5 the next morning. At 6 the security police arrived, and I was detained. I heard later that Trevor [Manuel, another senior UDF leader] was picked up that same morning.

Bulelani was taken to Fish Hoek police station, but members of the Black Sash were protesting outside and the station commander objected to this disturbance in his peaceful white suburb. He was moved to Newlands police station. After a few days he was moved again, this time to Grootvlei prison in Bloemfontein, where he found Trevor Manuel.

Bulelani and his colleagues had decided that in the event of their detention they would immediately embark on a hunger strike. This was Bulelani's third hunger strike in prison: the first followed Neil Aggett's death and the second took place in Victor Verster. The first three days are tough, he says, philosophically, but after that the body adjusts.

> We drank a lot of water with a little bit of salt in it. We were told it was important for our kidneys.

They called off the hunger strike on the 15th day when Bulelani received a visit from his wife and son, and Dullah Omar, who informed him that the leadership had said they should stop the hunger strike.

He was released on Friday 15 September 1989.

THE STING IN THE TALE: BULELANI NGCUKA

They told me they had no transport and asked if I would wait till Monday. I said no, they should open the doors immediately and let me go. They asked if I had any money and I said no, they should just release me, and I would make my own way.

As luck would have it, as I was walking out of prison, I bumped into Bonile Sandi, a lawyer from East London who was visiting his clients there. I waited for him, and we went to the airport together and he bought me a ticket to Cape Town.

Like many others, Bulelani was immediately issued with a harsh banning order. He was restricted to Gugulethu, and had to remain indoors overnight during the week and for the entire weekends. He was allowed only two visitors at a time, apart from the members of his immediate family who lived with him.

He decided to defy his banning order.

The Defiance Campaign, meanwhile, had continued unabated, with Cape Town the scene of extraordinary protests in August 1989, when Archbishop Desmond Tutu led thousands onto beaches reserved for whites. Police had gone to extreme efforts to try and contain the protest, cordoning off a five-kilometre stretch of the Strand with barbed wire and posting notices that read 'Danger, no entry, South African Police dog training' over the 'Whites only' signs.

On 2 September 1989 police used water cannons loaded with purple dye on thousands of protestors in central Cape Town. The purpose was to stain protestors for later identification and arrest, but things took a dramatic turn when one of the protestors got on top of the police vehicle and redirected the water cannon towards the local headquarters of the National Party (NP). Graffiti went up the next day saying, 'The purple shall govern.'

These protests took place a few days before the ill-fated general elections for a tricameral parliament on 6 September 1989 in which whites, so-called coloureds and Indians were expected to vote for representatives in separate houses of parliament, while the true power, of course, remained with the white parliament.

The elections did nothing to quell the protests, and resistance only grew. On 13 September 1989 there was a march of 20 000 people in central Cape Town, again led by Archbishop Tutu, and also Reverend Allan Boesak and Reverend Frank Chikane, and joined by the mayor of Cape Town, Gordon Oliver, as they made their way from St George's Cathedral to the city hall.

On a single day, 14 October 1989, as many as 150 000 people took part in 17 marches.[5]

That month, political developments took a leap forward with the announcement by De Klerk that Walter Sisulu and his fellow Rivonia triallists were to be released.

> Farieda Omar [Dullah's wife] phoned me and asked to come and see me. She was very excited and said she had taken [Mandela's son] Makgatho to go and visit Madiba, but Madiba had told Makgatho he couldn't see him because he was going to see Walter. 'Walter and others are being released. Madiba said I mustn't tell anybody. Dullah is away and I don't know who to talk to, so I'm telling you.'
>
> It was 10 October 1989, which was a public holiday [Kruger Day as it was known at the time], and we called all the UDF executive members, and those of us who were available met immediately and we agreed to hold a rally that same evening at UWC [the University of the Western Cape]. Bishop Tutu and Allan Boesak would address the rally. If they were released, the rally would be a celebration. If they were not, it would become a protest and we

would renew the call for them to be released.

By then word had spread and I remember [Walter's son] Zwelakhe Sisulu called me. He said there had been so many false rumours about their release. He asked if this one was true. 'We don't want to disappoint Mama [Albertina Sisulu],' he said.

Then De Klerk made the announcement that evening, but he didn't say when they would be released. Walter was being released with seven comrades – Andrew Mlangeni, Ahmed Kathrada, Wilton Mkwayi, Raymond Mhlaba, Oscar Mpetha, Elias Motsoaledi and Jafta Masemola.

There was this sitcom on TV at the time called *Eight is Enough* and in his speech Boesak played on these words: 'Eight is not enough. For as long as Mandela is in prison, eight is not enough. For as long as there are shacks in Khayelitsha, eight is not enough. For as long as there is apartheid, eight is not enough. Eight is not enough! Eight is not enough! Eight is not enough!'

He had the whole hall chanting with him.

Walter and his comrades were released on Sunday morning, 15 October 1989, and a national reception was organised for them that evening in Soweto.

❏

Thousands of ANC supporters attended a rally to welcome the released ANC leaders in Soweto on 29 October 1989, at which a message from President Tambo was read out, in which he said the way forward to a genuine political settlement in the country was spelled out in the Harare Declaration.[6]

The Harare Declaration was a declaration adopted by the

Organisation of African Unity calling for an end to apartheid, and calling on the apartheid regime to create the conditions for negotiations, which included the unbanning of political organisations, the release of political prisoners, ending the state of emergency and ceasing all political executions. The document also laid out a set of principles to be the basis of a new constitutional order in the country, including that South Africa should become a united, democratic and non-racial state with equal citizenship and a bill of rights.

The Harare Declaration had been signed at a summit of the Organisation of African Unity in August 1989 in Harare (hence its name). A UDF delegation led by Cheryl Carolus, then the Western Cape UDF representative, was at the Harare meeting.

The ANC impressed on the delegation the importance of getting the Harare Declaration endorsed inside the country. The UN general assembly was going to meet and was expected to endorse the declaration, and it would not look good if the declaration was rejected by the anti-apartheid movement inside South Africa.

> Cheryl came back and briefed us. It was agreed we must get this endorsed inside the country, so we convened a conference at the University of the Witwatersrand.

This was the December 1989 Convention for a Democratic Future. Its 4 600 participants representing over 2 000 organisations agreed on a manifesto adopting the Harare Declaration and calling for a constituent assembly to be established on a non-racial basis representing all the people of South Africa to draw up a new constitution for the country.

With some modification, the Harare Declaration was adopted on 14 December 1989 by the general assembly of the United Nations.

PART III
A New South Africa

PART III

9.
A year of hope

*'1990 was an exceptional year in the
history of South Africa. There was an air of hope.
Everything was possible.'*

'Ah! Finally, we meet!'

These were Mandela's first words to Bulelani in Victor Verster prison in 1989, when he visited as part of a delegation from Nadel that included leading anti-apartheid lawyers like Pius Langa, Linda Zama and Azhar Cachalia. Mandela had been in Pollsmoor prison with Ntobeko Maqubela, and also knew of Bulelani through their mutual connection to Dullah Omar.

Mandela took the group through the discussions he had held with the apartheid government and the document he had drafted outlining the steps that had to be taken to get to negotiations. He had also sent the document to the ANC NEC in Lusaka.

> We were overawed. Madiba was now on his own in Victor Verster prison and there had been rumours. People were concerned about his isolation. We were not clear what was being discussed with the regime and what kind of pressure he was under. He laid to rest any anxieties we had.

Early the following year, in January 1990, Bulelani was part of the delegation that accompanied Walter Sisulu and his colleagues to meet the ANC in Lusaka. Others who were part of the delegation included trade unionists and political activists like Cyril Ramaphosa, Sydney Mufamadi and Chris Dlamini, and Alfred Metele, a UDF leader from the Eastern Cape.

> When we landed in Lusaka, it was as if a head of state was arriving. It was so exciting. You had to be there to understand the feeling. The comrades in Lusaka were so happy. They could see now that they were going home.
>
> There was a meeting of the NEC with everybody present. Thabo [Mbeki] spent a lot of time with the delegation and there were journalists from around the world. Rumours were flying that Mandela was going to be released and would be arriving in Lusaka. Of course, that didn't happen.
>
> A mass meeting was held so that the comrades in Lusaka could meet their leaders who had been released from prison. They were so excited, especially when they saw commanders like Raymond Mhlaba. The MK guys greeted him as commander.

Things were moving fast, and the delegation had hardly returned to South African when De Klerk announced on 2 February 1990 that Mandela would be released and political organisations unbanned.

> We had been expecting it but were not sure how to respond. We were holding a rally on the Grand Parade [in Cape Town] when we heard the announcement.
>
> The leadership immediately went to Dullah's chambers to discuss our response to De Klerk's statement. There was a lot of debate. Some argued that it was not enough.

Popo [Molefe] responded in his usual sober manner by saying we should not respond like schoolchildren. 'This is a very significant development,' he said, 'and we don't want to appear to have been caught off guard. Madiba's release is a result of our struggle.'

We studied [De Klerk's] speech and continued arguing for some time. In the end we came up with a lukewarm statement. Indeed, we were accused of being caught off guard.

The day before Mandela was released, Bulelani was addressing a meeting in Somerset West.

I received a note asking me to cut my speech short as I was needed urgently in Cape Town. I continued speaking, then a second note arrived telling me that I was needed at a meeting with De Klerk. So I ended the speech and went home to change into a suit.

While I was there Saki Macozoma arrived, accompanied by Allan Boesak and Jesse Jackson. Saki was a member of the Mandela Reception Committee, along with me. The people were so excited when they saw Jesse Jackson – they thought it was Madiba. Boesak had to calm them down, saying, 'This is not Mandela'.

I met Dullah, Trevor and Valli [Moosa] and we went to meet the commissioner of prisoners, General [Willie] Willemse. He told us that Madiba would be released at 3 the following day and that Madiba had said he should contact us. He then asked us what our plans were for Madiba's release.

The reality is we didn't know what our plans were, but we told him we preferred to discuss them with Madiba first.

THE STING IN THE TALE: BULELANI NGCUKA

General Willemse introduced us to a Brigadier Griebenouw and said he would liaise between us and the government on security matters. He said President De Klerk didn't want anything 'untoward' to happen to Madiba.

We had to go and see Madiba and begin to mobilise our structures. We had to organise the mother of all rallies on the Grand Parade and had less than 24 hours in which to do so.

We contacted our comrades in the UDF like Cheryl [Carolus], Willie [Hofmeyr], Johnny [de Lange] and others, and said they had to get to work. It must be clear that this is a people's leader.

From there, we rushed back to Victor Verster, accompanied by the media all the way. When we arrived, we found Madiba in his pyjamas. We laughed about this and then discussed arrangements for the following day. Valli and Saki were asked to draft the speech.

We went back to Cape Town to get a briefing on preparations for the rally. By this time the announcement was out, and the world was waiting for Madiba. We had to do a lot of interviews. I don't recall us sleeping that night.

There were two major problems we faced. The first was that we could not find Winnie [Mandela]. She was at a funeral in Soweto and could not be contacted. Also, all the flights to Cape Town were full. Everyone wanted to be in Cape Town for Madiba's release.

The second problem was: where was Madiba going to stay? Some comrades argued that he should stay in the township. I had reasonable accommodation in the township, and they said he should stay with me. I was clear this was not going to happen – I knew my house didn't have the space or security that Madiba needed. So I told the media that Mandela would stay at the official residence of Archbishop Tutu in [the Cape Town suburb of] Bishopscourt. The only problem was that I had not spoken to Tutu at the time I made the announcement; he was in Soweto on leave and the house in Bishopscourt was closed. When I told Madiba about this, he just smiled and said I was a silly boy!

I finally reached Tutu. He managed to get a lift with the BBC on a chartered plane and arrived in Cape Town. We had also managed to make contact with Winnie by this time.

On the morning of Madiba's release we were at the airport with cars we had organised with the Western Cape Traders Association. We had a fleet of Mercedes-Benzes and BMWs lined up at the airport.

Cyril [Ramaphosa, chair of the Mandela Reception Committee] flew in from Port Elizabeth with Oom Gov [Govan Mbeki]. When Cyril saw the cars, he objected and said we couldn't fetch a people's leader in such an elitist vehicle as a Mercedes. So we changed cars, and in no time we had Camrys and Jettas in their place.[1]

On the day of Mandela's release, there was some disagreement between the Mandela Reception Committee and Winnie Mandela about where his first public address should take place. Arrangements had already been made for him to speak at the Grand Parade in Cape Town, but when Winnie arrived, she told the committee that she had come to collect Mandela and would fly back to Johannesburg with him, where he would be released from his house in Soweto.[2]

We didn't know what to do. The Grand Parade was already packed.

We drove to Victor Verster and Winnie made her case to Madiba. He turned to me and asked what we should do.

I told him, 'Tata, the people are waiting; the whole world is waiting.'

He turned to Winnie with a smile and said, 'Zamo,[3] I think my son is right. Let's go to the parade.'

We were now more than an hour late. We got Madiba into the car and drove to Cape Town. People were lining the streets from Victor Verster all the way to Cape Town.

As we entered Cape Town, there was Willie standing in the middle of the road and he stopped the car. His T-shirt was torn and tattered. 'Don't go to the parade,' he told us. 'We have lost control.'

One of the traffic cops said he knew the back roads and would help us. We followed him and he led us straight into the crowd. There were people on top of the cars. The only way we survived is because people didn't know Madiba[4] – they didn't know that he was in that car.

We finally got out of the crowd and Madiba was cool. All he said when we got out was, 'Bulelani, you welcome me with a bang!'

We then drove to the house of Saleem Mowzer's parents [in Rondebosch East]. Saleem was a UDF activist. Tutu [then arrived and] was clear we had to return to the parade. 'You must bring him back. If Madiba doesn't come to the parade, Cape Town will go up in flames today.'

This time we made it safely to the parade with the help of the police, who cleared the way. The police were monitoring our movements and it was Brigadier Griebenouw who had informed Trevor when we lost our way earlier. We arrived at the city hall and as Madiba was about to make his speech, we realised he didn't have his glasses. He took Winnie's glasses. So when he made his first speech after his release, he was wearing Winnie's glasses. Winnie had not brought extra clothing with her and she had borrowed an outfit from Phumzile who was one of the marshals in the crowd.

A crowd of 60 000 was on the Grand Parade to listen to Mandela's speech.

'Friends, comrades and fellow South Africans, I greet you all in the name of peace, democracy and freedom for all. I stand here before you not as a prophet, but as a humble servant of you, the people. Your tireless and heroic sacrifices have made it possible for me to be here today. I therefore place the remaining years of my life in your hands ...'

He ended the speech by quoting his own words from the trial that sent him to jail for life in 1964 with seven other comrades: 'I have fought against white domination, and I have fought against black domination. I have cherished the ideal of a democratic and free society in which all persons live together in harmony and with equally opportunities. It is an ideal which I hope to live for and to achieve, but if needs be, it is an ideal for which I am prepared to die.'

After the rally, Madiba was taken to Tutu's residence in Bishopscourt while the UDF leadership met at Dullah's house in Rylands Estate to gather their thoughts. While the group was in discussion the phone rang and Dullah's young daughter answered it.

'Daddy, you have a phone call,' she said.

'Who is it?'

THE STING IN THE TALE: BULELANI NGCUKA

'I don't know. He calls himself Bush.'

It was indeed President George HW Bush of the United States, wishing to speak to Mandela and congratulate him on his release.[5]

The following morning the group went to meet Mandela at Bishopscourt. He was due to fly to Johannesburg for his welcome there.

> Madiba was clear that he was not going to fly to Johannesburg until we had put our house in order. He did not want to see the same kind of chaos in Joburg that he had seen the day before in Cape Town.
>
> It was agreed that Cyril and others would fly back to Johannesburg to supervise the arrangements, and a rally would be held at FNB stadium to welcome Madiba.
>
> He then held his first press conference, at Bishopscourt. Cheryl had organised it and had her hands full. There were journalists from everywhere. It was the biggest press conference I've seen in my lifetime.
>
> It was a wide-ranging interview. They asked him about everything and he was just exceptional. At the end of the interview he got a standing ovation, and to get that from journalists is really something.
>
> We were tense and worried before this about how he would cope with such a big press conference after so many years alone in prison. He surprised us all.
>
> We had hardly finished with the press conference, and our people and the police were calling from Johannesburg. They said the stadium was already filling up and that Madiba had to come to Joburg that day. The same thing was happening that we had experienced in Cape Town: if Madiba did not arrive in Joburg that day, there

was going to be serious trouble.

All the plans we were making had to be abandoned and we had to get Madiba on a flight that same day. Brigadier Griebenouw contacted us that evening. He was frustrated and worried and said the police could help. We obviously didn't trust them and wouldn't accept their help. However, they did clear the way when we took Madiba to the airport to fly to Johannesburg.

Mandela addressed the FNB rally outside Soweto on 13 February 1990. After this he left for Lusaka, Zambia, to meet the ANC leadership, and toured Tanzania, Zimbabwe and Ethiopia; and then he visited Oliver Tambo in Sweden, where he was receiving treatment for a stroke.

❑

Mandela and the Rivonia triallists were out but thousands of political prisoners were still behind bars. The release of political prisoners became a major stumbling block in the negotiations between the ANC and the apartheid government.

FW de Klerk had followed up Mandela's release by releasing 100 political prisoners whose offences were deemed to be non-violent in nature. This included 50 political prisoners from Robben Island. The remainder, it was argued, would be released in phases, depending on the severity of their offences.

In March 1990, over 300 political prisoners on Robben Island went on hunger strike. This included ANC and PAC political prisoners. They demanded the immediate and unconditional release of all political prisoners.

Bulelani was among a group of lawyers selected by the prisoners to negotiate with prison authorities for their release.

Others in the group were Dullah Omar, Arthur Chaskalson, George Bizos, Pius Langa, Willie Hofmeyr, Dikgang Moseneke and Willie Seriti.

The prisoners had set up a committee which included Naledi Tsiki, who had been sentenced to 14 years in the 1978 'Pretoria 12' trial with Tokyo Sexwale and others; and Vincent Diba, who'd got 15 years on charges of treason and terrorism in 1983.[6]

When the lawyers visited Robben Island for the first time, the prisoners had not eaten for a week. Tsiki pulled Bulelani aside for a confidential discussion and told him that morale was high. He was, however, concerned that the ANC leadership should be properly informed.

A list of demands was handed over to the lawyers, who were tasked with seeing the minister of justice, Kobie Coetsee, on the prisoners' behalf. Central to the demands was the immediate and unconditional release of all political prisoners.

> We put a call through to Kobie Coetsee and asked for a meeting. A message came back that he would only see Dullah. He refused to meet with us as a group.
>
> At first Dullah refused but we said he should go. Dullah reluctantly went to see Kobie Coetsee on his own. Kobie said the prisoners should not put pressure on him and that the release of political prisoners was subject to negotiations.
>
> Off the record, this is [I was told] what he said to Dullah: 'Look into my eyes. I will release them. But not now. And not under these conditions. Trust me. But don't repeat what I've just said to you.'
>
> Before we could return and report back to Robben Island, Tata Sisulu phoned me and told me, 'Go and tell

Naledi Tsiki that I'm not a sellout. Tell him that we are handling this matter. They must eat. The president is handling this matter. I left prison a few months ago and all of a sudden I have changed? Who do they think they are?'

Shortly thereafter, Dullah Omar received a phone call from Mandela, who was visiting Tanzania. Both he and Sisulu were angry and hurt. They felt they had been snubbed by the Robben Island prisoners and clearly wanted to assert their leadership, Bulelani says. 'Go and tell those prisoners there are no lawyers who are going to negotiate the release of political prisoners. That's a matter for the ANC to handle, not lawyers. Tell them they must go and eat. They will get instructions from us. We are handling the matter.'

Dullah was concerned, Bulelani says. He pleaded with Mandela and said a more conciliatory approach was needed, that the prisoners' spirit should not be broken. 'We must give them something. Isn't there something we can tell them?'

'Tell them they must eat.'

The group now had to work out how to persuade the hungry prisoners on Robben Island to end the hunger strike and convey the message that their release was being handled by the ANC, without being able to provide them with any concrete information on what progress was being made and when they could expect to be released.

When the lawyers returned to Robben Island, they agreed it was important to meet with each group of political prisoners separately.

> We met with ANC representatives from the prisoners' committee and told them, 'Comrades, we're sorry, but the leadership has told us to tell you that you must eat

and that your release is being handled by De Klerk and the ANC, not lawyers. We've been told not to interfere.'

They agreed immediately. They were disciplined ANC cadres. But we realised that we had to give them something if we were to persuade the rest of the prisoners and the multiparty committee to agree. Prison conditions can always be improved, so when we met with the committee, we discussed the matter. They agreed and gave us a list of conditions that should be improved.

We had an open line to General Willemse, the head of prisons. He immediately agreed to the demands. In our discussions it had also been suggested that we, the lawyers, should address the prisoners, since we stood a better chance of persuading them to end the strike. Again, Willemse agreed.

Arthur, Dullah and I addressed the ANC prisoners. I remember facing this big group of hungry comrades who had now not eaten for more than ten days. Four had already been admitted to hospital. Arthur was genuinely concerned about their health. They had been on hunger strike for so long.

The only thing I could think of saying was that it was a revolutionary thing to eat! I also told them that we would never abandon them. 'No-one gets left behind,' I said. 'Some of my own co-accused are still among you here.'

When I finished speaking, I was holding my breath. We were not sure if they would agree. Then they all shouted, '*Lelethu!* It's agreed!'

All 300 of them then began singing *Nkosi Sikeleli*. I was in tears. The hall reverberated with their singing.

'You see, comrades,' we told them. 'It's the first time

you are meeting here on Robben Island as ANC prisoners with ANC lawyers. This in itself is a sign that things are changing. Your release is only a matter of time.'

In fact, it would take more than a year to get them all out, and there would be further hunger strikes before all political prisoners were released.

❏

The release of Walter Sisulu and other Rivonia triallists had unexpected consequences for political trials, as Bulelani found in several of the cases he was defending at the time.

One, in 1990, involved a woman and her daughter who were charged with harbouring a 'terrorist'. This had followed a raid on their home by the security police in which an MK cadre had been killed.

When Bulelani arrived at court, he was ready to start what he thought would be a long process. The magistrate, however, called both him and the prosecutor aside and asked the prosecutor, 'Why are you proceeding with this case? Can't you see what's happening in the country? The leaders of these people are being released from prison. You want to send more people to prison? I can't send more people to jail. It's a waste of time and state resources to proceed. So what are you going to do?'

The prosecutor was taken aback and not sure how to respond. In the end, it was agreed that the case should be finalised that day. The magistrate used whatever evidence he had before him and found the accused guilty. He gave them a suspended sentence.

A similar thing happened in the case of Madoda Daki, also an MK cadre, who had been arrested in Khayelitsha in 1989. The case had not yet started and, with current developments in mind, Bulelani decided to postpone it to see what would happen. In the end the matter was abandoned.

Bulelani remembers how puzzled Madoda was when they applied for bail and the court agreed.

> He had come to court not believing for one minute that he was going home. There was no-one at the court from his family because they were not expecting him to be released. He was so excited when we were driving him home after the bail had been agreed to.

In another case Bulelani handled in 1992, David Dlali, an MK operative and veteran trade unionist, had been arrested with an arms cache. Dlali pleaded guilty but the judge gave him a suspended sentence after hearing evidence from people like Penuell Maduna and Chris Dlamini, president of the Food and Allied Workers Union.

> The judge was impressed with all of this evidence and said that the court had to send a message that it was contributing to a peaceful transition and could not sentence a person like David to jail. The state wanted to use the case to demonstrate the ANC's alleged duplicity – talking peace on the one hand and collecting arms on the other – but we were able to outwit them.

❑

It was April 1990 and excitement was high.

> The UDF were preparing to receive our leaders from exile. They were arriving on Friday 28 April 1990 and we

decided to organise a big rally in Mitchells Plain that weekend. I was going to chair the rally and Dullah was going to be one of the speakers.

But the Wednesday before this, we received a call from Lusaka that Dullah Omar, Arthur Chaskalson, George Bizos, Lewis Skweyiya, Pius Langa, Essa Moosa, Fink Haysom and I must go to Lusaka that weekend.

I was disappointed, of course. But duty called and in fact one of the most exciting periods of my life was about to begin.

In Lusaka we met Zola, Kader Asmal, Albie Sachs, Penuell, and Brigitte Mabandla. That's how we were drafted onto the ANC constitutional committee. We had to meet and plan. Negotiations were starting and we had to work on the new constitution.

We flew back on Sunday evening, and Dullah and I had to report back to the ANC leadership in Cape Town, which included the delegation from exile who were staying at the Lord Charles Hotel in Somerset West. When we arrived, the police stopped us – the funny thing was the security police who had arrested and detained me were now the ones who were protecting our leaders. They stopped us and said, 'Wait here, we want to know if your leaders want to meet you.'

It was amazing to see how things had changed in such a short space of time.

The visit to Lusaka in May 1990 marked the start of Bulelani's fulltime work on constitutional matters. The committee agreed that it needed a base, and the Community Law Centre at the University of the Western Cape presented the ideal opportunity. Dullah Omar had recently been appointed director of the centre, and Bulelani became his deputy.

> UWC was a very special place in 1990. Exceptional work was being done at the university. The future of South Africa was there.

The university had assumed new prominence under the leadership of Professor Jakes Gerwel and was known at the time as the intellectual centre of the left.

Dullah and Bulelani were soon joined by their comrades from exile – Albie, Kader, Zola and Brigitte. They worked closely with legal experts and colleagues from both UWC and the University of Cape Town, including Hugh Corder, Dennis Davis, Christina Murray, Lovell Fernandez and Medard Rwelamira.

They were accommodated at UWC by Professor Renfrew Christie, the head of research, which gave them access to the law faculty. Renfrew had been sentenced to 10 years in 1980 for reconnaissance work he had done for the ANC on nuclear and electrical installations in South Africa, and was now putting his skills to good use by looking at what would be required in post-apartheid South Africa.

As part of the constitutional committee, Bulelani found himself grappling with issues like a constitutional court and the concept of constitutional democracy. They were not automatically accepted by all members of the ANC committee.

> We had been brought up with the notion of parliamentary sovereignty. Now there was this idea that when you have majority rule, you cannot do as you want. You must be subject to this thing called constitutional democracy. These were very contentious issues at the time.

It was not surprising that there were concerns about constitutional democracy and the role courts would play in such a system. The majority of judges had served during the apartheid era and showed very little concern for human rights. They had been appointed by the NP and the notion that it could be these same judges who would now be deciding on important constitutional matters didn't sit easy with many and only added to the discomfort that many felt about a negotiated settlement.

> Some of us were not convinced. We argued as only a bunch of lawyers can argue. But in the end, we agreed.
>
> Our leitmotif was that the constitution should not only serve us when we are in power, but that it needs to serve us when we are in opposition. We agreed that whatever we proposed, we had to keep in mind that there may come a time when we are not in power. When you are in power, you don't need the protection of the constitution. You need it when you are powerless.
>
> When I think back and look at what's happening in our country today, I realise once again how important the work was that we did.

Bulelani, who himself had been schooled in the Commonwealth system and had to do a '180-degree turn', credits Kader Asmal and Albie Sachs with being some of the strongest proponents of constitutional democracy.

The ANC was determined to consult as broadly as possible on all the positions it was developing on the constitution for a democratic South Africa, which meant that the committee spent a great deal of its time not only developing working papers but also organising workshops, conferences and meetings covering issues such as electoral systems, gender issues, local government, affirmative action, the judiciary and land.

> It was a real challenge. We wanted to carry the country with us but our people had not been exposed to these issues before. We had to think about how to mobilise them to participate in constitutional issues.
>
> Most of the people doing research on constitutional issues at that time were white professors in white universities and we had to look for black people to deliver papers. Many of the people I found then have gone on in life to occupy good positions.

An early challenge the committee faced was on the composition of the committee itself, which had only one woman in its ranks, Brigitte Mabandla. As a result, Bulelani pulled in a number of female lawyers who would later assume prominent positions in the public and private sectors, such as Pansy Tlakula, Mojanku Gumbi, Cawe Mahlati, Ouma Rabaji, Kgomotso Moroka and Cynthia Burhali.

> I remember when we were organising the land conference in Mpumalanga, I received a call from someone I had never heard of before. He told me we could not possibly organise a conference on land without dealing with the mining issue. He said he wanted a place on the programme at the conference.
>
> He told me his name was Patrice Motsepe and he was the only lawyer in the country who knew anything about mining.

Motsepe went on to become one of the biggest mining magnates in South Africa after the 1994 elections as the founder and executive chairperson of African Rainbow Minerals.

At the conference on the judiciary, which was held in Cape Town, Bulelani spoke on the issue of transformation. When his talk was over, he was approached by Arthur Chaskalson,[7] with whom he had a close relationship.

> 'Bulie-boy, how long do you think it takes to train a good lawyer?' he said.
>
> 'Four years for a junior degree, two years for an LLB, and some working experience, so maybe ten years?'
>
> 'No, no. It takes 15 years. At least 15 years. The future of South Africa', he said, 'is not going to be determined in 15 years. It's going to take much longer than that. Don't promote people into positions when they are not ready. Be patient. Don't tamper with the judiciary. We are moving towards a constitutional democracy. You mess with the judiciary and your country is gone.'
>
> All of us were young and angry and wanted this transformation to happen today, now. But Arthur was wise and told me it could not be done overnight. Because it was said by Arthur, I listened …
>
> Those were exciting times. We were learning. We would go into a meeting with one position and come out with different positions, all of us. To borrow some of the words of Charles Dickens, it really was the best of times, an incredible time, the age of wisdom … we had everything before us.

❏

The unbanning of political organisations and prospect of elections meant that the ANC had to work quickly to re-establish its branches and other structures in the country. The party held its regional conference in the Western Cape in 1991 at the University of the Western Cape.

THE STING IN THE TALE: BULELANI NGCUKA

When we went to conference, the ANC had not established itself properly in so-called coloured areas. Comrades like Amos [Lengisi, secretary of the ANC Western Cape] and Christmas [Tinto, president] had organised hard and mobilised branches in African areas. The majority of delegates at the conference were therefore African.

We had always grappled with this issue of the relationship between so-called coloureds and Africans, and who should be the driving force of revolution in the Western Cape.

There is a railway line that divides Gugulethu from Heideveld. It's more than a railway line. It epitomises the divide between 'coloured' and African people in the Western Cape. The divisions are huge and nowhere was this more apparent than in that first regional conference after the unbanning of the ANC.

We had always tried to ensure balance in leadership structures.

I could see when we got to the conference that we had a problem and I was worried about losing good cadres. I was worried about Trevor [Manuel] being snubbed. We wanted him to get the position of provincial secretary, but it was not going to happen, so I spoke to Dullah. He said we should speak to Trevor.

We explained the problem to Trevor. He had also seen the problem, of course. We told Trevor that we wanted to propose that he be appointed to the position of publicity secretary and that Randall van den Heever also be included. Trevor agreed and, fortunately, the conference also agreed.

We had a good executive. It was representative and included people like Johnny de Lange, Cameron Dugmore, Graeme Bloch, Johnny Issel – all hard workers and really committed comrades.

People were excited and wanted to work to build the ANC. We made a lot of mistakes, but we learned from them. We were grappling with this new environment. All this freedom! God almighty, we could mobilise freely and we were not used to this thing.

The early 1990s was a time of great expectations but also saw some of the worst violence. Like many areas of the country, the Western Cape soon had its own share of problems. Taxi violence flared up and what became known as the Western Cape Taxi War lasted for three years, from 1990 to 1992. It has been described as one of the most intransigent and politically motivated of South Africa's many taxi wars.[8]

The conflict played itself out between two rival organisations – the Langa, Gugulethu and Nyanga Taxi Association (Lagunya) and the Western Cape Black Taxi Association (Webta).

In those days taxis operated between townships. The routes to Cape Town were out of bounds because of apartheid.

Webta, however, defied [this] and started using these routes. They were harassed by police, but they fought hard and they won.

Of course, Lagunya then wanted these routes too. They were very profitable. And that's when the killing started.

The ANC was called on to intervene and Bulelani found himself working alongside Dullah Omar, Christmas Tinto and Amos Lengisi, attempting to get the two associations to agree to talks. Ex-Robben Islander Vincent Diba was also assigned to work with the associations.

> It was not easy. These guys were not staying at home. Webta were camping at the graveyard in Khayelitsha. Lagunya were camping in Site C. It was not easy just to get to where they were.
>
> They were armed. The police knew they were armed and were not disarming them. In fact, there were suspicions that the state was using the conflict to destabilise the region politically.
>
> On one occasion we went to see them and they eventually agreed to talk. So when we went to the other side, they said, 'Hey, you know those guys are going to kill us. Did you ask them for the hit list?'
>
> I was about to stand up and tell them that this was very silly – how could they expect those people to tell us who they're going to kill tomorrow?
>
> Dullah told me to keep quiet. He would handle it. He stood up and said, 'Comrades, I'm sorry. We made a mistake. We'll ask for it next time.'
>
> After that they vented their anger at us a bit, but they agreed to the talks.
>
> Dullah was able to read the mood. Me, with all my bravado, I just wanted to tell them they were talking nonsense.
>
> We managed to persuade them to talk but of course this issue of violence was going to flare up again and again, year after year, and bedevil the Western Cape, particularly in winter-time.

❑

While Bulelani was initially involved in running ANC matters on a daily basis, his involvement with the ANC constitutional committee took up more and more of his time. He realised that he was not going to be able to dedicate much time to his legal practice.

> I was too involved in politics. I realised it was a historic moment and I could not miss out, so I had to ask them [my partners] to release me. I was available to consult from time to time but could no longer be involved in the day-to-day work of the firm.

It was now nearly two years since Nelson Mandela had been released. Negotiations with the apartheid government had reached a critical point and in December 1991 the Convention for a Democratic South Africa (Codesa) talks began.

Bulelani was appointed to a working group chaired by Stella Sigcau which focused on the future of the apartheid homelands. Sigcau had been the first female prime minister of the bantustan of Transkei, before being deposed in a military coup in 1987.

In May 1992, Codesa deadlocked. One of the sticking points was the issue of the majorities required to adopt the new constitution.

The following month matters reached a crisis point with the massacre of more than 40 people in Boipatong. It was claimed that the SAP, in cooperation with the IFP, had organised the attack, which was carried out by armed men from KwaMadala Hostel, a nearby steelworks residence. The ANC formally decided to withdraw from negotiations. They sent a list of demands to De Klerk outlining what needed to be done before talks could resume.

Mass action followed, some of the most profound since the

1950s. More than three million workers joined a two-day national general strike called by Cosatu in August 1992 in support of the ANC's political demands – the biggest strike action in South Africa.[9]

In September about 80 000 protestors marched on Bisho, the capital of the homeland of Ciskei, calling for an end to the rule of Brigadier Oupa Gqozo. The march was led by senior ANC leaders including Cyril Ramaphosa, Chris Hani and Ronnie Kasrils. The shootings that earned the event the moniker the 'Bisho Massacre' took place when Kasrils led a group of marchers through a gap in the razor wire surrounding the Bisho stadium, believing this would allow them to reach Bisho town itself, which had been blocked off. Instead, they were fired on without warning by Ciskei soldiers. Twenty-nine people died and 200 were wounded. Most of those killed were shot either in the back or while running away, bending down or lying down, according to a ballistics expert.

An informal channel of communication between Ramaphosa and the NP's Roelf Meyer, the government's chief negotiator, was opened, and in September 1992 Nelson Mandela and FW de Klerk signed a Record of Understanding. This addressed issues such as the release of political prisoners and the agreement on an interim government of national unity.

Preparations to return to formal talks were under way, and after several bilaterals between the ANC and the NP, and a planning conference in March 1993, the multiparty negotiating process resumed on 1 April 1993. This time Bulelani served on the committee preparing for elections.

But tragedy was about to strike again. Hardly a week had passed when a lone gunman, Janusz Waluś, drove up behind Chris Hani just after 10 am on Saturday 10 April 1993, got out of his car and shot him at point-blank range on the doorstep of his home in Boksburg, Johannesburg.

It was later found that Conservative Party politician Clive Derby-Lewis had instigated the assassination and organised the weapon for Waluś. The police found a hit list that suggested Hani was only the third on Waluś's and Derby-Lewis's list, which also included the names and addresses of Nelson Mandela and Joe Slovo.[10]

> Chris's killers had hoped that his murder would throw the country into chaos and derail the entire negotiations process, but instead the ANC resolved that the process had to be speeded up.
>
> We were determined that Chris's death was not going to become a statistic, so we insisted that there must be agreement on a date for elections, and on 1 June 1993 the date was set: 27 April 1994.

10.
Rebirth of a country

*'This was the moment we had been
fighting for all these years.'*

It was the early hours of Thursday 18 December 1993 and the multiparty negotiating process had finally reached agreement on a package that paved the way for a new South Africa. This included an interim constitution, an electoral act and a set of constitutional principles.

Bulelani and his comrades were celebrating with a champagne breakfast when he was called aside by Valli Moosa, who told him to prepare to return to Cape Town immediately. He was to lead the process to prepare parliament to greet its first democratically elected MPs.

One of the first people he met in Cape Town was Alex van Breda, the NP's chief whip in parliament, who was a veteran of party politics and parliamentary procedure. The two men were to form a unique working relationship.

> When we met that first day, the NP and the administration were ready. They had a list of all the issues that had to be dealt with. I wasn't ready. I was there to listen.

Bulelani was a quick learner and was soon dealing with

matters ranging from rules for the national assembly, the senate and the constitutional assembly, to more practical issues such as organising seating for 400 people in the national assembly, and quantities of cutlery and crockery. He recruited Johnny de Lange to assist with the preparations.

Shortly thereafter, Sindiso Mfenyana from the ANC head office was appointed assistant secretary to parliament (a position he held until 1997, when he was appointed South Africa's first black full secretary to parliament).

> It was a strange time. We had to prepare but we also had to keep it quiet. It could not be known that the ANC and the NP were preparing for a handover, as if we had already anticipated the outcome of the elections.

Had the ANC fared better in the Western Cape in the 1994 elections, Bulelani's career might well have turned out very differently. The ANC won 62 percent of the national vote but only 33 percent of the vote in that province.

Bulelani was deployed to the senate. Kobie Coetsee from the NP was elected president of the senate and veteran Govan Mbeki deputy president; Bulelani was elected to the position of chief whip.

Coetsee had the wisdom to realise that, as a member of the NP, he had to allow the majority party to lead – but Mbeki was already 84 years old and delegated most of his work to Bulelani, so much of the responsibility for running the senate therefore fell on his shoulders.

Bulelani's work in parliament extended beyond the senate. The parliamentary staff knew him since he was the first person from the ANC they had worked with.

> The administration just didn't know how to relate to the

ANC and to black people who were confident and articulate and were there to assert themselves. They knew their work – they were well trained and disciplined – but they didn't know how to relate, so I had to assist in that area.

And Bulelani was determined to carve out a role for the senate.

> I wanted to make the senate relevant. It could not just be a rubber stamp for the national assembly but at the same time it was not there to second-guess the national assembly either. In fact, it was a house of deliberation and reflection.

In addition to stalwarts like Mbeki, members of the senate included veterans such as Professor Ernest Mchunu from the University of Zululand, Wilton Mkwayi, Dr Sam Motsuenyane, Isabella Winkie Direko, Henry 'Squire' Makgothi and Simon Makana. All of these individuals went on to occupy important positions – Motsuenyane as the country's first ambassador to Saudi Arabia in 1996 and founder of the National African Federation Chamber; Direko as premier of the Free State in 1999; Makgothi as chief whip of the national council of provinces in 1998; and Makana as ambassador to the Russian Federation in 1996.

Younger ANC members that Bulelani credits with playing an important role in the senate include Mohammed Bhabha, Siyabonga Cwele, Vuyiswa Tyobeka, Lassie Chiwayo, Mohseen Moosa and George Mashamba. And he mentions members from other political parties, such as James Selfe and Errol Moorcroft from the Democratic Party, Ray Radue, Alex van Breda and Kraai van Niekerk from the NP, and Musa Zondi from the Inkatha Freedom Party.

These were all good, quality people and I had the privilege to lead them in the senate in those early days in parliament.

Alex van Breda had also joined us in the senate. It was important that he was there. He was respected in the National Party. The Democratic Party, of course, hated him. They said he had been a terror in parliament as chief whip. However, we worked well with him, and I also had good working relations with James Selfe from the Democratic Party.

In all, I won the confidence of all political parties, and this was very important for the smooth functioning of the senate.

❏

Bulelani has never hesitated to tackle issues head-on and he soon found himself in conflict with no less a person than Nelson Mandela.

In the senate's first budget debates in parliament in 1994, he raised issues like the appointment of General Georg Meiring, who had been chief of the apartheid army, as the first chief of the South African National Defence Force, and the fact that Chris Stals remained governor of the Reserve Bank. Derek Keys, who had served in De Klerk's cabinet, was the minister of finance, and Pik Botha, another former NP minister, was now minister of minerals and energy.

The economic cluster was concentrated in the hands of the NP. This didn't sit easy with many and gave credence to the notion that the ANC had achieved political power, but economic power remained beyond its grasp.

There was unease about some of these appointments and a sense that Madiba was pandering too much to white people. Some of us understood but I thought this was an opportunity for the issue to be publicly aired and for Madiba to respond. I had spoken to Joel Netshitenzhe [one of the ANC's leading strategists and thinkers, at the time political advisor in the presidency] and he told me I should proceed and raise the matter.

So when I spoke in the debate, I first congratulated Madiba and said it was instructive that we were in the senate and had him as the president of South Africa with us, and Kobie Coetsee as the head of the senate – both midwives of the new South Africa. I then raised the issue of these appointments and said that I didn't want to be a populist, but the issue needed to be addressed.

He responded very coolly and said it was important that I had raised the matter.

The debate went well but the headlines in the papers the next day were 'ANC slams Mandela'. Madiba was livid and that afternoon he called Oom Gov, Stof [Arnold Stofile, chief whip of the national assembly], [ANC caucus chair] Mendi Msimang, Thabo Mbeki and me to his office at Tuynhuys [the Cape Town office of the presidency]. He said I had created the impression that the ANC didn't support him and asked why it was necessary for me to have raised the matter at all.

Before I could respond, Stof spoke and said I had in fact been quite moderate and that the issue was the subject of a lot of concern in the ANC ranks and had to be raised. He said they were happy with the way Madiba had responded in the debate.

Madiba wasn't happy, though, and wanted me to issue a statement withdrawing the remarks I'd made.

As he was speaking, a call came through from Bill Clinton wanting to speak to him. Madiba said he would call us back and we left.

Everyone I spoke to said I shouldn't issue the statement and that I must stick to my guns. From the ANC benches, comrades were adamant and told me to stand my ground and that Madiba was wrong. Thabo Mbeki said I had done nothing wrong in raising the matter and this gave me some reassurance.

Personally, I was conflicted. I wanted to make peace with Madiba but didn't want to back down because I believed in what I had said.

A few weeks later Madiba was addressing a meeting of mainly white people in Stellenbosch, and he attacked me publicly. I wasn't there but it was bad. He savaged me, said I was pandering to populism and so on.

Fortunately, others came to my rescue.

Barney Pityana [the chair of the first South African Human Rights Commission], for example, was very aggrieved about it and wrote a letter to Madiba telling him that he was being petulant and that it didn't befit him to launch an attack in the way he had. Jakes Gerwel also called me and said he had told Madiba to leave the issue alone.

Then Madiba wrote to me and said he wanted to see me. In fact, he later called and said I should phone Ismail Ayob, who was Madiba's lawyer at the time, and give him details of my trust account, and said I should handle all his financial affairs in Cape Town. So I did that and managed his financial affairs in Cape Town throughout his presidency.

I think he realised he had gone too far and was trying to make amends. We never discussed the matter again.

On the same day, Alex van Breda told Bulelani that 'in politics you must choose your enemies carefully'.

'You have a bright future,' he told me. 'You are a clever fellow and have a good future in politics. Now, let me tell you this, young man. Me, I believed in apartheid with all my heart. I joined politics in the 1950s at the time the leader was JG Strijdom. So let me tell you what I was told then by my leader.

'In politics there are people you cannot afford to make enemies of. It doesn't matter whether you are right or wrong. Mandela will never be wrong in this country. You will always be wrong.

'Go and make peace with Mandela. You need him more than he needs you. And don't tell me about your ego. This is politics. Take this advice from an old apartheid politician.'

It was a poignant moment in my life, getting advice from this old member of the National Party.

It wasn't the last time Bulelani would displease Madiba.
In 1994, the ANC caucus in parliament voted overwhelmingly to do away with the hated (at the time) springbok logo, which had appeared on the green-and-gold shirts of the South African national rugby team since 1906. Later, a press conference was held at which Stofile and Bulelani addressed the parliamentary press corps.

Madiba was away when we addressed the press that day, so he read about this issue in the media. He phoned me and Stof the next day and he was livid. He told us we couldn't implement the decision. This was before the 1995 World Cup. He wanted an opportunity to address the caucus himself.

'How can you treat a person who is your partner in this fashion?' he asked. 'Don't rub a person's nose in the dirt. Why must you make the Afrikaner feel vanquished?'

He was very, very angry. He addressed the caucus when he got back from overseas, and, as you know, the rest is history. Madiba wore the springbok jersey at the World Cup Final in 1995 and we became world champions.

Also in 1994, Dullah Omar, then minister of justice, introduced the Admission of Advocates Amendment Bill to parliament, to abolish Latin as a requirement for admission to the bar. The national assembly passed the bill without incident, but when it came to the senate, the ANC decided that Afrikaans should be abolished as a requirement along with Latin.

This caused a furore, with the Freedom Front's General Tienie Groenewald and advocate Rosier de Ville leading the fray.

In one of the meetings of the justice committee, De Ville complained, 'We can't have blacks not learning Afrikaans. Can you imagine that I have black people here in parliament calling me "Advocate Devil"! Do you know what it means to an Afrikaner to be called a devil?'

Prof Mchunu replied, 'I fully understand, Advocate de Ville. It is unacceptable but Afrikaners must also learn other languages. I have Afrikaners here in parliament calling me "Professor Msunu"! Can you imagine what it means to an African to be called msunu?' ('*Msunu*' means 'buttocks' in isiZulu.)

There was a lot of tension on the language issue in the early days of parliament. From the start, both the Freedom Front and the NP had insisted on speaking Afrikaans in committee meetings; in response, the ANC spoke in isiZulu, isiXhosa, Tshivenda, Sesotho and other African languages. In plenary sessions, notice was provided if MPs intended to speak a language other than English and interpreters were on hand. This procedure, however, was not always possible in committee meetings, and committee work was inevitably slowed down and delayed. These tensions were confounded by the bill and heated debate followed.

> Dullah called me and said he would have to withdraw the bill since [the senate] had introduced a substantive matter that needed cabinet approval. That weekend we were going to have a legal colloquium in Somerset West and we agreed that we would take the issue there. If we got the support of the colloquium, then he would take it to cabinet.
>
> We went to the colloquium. I was in the subcommittee dealing with the issue, and I spoke and said it was impossible to be objective. I told them that I was a graduate of '76 and after my experiences with Afrikaans Nederlands at Fort Hare, I couldn't just sit back now, in '95, and demanded a significant break with the past. I had no problems with Afrikaans, I explained, but it must receive the same treatment as other languages. We couldn't prescribe Afrikaans and say nothing about my own language. The subcommittee agreed and we reported back.
>
> Dullah said we must respect the sovereignty of parliament but that he had no choice but to withdraw the bill.
>
> I disagreed and said no, we have an opportunity now.

There is a bill before parliament, and we have the agreement of the colloquium. It was a very emotional issue for me, and I would not back down.

It was a public confrontation with Dullah, who was my best friend at the time, so it was not pleasant.

Who should intervene but Arthur [Chaskalson], who came to me and said, 'Bulie, give Dullah a chance.'

All three of us spoke again at the plenary. Dullah said the difference was that I wanted it done now and he would do it later. He was right. He had to follow protocols. But I stuck to my guns. I thought I was right. I had scars.

In the end, though, I had to give Dullah a chance, as Arthur said. We went back to parliament and allowed the bill to go through. And Dullah was true to his word: six months later, another bill came through and we did away with Afrikaans.[1]

The National Education Policy Bill of 1995 was one of the first big post-apartheid pieces of legislation to come before parliament. This bill was fiercely contested, with opposition parties arguing that it conflicted with the powers of the provinces. The bill was eventually passed by the national assembly and ended up in the senate.

The debate here took a different turn: opposition parties tried to block a vote on the basis of procedure and the debate ran late into the evening. Kobie Coetsee, head of the senate and a member of the NP, told the house he would deliver his ruling in the morning.

Early the next morning, at 7 am, he called Bulelani and told him he had had a sleepless night. 'For the first time in my life, I have to take a decision against my party. I think it's the right thing to do but my party is not going to like me after today. I'm going to allow this vote to be taken because that is the will of the majority, even though I think the bill is wrong,' he said.

> From that moment on we became friends and worked together without having to put party-political interests first each time. I could see he was wrestling with his conscience, but he took the right decision. It was a defining moment in our relationship in the senate.

❑

Among the structures the ANC set up in parliament was a political committee tasked with ensuring the smooth running of the institution. The committee included the speaker, Frene Ginwala, minister Zola Sweyiya, MPs and ANC heavyweights Baleka Kgositsile and Mavivi Myakayaka-Manzini, and parliament's chief whips, Arnold Stofile and Bulelani.

> There were many challenges. We were new, eager and clear that we were not going to do what had been done in the past. It didn't matter whether it was right or wrong. We wanted to set our own precedents. We recognised that this opportunity came once in a lifetime – to start from the beginning to shape an institution like parliament and not be inhibited by precedents and customs from the past.

MPs were responsible for nominating people to important institutions including the Constitutional Court. President Mandela had already appointed Arthur Chaskalson president of the court in June 1994.

He was also required to appoint four other members from the ranks of the Supreme Court and duly appointed Laurie

Ackermann, Richard Goldstone, Tholie Madala and Ismail Mahomed. He would appoint the remaining six judges after receiving nominations from the Judicial Service Commission (JSC).

The JSC is a 23-member body made up of judges, practising advocates and attorneys, academics, members of the legislative and executive branches, and presidential appointees. Bulelani was a member with Dullah Omar, Boyce Moerane, Wim Trengove, George Bizos, John Ernstzen, Kgomotso Moroka, Etienne Mureinik, Winkie Direko, Ray Radue and Professor Mchunu.

The JSC was tasked with screening a list of 100 candidates, which they reduced to a shortlist of 25 candidates who were interviewed in public hearings over four days in October 1994. There was an abundance of talent, Bulelani says, but the commission had to balance different interest groups. This Constitutional Court was going to certify the constitution, and have the ability to declare acts of parliament and the conduct of government unconstitutional.

> It was going to set the standard for the future, for our democracy.
>
> There was no argument about appointing [shortlisted] people like Pius Langa, John Didcott and Johann Kriegler, but when it came to people like Albie [Sachs] it was more difficult. There were some people who just didn't want him. They argued that he had never practised law, but we knew that it was politics and that they thought he was a terrorist.
>
> There were also those who argued that Kate O'Regan was too young. We had to do a lot of lobbying. People didn't know Kate. They didn't know Yvonne Mokgoro.

THE STING IN THE TALE: BULELANI NGCUKA

The six who were finally appointed by the president were Kriegler, Didcott, Langa, O'Regan, Mokgoro and Sachs.

> There were some good people who didn't make it, people like Zac Yacoob and Lewis Skweyiya. They made it later but not at the time.
>
> It was a good court. I was proud to have been a part of the process.

Bulelani speaks of Arthur Chaskalson's advice to him in later years, when it came to appointing judges.

> We were experiencing a problem of senior white advocates not wanting to apply for positions on the bench. They were opposed to being interviewed in public and believed that even if they made themselves available, they would be humiliated and not be appointed.
>
> On this one occasion, a senior white advocate applied. He interviewed very badly on issues of transformation. There was a streak of arrogance in him.
>
> In our discussions as a committee, I made it clear I was not going to vote for him. But Arthur called me later and said, 'You must vote for him, and tell your colleagues to vote for him. He's a good man. I know him.'
>
> I objected quite strongly but he was firm and told me, 'You're not going to play politics here. You must send the message that we appoint competent people.'
>
> I voted for him and I'm so glad I did. I was able to persuade my colleagues. We had a fight, of course, but I trusted a man like Arthur. We voted for him unanimously. Arthur was right and I was wrong. The man has gone on to become an excellent judge.

Bulelani was the chair of both the joint committee on the appointment of the South African Human Rights Commission and the joint committee on the appointment of the public protector.

The appointment of Dr Barney Pityana as chair of the South African Human Rights Commission was supported by most parties. He had solid credentials.

Things did not move so smoothly when it came to the appointment of the public protector, however. The ANC nominated Selby Baqwa – he had all the right credentials with the necessary legal qualifications, and was a prominent member of Nadel. But the NP didn't like Selby, who had a 'political profile' due to his involvement in many political trials in Natal during the apartheid days.

Bulelani finally approached Madiba, who spoke to De Klerk, and agreement was reached. With the support of the NP, Selby Baqwa was appointed as South Africa's first public protector.

❑

The new MPs not only had the business of setting up parliament but also had to draft South Africa's new constitution. In order to effectively deal with the wide variety of issues to be covered, six 'theme committees' were set up to work on different parts of the constitution, tasked with receiving and processing the views of political parties and the broader community, and compiling reports for discussion.

Bulelani was a member of the theme committee dealing with the relationship between the different levels of court; the composition and appointment of judicial officers; access to courts, including lay participation; traditional courts and customary law; legal education and the legal profession; transitional arrangements; correctional services; international law and interpretation; and attorneys-general. He was also a member of one of the most important decision-making structures, the 44-member constitutional committee, which reported directly to the constitutional assembly.

The new constitution had to be adopted by two-thirds of the constitutional assembly and this meant that all seven parties had to work together if they were to meet the deadline of 8 May 1996 and produce a constitution that was acceptable to all. It was not an easy process, and as the deadline crept closer, there were marathon all-night sessions as negotiators battled over issues such as property, education, the lockout clause and official languages.

The final agreements were reached at midnight on 7 May, and the constitution was adopted ten hours later.

It was on this occasion that Thabo Mbeki took to the podium and delivered his 'I am an African' speech: 'I am an African. I owe my being to the hills and the valleys, the mountains and the glades, the rivers, the deserts, the trees, the flowers, the seas and the everchanging seasons that define the face of our native land. I am an African!'

Bulelani could only marvel as he listened to Mbeki speak. He had been called in to assist in some of the deadlock-breaking, and as the two men parted late the previous evening, Mbeki had said to him, 'I must start on my speech now, Bulelani.'

> I couldn't believe it. He hadn't even started working on the speech when we spoke the previous evening, and look at what he produced!

With the adoption of a new constitution, a new body, the

national council of provinces (NCOP), was to replace the senate. Described as 'the institutionalisation of cooperative governance', the NCOP would be the only body in the constitution that brought together national, provincial and local government in one structure.

With his experience in the senate, Bulelani had legitimate expectations of being chair of the NCOP but remembers getting a call from Steve Tshwete.

> 'Hey, *kwedini* [young man], how are you? The president asked me to call you. The ANC has a problem and it's going to affect you. We're sending Terror [Lekota] to Cape Town to take over from Kobie Coetsee and he will make you his deputy. You must work with him.'

Steve told me that Madiba was concerned that I wouldn't accept the position of deputy chairperson.

'Madiba said we must ask you, but we told him you are a child of the ANC and will follow instructions, so I'm telling you. You're young, boy. Your time will come.'

11.

The 'poisoned chalice' job

'I recognise these fears [of political partiality]. It is going to be incumbent on me when I assume this post to demonstrate my impartiality and independence. It would be foolish of me to advance the ANC and to prejudice other parties. Certainly, I have no intention of doing that.'

In 1998, during an ANC-organised trip to Robben Island, Dullah Omar told Bulelani he wanted to recommend to the president that he be appointed as South Africa's first National Director of Public Prosecutions (NDPP). It was a job that would later be described as 'a poisoned chalice filled with a deadly cocktail of multiple interests: race, business, social, socio-economic, you name it; and the most fatal of them all, politics.'[1]

Bulelani told Dullah he was not interested.

That evening he got a call from Saki Macozoma, who urged him to take up the position. He shared his concerns with Saki, saying that the challenges of transforming the prosecution service were huge.

Saki had just left parliament to take up the position of managing director of Transnet, South Africa's state-owned rail, port and pipeline company, and he responded by saying that transformation was a challenge throughout South Africa and not one that Bulelani should shy away from. 'We are all dealing with the old guard,' he said. 'What's different about you?'

The difference with this position, Bulelani told him, was that if he did his job properly, sooner or later, he would run into problems with his own comrades.

'Well,' Saki said, 'if they have done wrong, and must face prosecution, so be it.'

Zola Skweyiya called Bulelani next, and didn't beat about the bush. 'Hey, *kwedini* [young man], why are you refusing to be deployed? You must reconsider.'

> I told him I would think about it.
>
> Then Dullah called me and said the deputy president [Thabo Mbeki] wanted to see me. We went to see him. He spoke about the challenges facing the country and why it was important that I take up the position. He said he didn't understand what was wrong with our family: Phumzile had refused the position of minister of labour when it was offered to her. [Phumzile had felt she was not well enough acquainted with labour matters.]
>
> It was clear to me after this meeting that I could not refuse.

The response to Bulelani's appointment was mixed. Douglas Gibson from the Democratic Party said that while Bulelani had shown himself to be 'a very able man' in parliament, the party condemned the appointment of 'someone who is knee-deep in politics to a post which should be non-political'.[2]

There was a similar reaction from Koos van der Merwe of the IFP. If it were all about individual merit, he said, there wasn't a better person for the job, but it was still 'wrong to appoint a politician to the job'.[3] The FF's Rosier de Ville called it 'an ill-advised political appointment while the NP's Roelie

Groenewald said, 'I have the greatest respect for him, but I fear he will have a political agenda.'[4]

But from within the ANC, unnamed sources noted that Bulelani had 'a reputation for independence of thought and integrity'. 'He has always been very much his own man, willing to take positions which are not popular, sometimes at a risk to himself.'[5]

Mandela told Bulelani after his appointment that he had initially opposed it; he had wanted someone more senior, but when Dullah pointed out that Bulelani had a Master's degree, he'd been impressed and told them to proceed with the appointment.

On the day his appointment was announced, Dullah took Bulelani to the Union Buildings for his first meeting with some of the attorneys-general who had served in the apartheid years. The only one he had met before was Frank Kahn from Cape Town. The others at the meeting were Jan d'Oliveira (who was eventually appointed one of the three deputy NDPPs), Les Roberts from Grahamstown and Andre de Vries[6] from Johannesburg.

Since 1992 attorneys-general had been independent civil servants with no ministerial or parliamentary oversight. 'Moreover, unlike courts, attorneys-general were not obliged to give reasons for their decisions, with the result that such decisions could not normally be subject to public scrutiny and debate.'[7] Under the new system, attorneys-general were no longer their own bosses. The NDPP would now set policy and issue directives, and could review decisions to prosecute or not to prosecute.

The only attorney-general who appeared to resist the change was Tim McNally from KwaZulu-Natal, who had also made himself very unpopular in the province. Bulelani made McNally an offer of a position in his office in Pretoria; he refused. This left Bulelani with no option but to ask for his resignation. Again, McNally refused, insisting that he had the trust of President

Mandela and wanted to speak to him directly.

A meeting with Mandela was set up and McNally arrived at the Union Buildings accompanied by a press entourage.

Mandela was scathing, and in a rare moment of anger tore into McNally. 'I am told you don't want to listen to my son,' he said, gesturing to Bulelani. 'You don't believe that he is acting in accordance with my wishes. You do not have the trust of the people of KwaZulu-Natal, Mr McNally, and you need to do what this boy wants,' he said gesturing towards Bulelani. 'That is all. You may leave.'

Even Bulelani was taken aback at the extent of Mandela's anger. He was clearly incensed by McNally's arrogance and his claim that he enjoyed the president's trust.

❏

Bulelani got advice and input from a variety of people in those early days.

Professor Lovell Fernandez from UWC's department of criminal justice and procedure, one of the foremost experts on prosecution in South Africa with a deep understanding of the criminal-justice system, told him, 'Get to know [veteran prosecutor] Jan Henning. If you bring him close to you, you will win the respect of the white prosecutors. He commands the respect of the majority of the white prosecutors. He has a very difficult personality but a razor-sharp mind.'

Neil Roussouw, the former Cape attorney-general, was also enormously helpful.[8]

> He knew the system inside out. Neil became the go-between between me and the former AGs [attorneys-general]. He was a good sounding board for my ideas. ...

When he retired, the government owed him a lot of money for leave he hadn't taken for many years. He didn't want the money. He donated it all to us to set up a library at the NPA.

Percy Sonn also paid Bulelani a visit.

Percy was a deputy in Frank's office in Cape Town. He told me he wanted to lead the Investigating Directorate on Organised Crime [IDOC]. He had prepared the terms of reference and had a list of the names of people he wanted to work with him. He was well prepared.

I was impressed. I consulted Dullah, who supported his appointment.

Percy was a character, of course, but he was courageous. I knew this was someone who would never leave you behind. This was someone you want to go to war with.

❑

In October 1998, close friends and acquaintances organised a dinner to celebrate Bulelani's appointment as NDPP.

When Saki Macozoma spoke on this occasion, he warned Bulelani of the tough times ahead but provided some words of encouragement too, reminding him that millions of South Africans shared 'the vision of a society in which criminals live in fear and give up crime altogether because they know there is a wolf at the end of the law – *ikhon' ingcuka*.'[9]

Bulelani's surname, Ngcuka, means 'wolf' in isiXhosa.

12.
Lawyers for the people

'There was nothing. No furniture. No phones. Nothing. Just empty offices. We had to start from scratch.'

In Pretoria, offices had been secured in Visagie Street, in the same building that housed the public protector. When Bulelani and his entourage arrived there, empty rooms greeted them. And there were obviously bigger things that needed Bulelani's attention.

Bulelani arrived in Pretoria with Sheila Figland, Hermione Cronje and Sipho Ngwema from his parliamentary office. They were later joined by Lungisa Dyosi from the Department of Justice and Neil Roussouw. Bulelani got down to business with this team of five people in his office.

There were four key issues he had to address and he wasted no time in dealing with them, all within a month of assuming office. Apart from establishing his office itself, these were the appointment of deputy directors and senior prosecutors, attending to the long-neglected matter of prosecutors' salaries and focusing on organised crime.

The NPA's first annual report made it clear how stark the challenges were. 'When we started the National Prosecuting Authority, we were almost overwhelmed by the enormity of the task that lay ahead. We had to develop and shape new structures, systems, a new identity and image, rules that were to govern the behaviour of prosecutors and a whole new way of doing things. In one way or another we had to start from the beginning ...

'It was never easy. The prosecution service was at its lowest point in its history. Morale was low, salaries and conditions of work were hopelessly inadequate, and frustrations were running high. While the rest of the country was grappling with issues of transformation, we seemed comfortable in our enclave and had not yet even begun to address such issues.

'Furthermore, commitment to the new order was indeed doubtful.

'The new dispensation required a new breed of prosecutors. Even though the faces in an institution could be changed, what was needed was a far more fundamental change in our orientation. We needed to see ourselves as "lawyers for the people".'[1]

❏

Before the NPA, what existed, as Bulelani says, was a country with '11 attorneys-general, each completely independent of the other. The result was an anomaly where, within a unitary state, each provincial attorney-general had his own prosecution policy and guidelines, applicable only to his area of jurisdiction. There were obvious differences in emphasis, content and approach.'[2]

An important task, therefore, was to ensure that a single prosecution policy be written and published.

The manual was completed in October 1999 and contained the prosecution policy, a code of conduct and a set of directives. These had been thoroughly debated and discussed at a strategic planning workshop for senior management in January 1999.

The NPA Act provided for a DPP at each of the high courts in the country. They are now divided into nine provincial divisions (with some having one or more local divisions). However, when Bulelani was appointed, he inherited seven attorneys-general from the high courts of 'white' South Africa – in Johannesburg, Pretoria, Cape Town, Grahamstown, Kimberley, Bloemfontein and Pietermaritzburg – and also former attorneys-general of the bantustans of Ciskei, Transkei, Venda and Bophuthatswana.

Bulelani initially kept all these in place, and things changed over time. For example, in Kimberley, Lungi Mahlati took over in 2000 when Charl du Plessis left; when Les Roberts in Grahamstown retired, he was replaced by Mzwandile Ntsaluba; and when Jan d'Oliveira quit his post in Pretoria and was promoted to deputy NDPP, he was replaced by Silas Ramaite. Frank Kahn maintained his position in the Western Cape, as did Andre de Vries in Johannesburg, Bethwell Manyuha in Venda and Johan Smit in Mmabatho. In Bloemfontein, Leonard McCarthy took over from Muller Van Der Merwe. Humphrey Lusu took over from Christo Nel in Umtata and Johan Bezuidenhout acted in Bisho after Leon Langeveld left.

Two of the biggest challenges Bulelani was confronted with were salaries – at the time, he had no budget for compensation[3] – and court performance. The biggest crisis was in the lower courts, or magistrates' courts, where the majority of prosecutors were found and up to 90 percent of all cases were heard. The system was clogged with awaiting-trial prisoners. Many had been charged for minor crimes but could not afford small bail amounts, such as R50, and ended up spending months waiting for their cases to come up in court, costing the state money.

While prosecutors didn't have full control over the finalisation of cases, they did have some say on the management of court rolls, so Bulelani promised to speak to prosecutors to review the matter of bail and reduce the number of awaiting-trial prisoners in return for an increase in prosecutors' salaries, which could, in turn, be funded from the savings from the number of reduced awaiting-trial prisoners. At the same time, performance targets, linked to increased salaries, included increasing court hours, increasing the number of finalised cases with a verdict, and reducing the cycle time for cases involving prisoners with bail of R1 000 or less.

Bulelani assembled a team and, once a formula had been devised which was acceptable to all, he approached the DPPs and asked them to go and speak to prosecutors and convince them about the proposal. He was taken aback at their response. They said there was no need to persuade anyone: he was the boss and should simply issue instructions.

> It was a different culture. I told them I came from a different background, and we needed to get buy-in from the prosecutors, so we had to consult them.

As it happened, however, the prosecutors were not entirely happy and argued that many issues were beyond their control. There were many role-players in the system – magistrates, interpreters, defence attorneys, police officers, correctional-services officials and so on, all of whom had an impact on their performance in court. However, Bulelani and his team persevered.

Jan Henning was brought in to head a newly established court management unit, for monitoring performance and ensuring that prosecutors kept to the agreements reached.

Bulelani noted in a 2004 address, 'As we were implementing this new system, we soon discovered that the system did not have statistics, let alone accurate ones, on which to base any managerial decisions. In a sense, the managers of prosecutors were managing in the dark. We immediately introduced a ... system that allowed for the collation of accurate statistics.

'For the first time in the history of our country, we now have a reliable picture of what goes on in our courts. We can account for the performance of every individual prosecutor. ... We now know where courts are under-resourced and need further assistance, we know who is working and who is not, and we know the extent to which other role-players in the criminal-justice system like magistrates, defence lawyers, court orderlies and court interpreters are hampering the effectiveness of the courts.

'This is groundbreaking stuff in the public service. Most importantly, this has enabled us to focus our attention on the management systems that we need to keep the momentum going and examine the effectiveness of managers.'[4]

It worked. Within six months, prosecutors had met their targets. The number of awaiting-trial prisoners decreased by 32.7 percent, well above the 10 percent target. Despite an increase in the number of cases going to the courts, prosecutors managed to work down the rolls, in district and regional court rolls, by 13 percent and 30 percent, respectively. The number of outstanding dockets also showed a dramatic drop, from 22 974 to 15 161 – a decrease of 34 percent.[5]

A task force was set up and deployed to trouble spots in areas like KwaZulu-Natal, Umtata and Mmabatho, where huge case backlogs were reduced within a matter of days. These 'rescue missions' were made up of some of the most experienced prosecutors in the country, and in many instances were led by Jan Henning himself. Some of the files these teams encountered, for example in Umtata, dated back to 1991. The team disposed of 900 files in the space of five days.[6]

In Mmabatho the team was confronted with 2 000 dockets, studied all of them and provided detailed written guidance on each of them. Likewise, in Pinetown and Verulam, 1 200 dockets were screened in five days and instructions given.⁷

Saturday courts and additional courts were set up in 2001 and 2002, further improving the finalisation of cases and decreasing court rolls. Between 2001, when they were first implemented, and 2004, they had finalised 57 000 cases.⁸

It was also important to attract new blood and ensure better training for prosecutors, as senior state advocate and Bulelani's legal advisor at the time, Lungisa Dyosi, explains. 'The skills level of prosecutors was very low. Prosecutors with an average experience of three years were having to stand up against advocates with 15 years' experience. We needed to attract the best. Even with the salary increases, we knew we could not compete with the private sector. So we introduced the Aspirant Prosecutors' Programme.

'Over 90 percent of our recruits came from underprivileged universities like Fort Hare, University of the North and so on. What we could offer graduates was four to eight hours in court a day. You will never get this kind of exposure and experience in any law firm. We were therefore able to attract the best graduates.

'We calculated that by year three we would lose 10 percent, who would leave for better pay in the private sector, and another 10 percent by year five, and yet another 10 percent by year seven. However, after 10 years, we would have retained 70 percent of those we trained, and this would be our core, our seniors with skill and experience. One must bear in mind, too, that the process was being repeated every year, so the numbers were increasing all the time. This is how we achieved transformation and built a core of skilled prosecutors at the same time.'⁹

When Bulelani was appointed, he also became aware of the frustration of senior advocates who had given up on hopes of promotion because of long delays in filling vacancies, and were leaving in droves.

I asked that all applications for prosecution posts be sent to my office and started with the posts for deputy directors. We soon filled all the vacancies for deputy directors – this is when we appointed people like Billy Downer, Gerda Ferreira and Phyllis Atkinson.

I was amazed when I interviewed one senior advocate in Frank Kahn's office. He wanted the position and qualified [for it] but he mentioned another candidate, Phyllis Atkinson. He said she had been discriminated against for a long time simply because she was a woman and deserved the position more than he did. He felt so strongly about it that he said he was willing to step aside for her to get the post. It was moving to find someone who was prepared to make that kind of sacrifice for a colleague. Remember, these people had waited a long time for promotions.

Of course, many of these positions were filled by white advocates – but their appointment opened up other spaces; we were able to move black candidates into positions below them. These appointments in turn opened up further vacancies. There was a lot of movement in the prosecution service, and this allowed for a lot of black appointments.

Slowly but surely the composition of the NPA changed. Between 1996 and 2000, white prosecutors dropped from 53 percent to 36 percent of the prosecution service, while the proportion of white male prosecutors dropped from 27 percent to 16 percent. The number of black, so-called coloured and Indian prosecutors and senior prosecutors increased from 47 percent to 64 percent. The proportion of female prosecutors and senior prosecutors increased from 41 percent to 44 percent.[10]

THE STING IN THE TALE: BULELANI NGCUKA

❑

There was a more fundamental challenge. 'During the apartheid years, prosecutors acquired the unfortunate reputation of being in cahoots with police in defending the policies of an illegitimate government. As a result, prosecutors were perceived more as persecutors of victims than as prosecutors of crime. ... Police and prosecutors lacked any legitimacy in the eyes of the public.'[11]

South Africa's new constitution required that prosecutors now function as part of a constitutional democracy and uphold a bill of rights that had won the admiration of many in the world. As Bulelani put it, prosecutors had to become human-rights activists.[12]

This would require a 180-degree reorientation. Nelson Mandela summed up the mind change that was required. 'The challenge for the modern prosecutor is to become a lawyer for the people. It is your duty to build an effective relationship with the community and ensure that the rights of victims are protected. It is your duty to prosecute fairly and effectively, according to the rule of law, and to act in a principled way, without fear, favour or prejudice. It is your duty to build a prosecution service that is an effective deterrent to crime and is known to demonstrate great compassion and sensitivity to the people it serves.'[13]

A victim-centred approach to prosecutions was championed by the Sexual Offences and Community Affairs Unit (headed by advocate Thoko Majokweni[14], whose flagship project was the establishment of the Thuthuzela Care Centres. '*Thuthuzela*' is isiXhosa for 'comfort'. The thinking was that these centres should embody all the feelings of 'warmth, freedom from emotional and physical concerns, safety, security, being pampered and care for and, above all, reinforcing dignity, hope and positive expectations.'[15]

The centres were staffed by prosecutors, social workers, magistrates, non-government organisations and police, and were linked to sexual offences courts, while the unit spent considerable time training prosecutors, magistrates, police officers, correctional services staff and traditional leaders.

By 2004, five of these centres and 51 sexual offences courts were in operation countrywide, reporting a conviction rate of 60 percent.[16]

❑

A number of other specialist courts[17] were set up, including a drug court in Durban, environmental courts in Hermanus (to deal with perlemoen [abalone] and crayfish poaching cases), and specialist courts to deal with bank robbery, cash-in-transit heists and hijackings, all of which were successful primarily because they allowed prosecutors and magistrates to get to grips with the specialised nature of the crimes they were dealing with.

Another innovation, the Community Courts project, kicked off in Hatfield, Pretoria, in 2004 to deal with the increased lawlessness in the country's central business districts, which ranged from petty crimes such as violations of municipal by-laws to serious crimes like rape, robbery, murder, drug-dealing and house breaking. The aim was to deal with offenders immediately, some within hours of their arrest. The model was based on a partnership between several entities, including the NPA, the South African Police Service (SAPS) and the department of justice.

THE STING IN THE TALE: BULELANI NGCUKA

The NPA also set up an Integrity Management Unit to ensure that the integrity of the NPA remained beyond reproach. The unit, which was led by Dipuo Mvelase, was responsible for, among other things, developing a management handbook, fraud response plan and anti-corruption strategy, providing training for management and staff, distributing and maintaining a gift register, overseeing the declaration of financial interests required in terms of the Public Finance Management Act, and conducting investigations into cases of corruption and maladministration involving employees of the NPA.

In 2001, the NPA had to take on a new responsibility when the minister of justice transferred the witness protection programme to the NPA. A senior prosecutor from the Western Cape, Dawood Adam, was appointed as head of the programme.

❑

The Specialised Commercial Crimes Unit was set up in 1999 under the leadership of advocate Chris Jordaan. This unit worked closely with detectives from the SAPS commercial crimes unit in Pretoria, and prosecuted all commercial or 'white-collar' crimes. By 2003 this unit had achieved a conviction rate of 96 percent, with sentences ranging from five to 17 years.[18] The unit started in Pretoria; a second unit was opened in Johannesburg in 2002, and a further rollout to Durban, Cape Town and Port Elizabeth was planned at the time of Bulelani's resignation in 2004.[19]

One of the cases this unit handled was the long-running Gary Porritt matter, which began in 2002 when Porritt and co-accused Sue Bennet faced over 3 000 charges including fraud and racketeering, and contravening the Income Tax Act, the Companies Act and the Stock Exchanges Control Act. The case is still not finalised even though two of Porritt's former colleagues, who are already serving time, turned state witness. Porritt faces 200 years in jail if convicted.

The unit also dealt with the headline-grabbing and long-running 'Kidneygate' case, involving international organ trafficking in which impoverished Brazilians were duped into selling organs to wealthy Israelis. It got under way in January 2004, with top surgeons and specialists facing charges of fraud, forgery, assault and contravening both the Human Tissue Act and the Prevention of Organised Crime Act. In a world first, a hospital group, Netcare, admitted guilt in November 2010 and was fined R4 million for its role in 109 illegal transplants.[20]

The Priority Crimes Litigation Unit (PCLU) was established in 2003, headed by advocate Anton Ackerman, who had distinguished himself working for the Goldstone Commission appointed in 1993 to investigate political violence and killings. The PCLU managed investigations and prosecutions dealing with weapons of mass destruction, mercenary activities, the International Criminal Court at The Hague in the Netherlands, national and international terrorism, and the prosecution of people who were refused or who had failed to apply for amnesty in terms of the TRC process.

This unit handled two cases involving mercenaries, one of which was a group of South African citizens arrested in March 2004 in Zimbabwe and Equatorial Guinea, along with 18 Namibians, 23 Angolans, two Congolese and one Zimbabwean, all suspected to be en route to overthrow the government of Equatorial Guinea. Those involved included Simon Mann, a former British Special Air Services officer and owner of the private security company Executive Outcomes, and Nick du Toit, a former member of the notorious 32 Battalion of the South African

Defence Force (SADF), involved principally in the conflict in Namibia and Angola but also in violence in townships in Gauteng in 1992.[21] The case led to the arrest of Mark Thatcher, the son of former British prime minister Margaret Thatcher, in August 2004, just after Bulelani's resignation.

Mark Thatcher, who at first denied any knowledge of the coup, pleaded guilty in 2005 to 'unwittingly' helping to finance the coup after South African police were able to prove that he had transferred about US$285 000 (about R1.9 million at the time) to the mercenaries who were to execute the operation, and had met and talked frequently to them prior to the coup attempt. He was given a four-year suspended sentence and a fine of about US$560 000 (about R3.7 million).[22]

The unit also played a key role in securing the evidence that led to the conviction of Asher Karni, a South African businessman who was arrested in 2004 in the USA on charges of exporting nuclear-arms technology to India.[23]

And the PCLU was involved in what was at the time thought to be the biggest case of international nuclear proliferation in the world. In 2004 police raided the premises of Tradefin Engineering in Johannesburg, where they discovered shipping containers destined for Libya with parts that would allegedly have allowed Libya to process enough enriched uranium for several nuclear bombs.[24] While trafficking charges against the company's director were later dropped, Gerard Wisser, a German engineer and former managing director of Johannesburg engineering company Krisch, reached a plea deal with the NPA in 2007 and was found guilty of seven charges of contravening the Non-Proliferation of Weapons of Mass Destruction Act and the Nuclear Energy Act, and two counts of forgery. In addition to house arrest of three years and a suspended sentence of 18 years, Wisser forfeited R6 million in cash and overseas assets worth about 2,8 million euros.[25]

Anton Ackerman and advocate Torie Pretorius handled one of the first major trials for apartheid crimes – that of Wouter Basson, 'Dr Death', the head of the apartheid regime's biological and chemical warfare programme. When the marathon two-and-a-half-year-long trial began in October 1999, two years after his arrest, Basson faced charges for crimes that were described as 'so grotesque, they almost seemed make-believe. The most vivid example was that he was alleged to have supplied the drugs to operators who administered them to political detainees before throwing them out of a helicopter into the sea off the coast of Namibia.'[26] The charges included 229 murders, conspiracy to murder, fraud totalling R36 million, and manufacturing drugs.

It was a difficult trial from the start, says Bulelani, and indeed one report noted, 'The state's case was fraught with problems. Many witnesses were reluctant to testify, some refused to do so at all, and others were openly hostile to the prosecution. The prosecutors had to rely on testimony from operators who had carried out murders many years before and whose accounts of the incidents did not always tally. Ultimately Basson's version of events was found to be the most believable by Judge [Willie] Hartzenberg.'[27]

In 2002 Basson was finally acquitted of all charges. The state's first appeal was dismissed but they took the matter to the Constitutional Court, which granted leave to appeal stating that the trial court had erred in dismissing charges against Basson regarding conspiracy to murder abroad. In the end, the Constitutional Court ruled against the NPA on the matter of whether the trial judge was biased or not but left it up to the NPA to decide whether to proceed with the conspiracy charges.[28]

Ackerman commented later that they 'concluded that the conspiracy charges had in fact been dealt with on the merits by the trial court on other charges relating thereto. As such, the principle of double jeopardy applied and consequently, the charges could not be reinstated.[29]

❑

The NPA was also involved in the Joint Anti-Corruption Task Team (JACTT), which was set up in 2003 to assist with the backlog of corruption cases in the Eastern Cape. It was led from the NPA side by Lungisa Dyosi and included representatives from the Scorpions (the agency that investigated and prosecuted organised crime and corruption), the Special Investigating Unit (SIU), the Asset Forfeiture Unit (AFU), the auditor-general's office and the intelligence services. The Scorpions were responsible for overall leadership of the project, which was one of the most successful mobilisations of different law-enforcement agencies at the time.

By September 2003 the JACTT was dealing with 374 cases, 144 arrests had been made, 18 convictions had been handed down and 113 people were facing trial.[30] By December 2004, it was reported that 60 percent of the cases finalised by the JACTT involved fraud and theft of social grants by paymasters working for the department of social development.[31]

When the Scorpions prepared papers for the 2005 Khampepe Commission,[32] they reported that the JACTT had arrested 380 people and convicted 110 people in 119 cases amounting to about R19 million of potential loss to various government departments. More than 200 people were on trial in 151 cases, with potential losses of more than R38 million to the state, while a further 228 cases of fraud and corruption with potential losses of more than R138 million were under investigation.

By 2006, the JACTT team had finalised 113 cases in court and registered a 93 percent success rate.[33]

The JACTT made use of the asset-forfeiture provisions in the Prevention of Organised Crime Act to reclaim money stolen from the state. In all, it was reported that by 2006 the AFU's JACTT-based investigation had confiscated about R5 million-worth of assets, with a further R15 million under restraint (the accused's property restrained before his/her conviction to ensure that it is available to be sold later to pay the confiscation order that may be made should the accused be convicted).[34]

Lungisa says that the JACTT'S work was an important exercise in inter-agency cooperation in law enforcement. 'There was collaboration taking place between the different agencies all over the country, but it really came together in the JACTT. The process threw up so many anomalies. In one of the cases, we knew that the SAPS, the National Intelligence Agency (NIA) and the SIU were all relying on the same intelligence source for their information, but they wouldn't believe us. So we arranged for a presentation and asked both the SAPS and the NIA to present what they had. The NIA went first. After the others heard this presentation, they refused and said no, they didn't want to present. They realised they had been had – they were all using the same source and this guy was using all three agencies, playing them off against one another. It was happening simply because they weren't talking to one another.

'From a law-enforcement perspective, we all came out of that experience enriched. There are many in senior positions in the

SAPS and the NPA who got valuable experience in the JACTT, including Sibongile Mzinyathi and Saks Mapoma. The NIA agent I worked with is now a regional head. There are police officers I worked with in the JACTT who have moved up in the ranks and occupy senior positions.'[35]

❏

Shortly after his appointment, Bulelani set up a working group led by Vincent Saldanha, who had served on the TRC and who went on to serve as a judge in the Western Cape, to review all the cases that had been refused amnesty by the TRC. The group drew up criteria to guide decisions on whether to investigate matters further or to make recommendations for prosecution.

Bulelani said he was obliged by law to prosecute where there was enough evidence to make a case, but at the same time part of him asked if it was worth it. Part of him wanted 'to go for them', but another part asked whether these apartheid perpetrators, many of whom were 'broken' or about to die, were really a threat to society.[36]

When the PCLU was formally set up in March 2003, hundreds of TRC cases were referred to it. Ackerman conducted an extensive audit and identified only 16 that he said were worth pursuing; and only three were ready for immediate charges.[37]

The first TRC-related matter the unit prosecuted was that of Eugene Terre'Blanche, leader of the Afrikaner Weerstandsbeweging, who was convicted on five counts of terrorism in 2003 for ordering at least five bombings before the 1994 elections. He had not applied for amnesty and this case did not require much investigation: those responsible for the bombings were already serving life sentences, and Terre'Blanche himself was already in prison at the time, for the attempted murder of a farmworker in 2001. He entered into a plea agreement.[38]

The highest-profile TRC prosecution Ackerman pursued was that of Gideon Nieuwoudt, a security policeman from Port Elizabeth with some of the bloodiest hands in apartheid history. 'Notorious Nieuwoudt', as he was called, was charged with the car-bomb murder in December 1989 of three black policemen and an askari – the 'Motherwell Four' – and sentenced to 20 years. He applied to the TRC for amnesty, was refused, and appealed. He was still waiting for a decision when he died in 2005. He was eventually refused amnesty, once again, in August 2005, about ten days after he died.

The TRC also refused to give amnesty to Nieuwoudt for the murder of three political activists from the Port Elizabeth Civic Organisation – the so-called 'Pebco Three', Qaqawuli Godolozi, Champion Galela and Sipho Hashe – who had been abducted, tortured and killed in 1985, and their bodies thrown into the Fish River. Two others were later charged with Nieuwoudt for the same killings – Johannes van Zyl, a security policeman from Port Elizabeth, and a former Vlakplaas member, Johannes Koole. Niewoudt, Koole and Van Zyl applied to court for a review of the TRC's 1999 decision to deny them amnesty, and this application was also outstanding when Niewoudt died in 2005.[39]

There have been questions about political interference preventing the prosecution of TRC cases, allegedly because the ANC feared that the NPA was intent on charging senior ANC leaders. But Bulelani emphasises that he was not subjected to any political interference during his time.

Some of the controversy about political interference related to a decision in 2004 not to prosecute 37 ANC leaders who had been denied individual amnesty. The commission had granted the group, which included then president Thabo Mbeki, collective amnesty, since they had claimed collective responsibility for all actions carried out by the ANC and MK between 1964 and 1994.[40] The NPA found there was no basis for prosecution, as there was no evidence that specific crimes had been committed, which attracted personal criminal liability.

Another TRC-related prosecution was the Bisho Massacre case, which got under way in 2001. The Bisho Massacre had taken place in September 1992, when Ciskei soldiers had opened fire on protestors. Those charged were the man who gave the order to his troops to open fire on ANC marchers, Lieutenant-Colonel Vakele Mkosana, and an ordinary rifleman, Mzamile Gonya. Both faced charges of murder, attempted murder, and culpable homicide. Both were denied amnesty.

When he announced that the two would be prosecuted, Bulelani said the prosecution would be asking for life imprisonment; quoted in a newspaper report, he said, 'It was a cold-blooded and brutal murder of people.'[41] The judge, however, accepted Mkosana's argument of self-defence and acquitted both men.[42]

In 2006 an insider noted that the unit's ability to handle TRC cases was severely hampered by a standoff between the Scorpions and the SAPS about who was going to investigate the cases, and said this matter had not been resolved at the time Bulelani resigned in August 2004. The PCLU itself didn't have any investigators.[43]

After Bulelani had quit the NPA, acting NDPP Silas Ramaite called a moratorium on TRC-related cases. Bulelani's successor, Vusi Pikoli, complained later about 'improper interference' in his work on TRC cases and said, 'Legally, I have reached a dead end.'[44]

The failure of the NPA to prosecute TRC-related crimes remains a sore point for many families and comrades of those who died at the hands of apartheid security forces.

13.
A balancing act

'It was clear that so much was wrong in the system, and that whatever decisions I took, I was going to face criticism and be lambasted from all sides.'

The constitution requires that the NDPP act without fear, favour or prejudice. At the same time, someone who simply stood up and said that politics was irrelevant would serve neither the NPA nor South Africa. If the NPA was to survive and function effectively, it needed a leader capable of navigating the tricky territory of politics, of being sympathetic to its nuances without compromising the independence of prosecutorial decisions.

In one of his very first cases, Bulelani was accused of advancing ANC interests.

The case of the 'Eikenhof Three' had been prosecuted in 1993 by then Transvaal attorney-general Jan d'Oliveira, subsequently one of two deputy NDPPs (Percy Sonn being the other). Sipho Gavin, Siphiwe Bholo and Boy Ndweni had been accused of the murder of Zandra Mitchley, her son Shaun and his friend Claire Silberbauer in Eikenhof, south of Johannesburg, in March 1993. Zandra had been taking the children to school when their vehicle was fired on by the occupants of a BMW that had been hijacked earlier.

The main evidence against the three was their 'confessions', which the judge found had been 'freely made', and the evidence of witnesses, three of whom were schoolchildren.[1] There was evidence during the trial about confessions being obtained by torture; this evidence was dismissed. The alibis of the accused were rejected.

All three were convicted. Sipho Gavin and Siphiwe Bholo were sentenced to death. Only Boy Ndweni, who was 17 years old at the time, escaped the death sentence.'[2]

But then things started to unravel.

In December 1996, a senior commander of the Azanian People's Liberation Army (Apla), Phila Dolo, applied to the TRC for amnesty for the very same attack. He had given orders to four trained Apla members, who had carried out the attack.[3] Dolo himself had been arrested in May 1993 and sentenced in December 1994 to life imprisonment for an attack on the Diepkloof police station in Soweto.

The Eikenhof Three appealed and applied for bail. Bulelani had been in the job for three months when the bail application came up before Judge Piet van der Walt. Prosecutors had already decided to oppose bail when Dullah Omar approached Bulelani and said, 'All is not as it seems. You should consider not opposing bail.'

Bulelani said he would consult the prosecutors involved. He spoke first to D'Oliveira, who dismissed the minister's concerns, saying Dolo was a liar and that he had only 'confessed' to the TRC to get the trio out of prison. He had intimate knowledge of the facts of the case and the three were definitely guilty, D'Oliveira assured Bulelani.

The senior prosecutor involved in handling the bail application also didn't agree to not oppose bail.

This is what Bulelani reported back to Dullah, saying that

on the basis of this information, he would have to oppose bail.

Dullah then advised Bulelani to speak to Sydney Mufamadi, minister of police. What he heard was startling. Gavin, Bholo and Ndweni, feeling absolutely secure in their innocence, had handed themselves over to the police with the assistance of the ANC a few weeks after the Eikenhof attack. Following Dolo's application to the TRC, further investigation revealed that no fewer than five witnesses who had been in the area at the time of the attack had failed to identify the Eikenhof Three as being the attackers and, after being shown 300 photographs, had instead identified two people who were known by police to be Apla members. This evidence had not been made available to the defence during the trial and D'Oliveira had not called any of these witnesses.

The weapon in Dolo's possession when he was arrested in May 1993 had been tested and had proved to be the one used in the Eikenhof attack. In addition, Dolo had referred in his amnesty application to documents that had been seized by police in an Apla house in 1995, which had included a report of the Eikenhof attack; and the first security police reports after the attack had, unsurprisingly, concluded that Apla was responsible.[4]

In these circumstances, Bulelani decided, he could not oppose bail, and he instructed prosecutors to withdraw their opposition. He told D'Oliveira he was free to argue against the three convicted men's appeal when this came up but that it was not correct to oppose bail in light of what had emerged about the way the matter had been handled.

There was an immediate backlash.

Judge Van der Walt said Bulelani's decision was 'extremely unfortunate, ill-considered and extremely unwise' in the light of his 'connection' to the ANC. 'He himself is an ANC member, appointed by an ANC government. Any person in his position should be extremely wary to take a decision of this nature,' he said.⁵

Bulelani was stung by this criticism. His first inclination was to hit back, but he received a call from Arthur Chaskalson, who was now president of the Constitutional Court. 'Don't say too much, Bul. You'll be vindicated by the Supreme Court of Appeal,' was Arthur's advice, Bulelani says.

And, indeed, in August 1999 the Appeal Court set aside the sentences and convictions, and said it was up to the NPA whether to proceed with a retrial.

The ball was back in Bulelani's court. He decided to withdraw the case and the Eikenhof Three were finally released in November 1999. They had spent six years in jail for a crime they had not committed.

The Eikenhof Three case demonstrated the size of the challenge ahead and, says Bulelani, gave him 'a taste of what it was going to be like'.

> On the one hand I knew I would constantly be told I was an ANC lackey, but I would also be heavily criticised for not moving fast enough to transform an organisation that had been an instrument of oppression throughout the apartheid years.

One of those who came to Bulelani's assistance after he was attacked by Judge Van der Walt was Anton Ackerman. Bulelani had just been appointed and did not yet know Anton.

> He phoned me out of the blue and said he had investigated the matter. He said he had spoken to witnesses and it was clear to him they had been coached by police. He gave me an affidavit and said he would testify if necessary.

THE STING IN THE TALE: BULELANI NGCUKA

> In the end this wasn't necessary but he told me I had done the right thing by not opposing bail.

❏

Bulelani faced a test of a different kind with the prosecution of Tony Yengeni, the ANC's chief whip in the national assembly, and a former MK commander.

In 1998 Yengeni, at the time serving as the chair of the joint standing committee on defence, had received a 47 percent discount on a Mercedes-Benz 4x4 bought from DaimlerChrysler.[6] The news of the 4x4, and what the media dubbed the 'cars for VIPs' scandal, broke in July 2001. Yengeni immediately took out several full-page newspaper adverts denying that he had ever received any extraordinary discount. He said he had received a 26 percent discount for a damaged vehicle. He also did not disclose to parliament that he had received such a benefit – and this was what snared him.

Bulelani was called to a meeting by minister of justice Penuell Maduna to discuss 'an important matter'. He did not tell him what it was about.

When he arrived at Maduna's home, Bulelani found Tony Yengeni there. Yengeni put his case to Bulelani, who responded by advising him to speak to his lawyers and to tell them to arrange for a meeting with the NPA.

> The case was being handled by Jan Henning and Gerda Ferreira. Gerda was spitting fire. Remember, Tony had been running a media campaign and attacking everyone involved in the case.
>
> Jan was in hospital at the time so when the lawyers set

up the meeting, I asked Leonard McCarthy [head of the Scorpions] to join me. They offered us a plea of guilty to the fraud charge, as an alternative to the principal count of corruption.

Then I had to go to the prosecuting team to discuss it with them. I knew Gerda would accept it if Jan accepted it, so we went to see Jan. He agreed with the plea, and we went to court. The court accepted the plea.

I had told Gerda at the time that I believed the appropriate sentence was a suspended sentence. I did not believe then, and I still do not believe, that the crime deserved a jail sentence. However, Gerda was bitter, and while she didn't go as far as asking for prison time, she made it clear in the way she argued in court that she felt he should go to jail.

Magistrate Bill Moyses also did not agree with the NPA's position on a non-custodial sentence, saying that Yengeni had abused his position of trust and that the example he had set as chief whip of the ANC was 'shocking'. 'What makes the crime even more serious is the planning and ongoing deceit after the benefit became public knowledge. Not only did you not disclose the benefit, but [you] thereafter covered up your tracks.'[7]

And Moyses expressed annoyance with the manner in which Yengeni had conducted himself in court. 'You held this court at ransom for a long time with all sorts of fanciful defences.'[8]

In his guilty plea, Yengeni acknowledged that the discount he had received was not available to the public or dealers, and admitted that it 'was highly unlikely that I would have received the benefit had I not been a high-profile person and chairperson of the joint standing committee on defence.'[9] He also admitted to not disclosing the benefit to parliament, and to making misrepresentations once the deal had become public knowledge, including signed backdated documents for a sale of agreement for a falsely inflated amount. He had also taken out an advertisement, he conceded, in which he had 'falsely attempted to give out that there was nothing improper about the benefit.'[10]

The judge sentenced Yengeni to four years in prison.

> Tony appealed against the sentence, and I had a fight with my team. I believed then, and I believe now, that the sentence was not justified.
>
> Jan's argument was that the convention is that once an accused person appeals, whatever the sentence, the prosecutor must defend the magistrate and the sentence handed down.
>
> I said, 'No, Jan, that can't be correct.'
>
> 'So,' he said, 'does that mean we must throw in the towel?'
>
> 'Yes,' I said. 'The sentence is unfair. It is too severe.'
>
> We had a big fight about it. I stood my ground. Well, in that case, he said, he can't go to court, and I must find another prosecutor.
>
> Okay, I said. I found another team to handle the appeal.

During the appeal, the issue of the meeting between Maduna, Yengeni and Bulelani in January 2003 came up. Yengeni argued that Bulelani and Maduna had agreed he would be sentenced to no more than a fine of R5 000 if he pleaded guilty to the alternative count of fraud.

No agreement had been reached at the meeting. Bulelani had simply told Yengeni to tell his lawyers to make an appointment with the NPA and discuss the matter there.

Yengeni was angry.

> He attacked me viciously. I chose not to respond.
>
> Tony was the first comrade I prosecuted. It was very sad, actually. However, the fact of the matter is I still believe the sentence was unfair. Tony was being sentenced because of his behaviour in court. The magistrate was angry. I still don't think it's right, even today.

After losing his final appeal, Yengeni went on to serve only four months of his sentence and was released on parole in January 2007.

Yengeni is one of the people who are critical of the fact that former apartheid security police served in the ranks of the Scorpions. Bulelani is upfront about this and says that Yengeni is not the only one who has criticised him for this. He says there were other friends and comrades who also found this uncomfortable.

> We had to be mature about this. We couldn't build a country and move forward without burying the animosities of the past.
>
> I accept that people felt very bitter about the actions of the security police, but former apartheid operatives didn't only exist in the Scorpions. They remained active in all arms of law enforcement, including the SAPS.
>
> The few we had in the Scorpions delivered. I was challenged at times about their presence but I can honestly say these guys delivered.
>
> They were not my friends.
>
> They were investigators and some of them were very good investigators. There were crimes we would not have

THE STING IN THE TALE: BULELANI NGCUKA

solved without them, for example, the urban terror and bombs in Cape Town.[11]

❏

Another politically charged case that Bulelani had to deal with early on was that of Winnie Madikizela-Mandela, struggle stalwart and president of the ANC Women's League. The case revolved around the use of ANC letterheads with Madikizela-Mandela's signature on them to obtain loans from Saambou Bank for 60 people who were not ANC employees, and the deduction of money from accounts for a funeral policy that wasn't underwritten.

Madikizela-Mandela was convicted in April 2003 on 43 fraud charges and 25 theft charges, and the court imposed a five-year prison sentence despite the fact that the prosecution had argued against a custodial sentence.[12] Winnie, who was 67 years old at the time, resigned from parliament after her conviction.

Madikizela-Mandela was one of the most popular and celebrated figures in the struggle against apartheid and so Bulelani knew there would be 'feedback'.

> There were people who tried to pressurise me. I received calls from a number of people, including cabinet ministers, saying Winnie should not be prosecuted.
>
> And then Winnie texted Steve [Tshwete, then minister of police], 'When I hit a bird, I hit the tree as well.' Ostensibly, she was saying that she will hit Steve and whoever is behind him.
>
> He responded, 'When you hit me, I will be holding a plough.' He meant that he would hit back.

He called me immediately and told me about this conversation. He wanted to know where the case was and said I must make sure she goes to jail.

I said, no, we must be consistent. When it was Mangope, we said our view in this dispensation is that we don't send grandmothers and grandfathers to jail.[13] It's not right to give her a custodial sentence.

It was a fairly complicated case and so the prosecutors kept me informed throughout the trial. My position was that we should go for a non-custodial sentence and fortunately the whole team supported it. In fact, the prosecutors ended up making a strong case for mitigation of sentence.

Those are some of the things that were very difficult. I had known Winnie for a long time and worked with her in the struggle days, and respected and liked her as a person. So prosecuting her was not a nice thing. But that's the law. The law applies to everyone, even the people you love. That's the nature of the beast.

❏

Bulelani also came under fire in the case against Allan Boesak, another popular figure in the anti-apartheid struggle. This case shocked many because of Boesak's high political profile, and the fact that the ANC continued to maintain he was innocent even after his conviction.

A prominent anti-apartheid fighter in the 1980s, Boesak was elected chair of the ANC in the Western Cape in 1991 and was appointed MEC of economic affairs in the Western Cape in 1994. He and Bulelani had worked together during the UDF days and setting up ANC structures in the early 1990s. He was a former president of the World Alliance of Reformed Churches.

THE STING IN THE TALE: BULELANI NGCUKA

In the early 1990s, donor funds had disappeared or been misused and Boesak was the accused. An investigation was ordered by Deputy President Mbeki, and Boesak was cleared. But the donor agencies ordered a further investigation and this led to Boesak being charged in 1996; this was a case Bulelani inherited on his appointment two years later.

In 1999 Boesak was convicted of fraud and theft[14] and sentenced to six years' imprisonment. This was reduced to three years on appeal when one of the convictions was set aside.

In September 2000, Boesak applied to be released on correctional supervision, serving a community-based sentence under the control and supervision of correctional officials. The national commissioner of correctional services contacted Bulelani and asked if the state would oppose the application once it went to court. Bulelani said he didn't think so but that he would need to consult Frank Kahn, since the case had been handled in the Western Cape. Kahn supported the application and it went to court.

At the same time as his parole application was being considered, Boesak's cell was searched and a cellphone was discovered. When he was asked about the phone, Boesak said he had brought it into prison with him when he was sentenced and had not used it. However, an examination of the phone's records showed that it had been used by Boesak during his imprisonment to phone a cabinet minister, an aide to President Thabo Mbeki and his wife. Boesak had therefore lied to the prison authorities. It also emerged that the phone was a stolen one.

The judge handling the application agreed that Boesak should be released for correctional supervision but that he should be charged for possession of the phone.

> When I was in prison, we smuggled in many things, newspapers and so on. Allan had been punished and it was enough.

A BALANCING ACT

> We didn't want to be seen to be vindictive. We discussed it with Frank and agreed Allan shouldn't be charged.

In a statement issued at the time, Kahn said there was no evidence that Boesak knew the phone was stolen, and that while Boesak had said he hadn't used the phone, contrary to evidence, the decision was not to proceed with a prosecution.[15]

Boesak was released in May 2001 having served just over a third of his sentence.

> Allan was released and in the first statement he made after he was released, he hit out at me. He was very emotional. What would I like to be in the next life? What would I like to be? Maybe I should be a white cricket captain who gets pardoned by the prosecutor general even before he's charged. He was referring to the Hansie Cronje matter, of course. But what can you do? You roll with the punches.

❏

The Hansie Cronje case was one that shook not only the international cricketing world, but also South Africa, where Cronje, captain of the national cricket team, the Proteas, had been held up as the golden boy of the sport.

Cronje was charged by Delhi police in April 2000 with match-fixing. The police released transcripts of a conversation between Cronje and an alleged bookmaker and Indian businessman, Sanjay Chawla, in discussion about who was playing and the amounts to be paid to Cronje and his teammates to sabotage the match in India's favour.

At this point in his career, Cronje had played in 68 Test matches and captained 53 of them.

THE STING IN THE TALE: BULELANI NGCUKA

Shortly after CNN announced that Hansie was accused of match-fixing in India, Percy [Sonn] phoned me. He was the president of Cricket South Africa at the time.

'Boss, we've got trouble,' he said. He said that Hansie had woken him at 3 am and confessed to him. He was in Durban, preparing to play the [one-day international] against Australia.

Percy said he got the shock of his life. He told Hansie to get some sleep and they would talk later.

Percy woke everyone up and convened an urgent board meeting of Cricket SA. They removed [Cronje] as captain and appointed Shaun Pollock [in his place].

They were looking for Hansie. He was nowhere to be found. Then he appeared in Cape Town with Ngconde Balfour, who was the minister of sport. Ngconde pledged his support for Hansie. I think he even used the words 'captain, my captain'.

My son, Olwethu, was playing cricket at the time at Pretoria Christian Brothers. Hansie was his hero. When I got home from work, he wouldn't talk to me. 'It's you,' he said. 'My friends won't talk to me because of you. It's not him. Hansie is innocent. It's those Indians who are corrupt.'

I told him we hadn't even started an investigation yet.

A week or so later, Cricket SA said they wanted to approach the minister of justice to set up a commission of inquiry, and they wanted Judge Edwin King to head it up because he understood cricket. They wanted my support. [But] if there was going to be a prosecution, there couldn't be a commission. They appealed to me to hold off on prosecutions. It was about the integrity of the national team. They needed to get to the bottom of it.

We were not getting much cooperation from India and there was no evidence.[16]

I was told the commission was going to be a whitewash. It would rely on what the cricketers said. There's a law against self-incrimination.

I chose Shamila Batohi as the evidence leader. People questioned her appointment because she was a woman and Indian. They thought I was protecting the cricketers. I wanted a woman leading the process, a black woman, and I knew Shamila could do the job.

Shamila came back to me and told me the cricketers wouldn't testify without indemnity. The judge agreed that it was a problem. The proposal was that we offer them indemnity on the same basis as Section 204 witnesses: on condition that they tell the truth to the satisfaction of the commissioner.

So we all agreed – myself, Balfour, Penuell and Shamila – to offer them indemnity on condition they tell the truth, and it was communicated to the lawyers representing the cricketers.

The next thing it was leaked to the newspapers and I got a call from a journalist. I explained how Section 204 of the Criminal Procedure Act worked [it is used when the state requires a person who may have been a party to a crime to testify against others] and said this was something we did all the time. There was nothing unusual about it.

During his testimony, Cronje confessed to taking about US$100 000 (about R400 000 at the time) in bribes from various individuals since 1996 but maintained that he was 'simply playing along' and 'forecasting', and had no intention of throwing any matches. His reasoning remained confused, but

THE STING IN THE TALE: BULELANI NGCUKA

under repeated questioning by Shamila, he admitted to having received money from Indian bookmakers as a 'deposit' in return for delivering the results they wanted – a 'fixed' match.[17]

> It was only when Shamila started cross-examining Hansie that the whole world started to take notice of her. She did a great job. The newspapers spoke about it. They called her 'the woman who made Hansie cry'.

In the end, King did not rule on whether Cronje had 'come clean' or not. Bulelani appointed Frank Kahn to investigate whether Cronje had met the conditions for indemnity or not. The matter was still being investigated at the time of Cronje's death in June 2002.

Cronje had earlier, in October 2000, been banned from the sport for life by the United Cricket Board of South Africa.

❑

Bulelani was once again in the firing line in the case of Billy Rautenbach, one of the murkiest cases in the history of South African law enforcement. It does not appear to be a political case on the surface but it is entangled with that of, among others, Jackie Selebi, the first black national commissioner of police and a senior political figure.

Rautenbach had business interests across the continent, earning him the title 'the Napoleon of Africa'. He took advantage of a loophole in tax regulations in 1993, establishing Hyundai Motor Distributors and setting up an elaborate scheme to import vehicles through Mozambique as fully assembled vehicles, then stripping them to comply with import rules, and then shipping them to Botswana, where they were reassembled. He was paying a 23 percent import duty to bring the vehicles into

Botswana, then exporting the finished vehicles to South Africa and paying no additional tariff; local South African manufacturers were paying a 115 percent tariff on imported cars.[18]

Rautenbach was making a killing, but it didn't last. By 1999, not only was the market declining but he was being investigated for fraud and corruption. His company was in trouble and banks were threatening to seize his assets. In January 2000 Hyundai Motor Distributors went into liquidation.

According to Bulelani, Rautenbach had been a person of interest for intelligence agencies in South Africa for some time; they suspected he was funding rebels in the war in the Democratic Republic of Congo. He also appeared on the list of the top 20 criminal suspects that the Scorpions were looking at, compiled in consultation with intelligence agencies and the SAPS.[19]

After finalising this top 20, Bulelani announced to the media that the Scorpions now had their targets and would be pursuing them. No names were mentioned in the press briefing. However, the media contacted Willie Hofmeyr, head of the AFU, and asked specifically if Rautenbach was on the list. He said he was, but the media were not satisfied: they wanted the NDPP himself to confirm the matter before they published the article.

> Willie went ahead without consulting me and told them I had said Rautenbach was on the list. I first heard about the matter when I read it in the *Sunday Times* the following day.
>
> I told Willie he was out of order but of course we received threatening letters from Billy's lawyers. We told them we would defend the matter in court. The investigation was already at an advanced stage.
>
> Madiba called me at about this same time. He told me

that he liked what we were doing in the Scorpions and asked if there was anything he could do to help. I told him we needed unmarked cars to use for surveillance purposes.

A few days later he told me he had secured four cars, two from Delta Motors and two from Hyundai. Madiba was unaware of the investigation and Hyundai was, of course, Billy's company. I told Madiba we could not accept cars from Billy. We were on the verge of charging him but needed to conduct a search of his business premises first.

Madiba kept quiet for a while and then he said, 'Take the cars and then charge him.'

And that's exactly what we did. We collected the cars and a week later, in November 1999, a search was conducted at Billy's offices. During the search, Billy kept telling Gerrie Nel that he was making a mistake and that he was 'very close to Mr Ngcuka'. Gerrie told him he could phone me, but he would continue with the search.

We got the evidence we needed.

Three truckloads of records, documents and data were seized in the raids.

Immediately after the search-and-seizure operation, Rautenbach challenged the constitutionality of the relevant provisions of the NPA Act. He won his case when Judge Brian Southwood declared the provisions unconstitutional and ordered that the documents seized during the search be returned. (The Constitutional Court later set aside this judgment.)[20]

Days after the search, Billy ran and left the country for Zimbabwe.

It was going to take a bit of time to sift through the

documents, but it was clear we had a good case and that we were going to charge Billy.

A week or so later, I was returning from a trip to Zurich when a man came up to me on the plane and introduced himself as Glenn Agliotti. He came to see me a short while later in my office. He told me he had come to see me about the Billy Rautenbach case and that Billy wanted to return to South Africa. He was basically pleading on Billy's behalf for some kind of arrangement to avoid a jail sentence.

A short while later, Bulelani was approached by a lawyer from London who said he was representing Rautenbach, who wanted to reach some form of arrangement. Rautenbach, he said, had a lot of assets, which could be 'made available' to both Bulelani and the South African government.

When Bulelani cautioned him against what appeared to be the offer of a bribe, he backed off and said he had been misunderstood and that the assets were only being offered to the government in return for an agreement that Billy would not be prosecuted.

> By then Rautenbach's name was on the list of those who could not travel, and the net was closing in on him. 'No way,' I said. We were confident of our case. 'Billy will go to jail. *Qha!* Period. Billy must be counted before he sleeps.' In Xhosa, when you talk about people in jail, you say *'ulala ubaliwe'*, 'you are counted before you sleep'.
>
> The lawyer left, then came back and said that Billy had information that might be very useful to the South African government and was willing to offer this. I said I would think about it and consulted with ministers in the security cluster. They said I should test him first. So the

THE STING IN THE TALE: BULELANI NGCUKA

NIA drafted a letter asking Billy a number of questions and I sent him the letter. He responded positively and said he would share information with us.

We then set up a meeting in Mozambique with Pete Richer from the Scorpions and Jeff Maqetuka from the NIA. The purpose of this meeting was to assess the type of information Billy claimed to have. I was still adamant he should be charged but I was obliged to take the security interests of the country into account too, so that intelligence could assess the information he said he had.

We met with the president after the Mozambican trip and debriefed him. It was agreed that this information was nothing new and that there was no point in trying to reach any arrangement with Billy. Of course, we knew Zimbabwe would not extradite him.

In September 2000, the AFU moved in and seized R60 million of Rautenbach's assets in South Africa. These included a private Falcon jet worth R15 million, a Bell helicopter worth R8 million, a house and several apartments in Johannesburg, a wine farm in the Western Cape and another farm in KwaZulu-Natal.

Willie Hofmeyr explained at the time that Rautenbach appeared to have no assets of his own and that the assets were instead owned through front companies and trusts. The jet, for example, belonged to a company called Wheels Aviation, which was in turn owned by Airlex, a company based in the British Virgin Islands, which was controlled by Sefta Trustees in Jersey in the Channel Islands, which was owned by the El Hara Trust. 'Behind all of these are Rautenbach,' Hofmeyr explained. 'That is why it was important to convince the courts to strip away the corporate veil that hid his assets. ... If he [Rautenbach] wants to contest this, he will have to choose between his property and his liberty.'[21]

Hofmeyr said that in addition to fraud and the customs charges, Rautenbach was being investigated for money-laundering through what he called 'the family payday', in which millions were paid in cash to family members and friends after one of Rautenbach's companies had invoiced another for fictitious services and then issued cash cheques.[22]

In 2002 the Johannesburg High Court ordered that Rautenbach's assets be returned to him. Everything then seemed to come to a standstill until Rautenbach, who was keen to return to South Africa, finally struck a deal with the NPA in 2009. He pleaded guilty to 326 charges of fraud and was ordered to pay a R40-million fine. An NPA spokesperson told the media that the NPA had attached his farm in the Western Cape valued at R30 million in case he reneged on the agreement.[23]

But this was not the end of the matter. Rautenbach went on to testify against Jackie Selebi, whose trial got under way in October 2009, and again Bulelani was pulled into the fray.

Selebi was facing charges of corruption and defeating the ends of justice. Among other accusations, it was alleged that he had taken money from Glenn Agliotti – the same man who had introduced himself to Bulelani on the plane, and a self-confessed drug dealer – in return for agreeing to use his influence in the investigation into Rautenbach's case.

Agliotti was a long-time acquaintance of Selebi, going back to the unbanning of the ANC and the return of political exiles in 1990. Agliotti had been introduced to Rautenbach in Zimbabwe in 2003 as 'someone who could assist in moving Rautenbach's Hyundai matter forward in South Africa'.[24] Agliotti had first demanded R1 million as a fee from Rautenbach for his assistance in facilitating access to Selebi, which Rautenbach had said was exorbitant. Rautenbach had finally agreed to pay US$100 000 (about R800 000 at the time)[25] on the understanding that Selebi had the necessary contacts to 'resolve' his matter since 'the doors of the NPA were closed.'[26]

During the trial an email emerged in which it became clear that in his discussions with Rautenbach's business partner, Selebi had suggested that Bulelani was controlled by British intelligence and that they were 'using what they knew of his role as an informant during the apartheid era to blackmail and control him'.[27] He had tried to use the letter Bulelani had sent to Rautenbach earlier on the advice of NIA as proof that Bulelani had attempted to solicit a bribe, but this was rejected by the court.[28] The bribery allegations were false, the judge said, and Selebi hadn't even proven that Bulelani knew that Selebi was in possession of the letter.[29]

Bulelani responded with an angry statement saying that Selebi's claims that he had attempted to secure a bribe from Rautenbach were 'an outright lie.' In a statement he said, 'It is baffling why Mr Selebi, the most senior policeman at the time, did not charge me following his alleged discovery. If Mr Selebi or anyone else has evidence of my criminal involvement, they may present it in court.'[30]

Selebi was sentenced to 15 years and released on medical parole in 2012. He died in January 2015.

14.
Bombs, arms caches and carjackings

*'We had to take action before New Year's Eve.
That was just a week away ... We couldn't
risk any more bombings.'*

It was Christmas morning, 25 December 1999. Bulelani, at home in Cape Town, was up early.

The previous night's celebrations had been dampened by the news of yet another bombing in Cape Town. Seven police officers had responded to an anonymous tip, and had been injured when an explosive was triggered remotely, exploding in a bin at 10.30 pm outside a restaurant in Green Point.

It had been a bloody year in the Western Cape, which was in the grip of an urban-terror campaign, with bombs exploding at police stations, restaurants, fast-food outlets, night clubs and a synagogue.

A pipe bomb had exploded at St Elmo's pizzeria in Camps Bay in November, injuring 48 people, among them a 16-year-old schoolgirl who lost a leg. A few weeks before this a popular gay bar in the city centre had been bombed and nine people injured.

Three police stations had been bombed in 1999 – Athlone, Woodstock and Caledon Square; 11 people were injured in the Caledon Square bombing.

THE STING IN THE TALE: BULELANI NGCUKA

A car bomb had exploded on New Year's Day, 1 January 1999, at the Victoria & Alfred Waterfront, injuring two people.

And 1998 had been just as bloody. The Wynberg synagogue was bombed in December of that year, while in August 1998 two people had been killed and 26 injured in a blast at the Planet Hollywood restaurant at the Victoria & Alfred Waterfront.

Also in August, the Bellville building housing the police unit investigating People Against Gangsterism and Drugs (Pagad) had been bombed, with one person killed and another injured. The head of the unit, Schalk Visagie, had narrowly escaped death in this bombing – and again when he was fired on in heavy traffic while driving on a Cape Town highway. Seriously injured, he had managed to scramble out of his car still under heavy fire and take cover in a ditch next to the road.[1]

In January the next year, police detective Ben Lategan, who had been investigating Pagad-related crimes, was assassinated in Mitchells Plain while driving home in the early hours of the morning after a raid. He was shot ten times at point-blank range.

It was this reign of terror, Bulelani says, that was on his mind when he received the call from Steve Tshwete after the Christmas Eve bombing in December 1999.

> When I received the call on Christmas Day, Steve said the president said we should visit the scene of the bombing immediately. I left home and on my way I called Percy [Sonn] and the rest of the team, and they joined me.
>
> From the bombing scene, we went to the hospital to meet some of the victims, and then we went to the IDOC offices in Plein Street. We had everyone in the room with us, including the NIA, the SAPS and military intelligence.
>
> 'But we know who is behind this,' one of the team

members said. 'The brains behind all of this is a guy called Abdus Salaam Ebrahim.'

I told him, 'We have the intelligence. It must be converted to evidence.'

Ebrahim was the national coordinator of Pagad, which had started with protest marches: the movement was a reaction to community frustration with what they perceived as police inaction and was ostensibly intended to rid communities of gangs, druglords and merchants, but the focus shifted quickly from community vigilantism once a military wing known as 'G-Force' was established. By 1996 it was operating in small cells suspected of involvement in virtually all of the Cape Town bombings.

The team believed they could successfully prosecute Ebrahim for the murder of Rashaad Staggie, alleged leader of the Hard Livings gang. When a march to Staggie's home in Salt River in August 1996 turned violent, Staggie, who had been arrested more than once on drug and gang charges (at the time he was killed, reportedly making R100 000 a day selling drugs[2]), was beaten and shot, then had petrol poured over his body and was burned. The news media were present and images of Rashaad's burning body were beamed across the world.[3] Ebrahim was caught on camera during the killing.

> 'We have a case against him. Why not prosecute him for murder now? He's acting like he's a law unto himself. We know he is behind these bombings.'
>
> These were the arguments that were put forward as we debated the matter. We discussed it for a long time, and then they all turned to me and said, 'It's your call, boss. We can arrest Abdus now and charge him, but you must

know that we are going to have a running battle with the media to get the tapes.'

'Okay,' I said. 'Let's cross that bridge when we get to it. I can't in all good conscience allow this to continue.'

One of the journalists who had [still] pictures was freelance photographer Bennie Gool. Percy Sonn spoke to him. He was very sympathetic but refused.

After midnight I called Steve [Tshwete] and told him that we had decided to arrest Abdus.

The following day he called me. '*Uyabamba, toto?*' [Are you going to arrest him?]

'*Ewe, Bhuti.*' [Yes, brother]

'*Nini, toto?*' [When?]

'Thursday, *Bhuti.*'

'No, no. *Kwedini. Ngoku, kwedini. Ngoku.*' [No, no. Now, young man. Now.]

Then I had to explain about [the time it would take to investigate, draw up] the charge sheet, [get] the warrant and so on.

I had the same conversation with Steve the next day, and the next. He kept on calling until we arrested Abdus a few days later.

We had to find a secure police station that Pagad could not target for protests or anything else, so we took him to Khayelitsha C Section. We knew they would not dare go and protest there. He appeared in court and was denied bail.

The team still needed the tapes of Staggie's killing to proceed with the trial against Ebrahim. The two media houses that had footage were Reuters and the SABC. The team ultimately lost a case against Reuters for its tapes.

BOMBS, ARMS CACHES AND CARJACKINGS

The SABC also had tapes, so I spoke to [political editor at the SABC] Phil Molefe. I told him we didn't want to create the impression that they were cooperating with us, and that if they simply told us where the tapes were, we would come and take them. He agreed, but then every time we arrived, there was a delay. Finally, by the third day, we lost patience and went in and searched. We found nothing.

The day we searched was 19 October, International Press Freedom Day, and the anniversary of the banning of many Black Consciousness organisations in 1977, including newspapers like *The World*. I didn't pay special attention to the date when we raided the SABC, Reuters and Associated Press, and got a beating in the media. I think the *Sunday Times* made me 'Mampara of the Week'. [Mampara is a colloquialism referring to a person without intelligence or sense.] I was called 'a bull in a china shop' and all sorts of things.

Then Bulelani received a call from Snuki Zikalala, a former MK combatant and executive editor in charge of input at SABC news.

> 'Why are you going to those people?' he asked me. 'They know nothing about the struggle. We fought for this country, and we will not let it go to the dogs. What do you need?'
>
> I told him I needed the tapes. He made sure I got them. Snuki came to the rescue.

After Ebrahim's arrest the team began to find links between Pagad and the bombings. Further raids followed and two more Pagad leaders were arrested.

One of the things the team discovered was that the bombers had used cellphones to detonate the bombs. Saki Macozoma was

THE STING IN THE TALE: BULELANI NGCUKA

the chairperson of cellphone company MTN at the time, and Wendy Luhabe was the chair of Vodacom.

> So I called both of them. We wanted both companies to issue a statement that day to say that from now on no-one will ever be sold a SIM card [the computer chip that enables a cellphone user to connect with their network] without an ID card.
>
> Both companies came to the party and issued a pledge to South Africans at midnight on 25 December 1999, not to sell SIM cards without recording buyers' identity numbers.
>
> I didn't know what a headache this would cause in the cellphone industry. I knew it would take time to implement but we needed them to make the statement immediately, so that the message got out and the guys would be afraid to go and buy more SIM cards.

The Cape Town team became one of the most successful prosecution-led investigation teams in the country. And this was critical, says Bulelani, since it was this team that was going to set the precedent for the rest of the country.

> There had been 166 pipe-bomb incidents that year [1999] without a single prosecution. The agencies had been working in isolation. Police were working on their own and dockets were stuck in prosecutors' offices. It became clear that we had to form partnerships; we had to work together with the police and intelligence services.
>
> We didn't have the money and personnel to tackle these huge problems. Sydney [Mufamadi] was minister of police [until Steve Tshwete took over the post in June 1999] and a close friend. We had a common vision, so this

helped a great deal. Joe Nhlanhla [deputy intelligence minister] played an important role. And, of course, Dullah [Omar] and Zola [Skweyiya] also played a central role. I started off with the backing of these comrades.

They were not just comrades but my personal friends and it mattered a great deal. I could walk over to them at any time of the day or night when I had a problem and resolve matters. They constituted the core of people I worked with.

I also found a trusted and dependable ally in [national police commissioner] George Fivaz [who was succeeded in 2000 by Jackie Selebi]. He was somebody who was willing to solve problems.

We all agreed we had to work together. Everybody wanted results. I had brought in Percy Sonn. He brought in Willie Viljoen, Connie Erasmus, Adrian Mopp, Dawood Adam and Faiek Davids from the NPA.

We selected the police we wanted to work with. We drew up a list of who we wanted the police to second to us and gave the list to George. He said, 'Look, I will give these guys to you if you want them, but I don't think they are the right people.' He gave me good reasons. So he removed half of the people from the list. I'm glad he did because later he was proved right.

We ended up with a white team. I wasn't bothered but I knew I would be criticised. The situation was critical, and I wanted results and would have to deal with transformation issues later.

By October 2000 suspected Pagad members were facing 43 counts of murder, over 100 of attempted murder and a number of possession of explosives and bombs.[4]

This included the case of Ismail Edwards, an alleged hitman who had murdered an alleged drug dealer. Magistrate Pieter Theron was presiding over Edwards' case when he was assassinated in the driveway of his home, shot five times in the head. The trial had to start all over again, but Bulelani said the team would not be intimidated and that it was clear Theron had been 'taken out for the work he was doing'.[5] (Edwards was also charged for the murder of police detective Ben Lategan, but acquitted; the murder of Lategan was never solved.)

Ebrahim Jeneker, another top Pagad hitman, was charged in December 2002 (along with others), with murder, attempted murder and armed robbery. There were moments of high drama during this trial when seven of the accused, including Jeneker, escaped from a courthouse cell during a lunchtime break, overpowering a police officer and seizing his gun. A dramatic shootout ensued through the city centre of Cape Town. The escaped prisoners stole a car and fled for the suburbs, and a further shootout took place in Athlone. Jeneker was slightly wounded in the shooting but all were eventually rearrested.[6]

Lengthy sentences were imposed, as in the case of Mansoer Leggett, who received 11 life sentences in March 2001. The killings he was convicted of had taken place over a six-month period, between May and October 1999, and included gang members, and shebeen owners and customers.[7]

Abdus Ebrahim finally went on trial in May 2001. He was found not guilty of murder – Judge John Foxcroft said there was not enough evidence to link him to Staggie's actual killing, as the videotape footage shown in court did not show the source of the shots that had killed Staggie. But Ebrahim was convicted in 2002 for public violence and received a sentence of seven years.

BOMBS, ARMS CACHES AND CARJACKINGS

IDOC was set up in 1998 to deal with, among other things, the urban terror in Cape Town, says Bulelani.

> IDOC had never been used before. It was on the statute books but had never been used. We set up to deal with the urban terror in Cape Town, hijackings and the violence in KwaZulu-Natal. Percy Sonn was the overall head and led the Cape Town squad. Gerrie Nel led the Gauteng unit that dealt with car hijackings and Chris Macadam headed up the team in KwaZulu-Natal.

In Gauteng, as Bulelani explains, the concept of prosecution-led investigations was also put to the test.

It was reported that 65 000 cars had been hijacked between 1996 and 1999, and 61 percent of these incidents were taking place in Gauteng alone.[8] A task force to investigate and prosecute carjacking syndicates was established in March 1999, led by Gerrie Nel, head of the Scorpions in Gauteng.

Prior to the establishment of the task force, most cases were simply closed, as no arrests could be made. When arrests were made and cases eventually brought to court, it was taking seven to nine months to get a trial date. There was little communication between investigating officers and prosecutors, resulting in lengthy delays, remands, and withdrawals due to lack of evidence, witnesses and cooperation. And the conviction rate in Johannesburg was less than 10 percent of all cases charged.[9]

All carjacking cases, up to this time spread throughout dozens of courts and police stations in Johannesburg, were now routed to the task force, which started off with just three prosecutors and an administrative officer based at the Johannesburg magistrate's office. The goal was to introduce police and prosecutors early on in the process, offering a more victim-centred approach, and involve and disseminate crime information to communities most affected by this crime.[10]

The approach brought about profound results. 'In its first year of operation the task force succeeded in raising convictions to more than 40 percent ... Cases brought to the task force are finalised in an average of four to five months, and the task force has secured sentences ranging from the minimum of 15 years to a maximum of 45 years for armed robbery (hijacking).'[11]

Task force members were on a number of occasions offered bribes in return for destroying dockets. Special measures were put in place to protect dockets and it's a measure of the success of the project that not a single docket was lost.

By 2000 the unit had closed down five international syndicates and arrested an international syndicate boss within an hour of a hijacking incident. They had a 100 percent success rate in opposing bail and 100 percent success in convictions.[12]

One of the most important aspects of the programme was its victim-empowerment component, which referred victims for counselling and ensured that witnesses were provided with court-preparation services. Prosecutors kept special days open to consult with complainants and victim-liaison officers were responsible for keeping complainants updated about their cases.

Reflecting on the success of the project, a report from the Bureau of Justice Assistance (an agency in the US providing assistance to the NPA at the time) commented that 'prosecutors have become leaders of multi-agency solutions to crime problems rather than legal technicians operating solely in the courtroom'.[13]

BOMBS, ARMS CACHES AND CARJACKINGS

❏

In KwaZulu-Natal, an enemy of a different kind was being confronted. In the dying days of apartheid, there had been constant allegations and suspicions that the NP government was supplying Chief Mangosuthu Buthelezi's IFP with weapons. The Goldstone Commission, which looked at the role of the SAP and the government in violence in KwaZulu-Natal, stated in 1994 that the IFP had indeed been the recipient of covert funding and training from the military intelligence corps of the SADF. These reports had always been denied both by the IFP and the apartheid government.

However, in 1996, the commander of the security police death squad base at Vlakplaas, Eugene de Kock, or 'Prime Evil', as he was called by his colleagues, blew the whistle. During his trial, De Kock said he had personally supplied truckloads of hand grenades, machine guns, mines, ammunition and AK-47s to senior IFP officials, including former IFP senator Phillip Powell, and trained Inkatha's 'self-protection units' at a secret camp in KwaZulu-Natal.[14] Powell denied receiving weapons.

Shortly after his appointment Bulelani was approached by deputy minister of intelligence Joe Nhlanhla.

> *Mntaka Ngcuka [child of Ngcuka],* he said to me. Please find those weapons De Kock says he gave to the IFP. This country will know no peace until those weapons are found.

Bulelani put together a team consisting of NPA personnel and some from military intelligence. Up to this point the intelligence agencies had not been able to locate any of the weapons.

> We knew Powell was the key. We started monitoring him, and sure enough, he gave in to the pressure and went to

THE STING IN THE TALE: BULELANI NGCUKA

see Mpshe [Mokotedi Mpshe, DPP in KwaZulu-Natal] and said he wanted to confess.

Powell asked for indemnity in return for pointing out where the weapons De Kock had supplied to him were buried. Mpshe phoned Bulelani, who told him to work with Powell, but Mpshe did not indicate that Powell had asked for indemnity – and that he intended giving it to him.

In May 1999 – less than a month before the country went to elections – Powell led the NPA to a cache in Nquthu in KwaZulu-Natal, about 30 kilometres from Ulundi, containing six tonnes of arms including rocket launchers, grenades and anti-personnel mines. However, De Kock revealed in 2013 that he had told the special investigating unit in charge of the search that Powell had pointed out only a fraction of the weapons he had supplied him with in preparation for possible war during the 1994 elections: according to De Kock, 64 tonnes of the massive arms cache was still missing. He said he had given the investigators this information while he was in prison, and had supplied a list of arms, ammunition and explosives after he was informed what arms had been pointed out by Powell.[15]

Shortly after Powell's Nquthu revelation, a routine meeting of the DPPs was taking place in Pretoria when one of those present mentioned, almost in passing, that Powell was apparently to get indemnity in return for pointing out the weapons. Bulelani responded that 'my father will turn in his grave if Powell is not prosecuted'.

That evening Bulelani received a call from Mpshe, who said he needed to see him urgently. When Bulelani arrived at Mpshe's hotel room the next morning, to his astonishment, Mpshe asked Bulelani to join him in prayer. During the prayer, Mpshe asked God to 'enter Bulelani's heart': he had made a mistake, he said, and had granted Powell amnesty, and appealed to Bulelani not to fire him.

Bulelani was nonplussed for a minute or two but soon regained his composure. He told Mpshe that he shouldn't worry.

> You're not fired. You are lucky. The final decision rests with me, not you. I will review your decision. Hand the file to Chris [Macadam].
>
> We wanted all the weapons, and we wanted all the people involved, because clearly [Powell] was not acting alone.

Powell left the country in 2000 while still under investigation. The remaining weapons referred to by De Kock have never been found. De Kock claimed that while he had supplied the weapons, he did not know where they had been buried.[16]

❑

Violence in Kwa-Zulu Natal was another issue the NPA had to deal with at the time Bulelani was appointed. In November 1998 he announced the formation of a special crime-busting team in an attempt to bring an end to the political violence in KwaZulu-Natal. The new unit would take a multidisciplinary approach to investigating politically motivated crimes, Bulelani said in a statement. Advocate Chris Macadam, the province's former deputy attorney-general, would head the investigating directorate, with the title of deputy DPP.

Violence had continued in areas such as Shobashobane on the south coast, Richmond in the midlands, and Nongoma in the north. At one point there were said to be 20 000 refugees in Richmond, living in tents and shelters on the streets, who had fled the violence in surrounding areas.[17]

One of the key players was a senior ANC leader in the midlands regions, Sifiso Nkabinde, who had led the formation of 'self-defence units' in the struggle against apartheid. Nkabinde had defied an order from the ANC after 1994 to disband the self-defence units, and was expelled. He had declared war on the organisation. Bloodletting followed and the ANC deputy mayor of Richmond, Rodney van der Byl, was assassinated in 1997. In July of the same year, five newly elected ANC councillors were executed.

The SAPS succeeded in charging Nkabinde but he was acquitted on technical grounds in January 1998.[18] The killing continued and communities were now openly hostile towards the police, accusing them of working with Nkabinde and his men. Witnesses came forward who said they had seen police distributing weapons with Nkabinde, and demanded that the police be investigated for colluding with Nkabinde.

After the murder of the new deputy mayor, Percy Thompson, in July 1998, along with ten other people, police commissioner George Fivaz closed the Richmond police station, saying that the police had lost the confidence of the community.

In January 1999, Nkabinde himself was gunned down in the centre of Richmond. This was followed by the Ndabazitha massacre, in which 11 members of a single family were killed, including an 82-year-old grandmother.

Andrew Ragavaloo, who was mayor of Richmond at the time, says in his book *Richmond: Living in the shadow of death*, that he met with then KwaZulu-Natal attorney-general Tim McNally (who would later earn a scathing rebuke from Mandela) early in July 1998 and pointed out that investigators were botching evidence because they lacked legal guidance. He suggested that prosecutors be attached to the investigating teams but McNally dismissed the proposal.[19] However, it was this very same approach that the NPA brought to the table once Bulelani deployed deputy director Chris Macadam and the team from IDOC to the area in January 1999.

Ragavaloo says that by early 2000, Macadam and his team had solved most of the cases. It was the first time since the violence had begun three years earlier that killers were being arrested and sentenced, and it brought the community new hope.[20]

By 2002, 25 suspects had been convicted and at least 69 life sentences imposed. The endemic violence in Richmond came to an end.[21]

❏

The prosecution-led approach also succeeded in quelling taxi violence in the Eastern Cape, when a task team was set up in September 1999. At least seven people had been killed and more than 30 injured, and 20 minibus taxis burned, by the time the Scorpions arrived.

> After the '99 elections, Dullah had moved and was now minister of transport. There was a problem with taxi violence in the Eastern Cape. People were dying and Dullah asked me to deal with it.
>
> I asked [investigator] Casper [Jonker] to go to East London and look at all the cases and dockets and bring them back to Pretoria and review them. He did and found that there had simply been no prosecutions.
>
> There was one fellow known as Hitman who appeared to be untouchable. We decided to make an example of him.

THE STING IN THE TALE: BULELANI NGCUKA

When we arrested him, we wanted the media to be there. But they said they would only come if I was there. Otherwise, it wasn't newsworthy.

We debated it for a while. Obviously, my presence meant it would really get a lot of media attention. Some people argued it was not right to expose people before they were charged – what if they were acquitted?

But in this instance, we wanted to send a message to the people of East London. We wanted them to see we were taking this seriously. So we agreed.

It happened to be on a Sunday. There was a match that evening – Bafana Bafana were playing in some other country. I arrived and sat around with friends until late, and then said I had to go to sleep. I was pretending, of course. We had agreed to move at 2 am. I went back to the team.

This was a joint operation with the SAPS. Sipho [Ngwema, NPA spokesperson] went to collect the media.

The arrest was on *Morning Live* on SABC TV. That created an aura of fear. It was good because it sent a message.

I went to court. I was ready to oppose the bail application. I wanted to do it myself.

One of the things that touched me was that some of the journalists approached Casper and asked him about me: 'Is he not going to be in danger?' He said, No, we will give our lives for our boss. He didn't say it to me – the journalists told me about it afterwards. They said, 'Wow, you have been able to get so much loyalty out of these guys. They are willing to lay down their lives for you.'

That touched me.

Bulelani acknowledges the criticism of what has become

known as the Scorpions' 'Hollywood style' of arrests but believes it served a purpose.

> It was always a tricky balance between public perception and the [public's] right to feel safe, versus individual rights. We were aware that there were those who felt we were sending the message that they were already guilty before they were convicted. We were not doing it indiscriminately and would select the targets.
>
> In this case, this man believed he was untouchable, and we had to send a message to those behind the violence: 'You are going to be stopped, you will be arrested, shown in public, and everyone is going to see that you are going down.'

Some of those who took part in this operation had been part of the 'D'Oliveira Ondersoekspan' (D'Oliveira Investigation Team) appointed by the Goldstone Commission to investigate 'third force' murders by apartheid police and military agents. They were responsible for investigating, among others, Eugene de Kock, commander of the infamous Vlakplaas unit, who was ultimately given two life sentences and 212 years in 1996.

The East London operation was part of a much wider operation by the Scorpions against taxi violence in the Eastern Cape, and led to more arrests and convictions. In Umtata, the Scorpions successfully infiltrated two syndicates involved in taxi violence and cash-in-transit heists.

After these arrests, and with most of the top hitmen either dead or in prison, taxi violence came to an end in the Eastern Cape.

PART IV

Fighting Organised Crime

15.
Taking the profit out of crime

'I knew that once Willie set his mind on something, he would work day and night, and he wouldn't give up until he made it happen. And he was passionate about making sure that people paid for their crimes.'

Many criminals, including crime bosses, saw time behind bars as an occupational hazard but, as Willie Hofmeyr argued before parliament in 2002, putting their families on the street, and removing their favourite playthings and their 'pensions', usually the proceeds of a life of crime, would cause them real pain. 'If the parent was to be poor but for the proceeds of crime, then the child must learn to live like a poor child,' he said. 'Criminals must realise that that their families will suffer.'[1] In addition, seizing their assets would ensure that the proceeds of crime would not remain behind to be used by a new leadership or generation of crime bosses.

Partly to this end, in 1998 parliament crafted a new weapon against crime: the Prevention of Organised Crime Act.[2] It was 'a complex piece of legislation enacted to deal with complex criminal activities'[3] and was bound to intimidate most prosecutors. It was clear that a specialist unit would be needed to ensure that the full provisions of the act were put to good use.

Bulelani had known Hofmeyr, one of the chief architects of

THE STING IN THE TALE: BULELANI NGCUKA

the legislation, and parliamentary advisor to the deputy president at the time, for many years; they had been UDF and ANC comrades.

> No-one knew this Act better than Willie. More importantly, I knew that Willie was a fighter. ... I decided that he was the person to implement this legislation.

Hofmeyr was appointed special director and head of the AFU in May 1999.[4]

In terms of the Prevention of Organised Crime Act, No 121 of 1998, the state can pursue both the criminal and the civil route to asset forfeiture.[5] After securing a conviction in a criminal court, the state can apply to have the benefits of the crime seized and ultimately forfeited to the state. However, the state also has a much more powerful weapon: in wording that explicitly separates the criminal process from the civil forfeiture process, the act allows the state to seize assets using the civil route, even when there is no prosecution.[6] This is focused not on 'wrongdoers, but on the property that has been used to commit an offence or which constitutes the proceeds of crime. The guilt or wrongdoing of the owner or possessors of the property is, therefore, not primarily relevant to the proceedings.'[7]

It was this that gave many cause to doubt the fairness of the new legislation, but both Willie and Bulelani were adamant: unless they could increase the risk and decrease the profits, it would be impossible to deal effectively with crime. Targeting the proceeds of crime would hit criminals, and organised crime in particular, where it hurt the most – in their pockets.

Five years after its establishment, the AFU had successfully used both routes, and had done roughly 47 percent of its cases in terms of criminal procedure, and 53 percent in terms of civil processes, illustrating the importance of both routes.

The unit grew rapidly, increasing to a staff component of 91 by 2004, which included 44 lawyers. Offices had been established in Cape Town, Durban, Johannesburg and East London, with further offices planned in Port Elizabeth, Bloemfontein, Kimberley and Pietermaritzburg.

In those first five years, the AFU obtained about 500 court orders to seize criminal assets worth more than R600 million, and had proceeded to the second stage of applying for forfeiture in 173 cases involving R155 million.[8] It had won 129 forfeiture orders worth R76 million.[9] R55 million had been paid into the criminal assets recovery account (a separate account within the National Revenue Fund into which monies and property are deposited following a judicial forfeiture or confiscation order) and R100 million had been returned to victims of crime, which included private individuals and entities, and government departments that were victims of fraud and corruption.[10]

❏

While one of the unit's early strategic objectives was to test the law, Lungisa Dyosi points out that Willie was just as adamant that the legislation had to be used as a weapon to disrupt organised crime. 'Willie said that if he took on 20 cases and won only two, but succeeded in disrupting crime syndicates, he would be happy.'[11] However, it was an uphill battle, and the unit lost three of its first six cases.

The first test case was that of Gavin Carolus, businessman and alleged drug 'kingpin' from Milnerton, Cape Town. The seizure of several properties, luxury vehicles, furniture, jewellery and cash took place in full view of the media. His bank accounts were frozen and several businesses, including a restaurant and transport service, were also seized, and curators appointed. The message was clear: crime doesn't pay.

But the AFU soon found itself in hot water, losing three cases in quick succession over the next six months. First, Carolus took his case on appeal on the issue of 'retrospectivity', arguing that all the alleged facts relied on when they obtained the order to seize his property had occurred before 21 January 1999, when the Prevention of Organised Crime Act came into operation. The court agreed and said that the legislation did not apply before 21 January 1999. The NPA, of course, immediately appealed, but the appeal judge found that parliament had been very clear when it said the criminal route to asset forfeiture was to be applied retrospectively, but not the civil route.[12]

The unit was again challenged on the issue of retrospectivity in its second case, in July 1999, when it seized the property of Piet Meyer, the suspended deputy head of the Durban organised crime unit. As with Carolus, the court ordered that the act could not be applied retrospectively and ordered that his assets be returned.

Then, in the third matter, in August 1999, a court again found that the act could not be applied retrospectively and ordered that the assets of Wouter Basson be returned. 'Dr Death' was on trial facing 64 counts of murder, theft and fraud. His seized assets worth about R44 million included a company in the United States, homes in South Africa and the United Kingdom and money in various foreign bank accounts.[13]

As fast as assets were being seized, they were being returned. Cartoonists had a field day. When asset forfeiture had started, one cartoonist had drawn a picture of a removals truck with

Willie Hofmeyr seated on top, dubbed 'Ngcuka's secret weapon: Willie's Removals'. Now, the cartoonist Zapiro was joking about the 'secret weapon' – the 'asset-freeze gun' – itself being frozen.[14]

Parliament was angry. Johnny de Lange, the chair of parliament's justice committee, said that for the judges to rule that the law did not apply to crimes committed before January 1999 was 'effectively saying that there will be an amnesty for all assets stolen before January 1999', leading to 'absurdities'.[15]

Bulelani received a phone call from a concerned President Mbeki: 'No more seizures, please. This is looking bad. Fix the problem first.'

So Willie and Bulelani went back to parliament and made sure that all the loopholes in the legislation were closed, including the issue of retrospectivity.[16]

> It was one of the fastest pieces of legislation to go through parliament. All the political parties agreed. No-one opposed it.

After the amendment of the law, things improved, but they would still find themselves challenged in court: in 2001, the unit had to defend the new legislation on no fewer than 30 different legal and procedural issues.[17] One example was the case of Simon Prophet, who had been arrested at his home, which the court described as a 'mini-laboratory', in Woodstock, Cape Town. Chemicals used to manufacture the cheap and popular street drug tik (methamphetamine) were confiscated during the raid. His property was seized but Prophet argued against a forfeiture order in July 2001 on the grounds, among other things, that it had not been proven that the property was an instrumentality of an offence. His arguments didn't convince the court and the forfeiture order was granted in May 2003.

Prophet was acquitted on a technicality on criminal charges, but Judge Erasmus commented that 'there is no doubt that civil forfeiture is a controversial mechanism but it has been accepted by many nations as a legitimate law enforcement tool to combat serious crime. Forfeiture both prevents further illicit use of the property and imposes an economic penalty, thereby rendering illegal behaviour unprofitable.'[18]

Prophet took the matter to the Appeal Court and lost in 2005; then he took his case to the highest court in the land, the Constitutional Court, where he lost again.[19]

Still, by 2002, the unit was on a successful streak, winning 17 of 19 applications, a success rate of 85 percent.[20] The success rate in seizure actions increased to 94.4 percent the following year, and the unit began to move to the second stage, applying for forfeiture of frozen assets, where it had a 100 percent success rate.[21] In June 2002 Bulelani was able to report for the first time that the AFU was bringing in more money than it was costing.[22]

Hofmeyr reported to parliament in the same year that 34 percent of the AFU's cases were about economic crime, and that this category constituted 50 percent of the assets seized because of the large amounts of money involved. Drug cases, which made up 31 percent of the cases, constituted only four percent of the assets seized. Corruption cases were 16 percent of the cases taken on and constituted seven percent of the assets taken; natural resources (like perlemoen smuggling and overharvesting) made up six percent of the cases and 18 percent of the assets, while cases involving violence were seven percent of the cases and two percent of the assets.[23]

❑

Asset forfeiture was also used against some small or so-called 'ordinary' criminals. Lungisa Dyosi and Hermione Cronje, both of whom worked in Bulelani's office, took on some of the first asset-forfeiture cases in the NPA. 'We approached the directors of public prosecutions in the provinces and the Scorpions, and picked up a few cases with asset-forfeiture potential. Prosecutors were very wary at that time. They were a bit intimidated,' Lungisa says.[24]

Lungisa took on a case in Idutywa in the Eastern Cape involving Nolundi Yanta and her husband, Petrus Peter, who were convicted of more than 800 counts of pension fraud in November 2000. Yanta was also convicted for the murder of a government employee from the department of social services who was shot dead at a government grants paypoint; she ultimately received a life sentence for fraud and conspiracy to commit murder.

The assets seized included a house, a bottle store, a fashion boutique and the loan book from a *'mashonisa'* [small loans] business that Yanta ran. The loan book yielded nothing because customers refused to pay up, and the boutique was boycotted by customers after Yanta was convicted, and curators were forced to put the goods on sale and eventually close down the business.

The judge who sentenced Yanta and her husband on the fraud charges was unequivocal about asset forfeiture. 'The court has been informed that you have been left with virtually nothing after both your movable and immovable properties were attached. The entire amount stolen from the government by you will be recovered up to the last cent when your properties get auctioned.'[25]

Yanta was the mastermind behind the whole scheme, Lungisa says. 'During the investigation, we learned that she had recruited a former Apla fighter to assassinate two Scorpions investigators working on the case. We set up a sting operation with the assistance of an agent from the National Intelligence Agency. The would-be assassin was arrested while trying to buy a firearm from the NIA agent. When he was arrested, he was found with a piece of paper with the names of both Scorpions investigators on it.'[26]

Another early successful case in the Eastern Cape that Hermione Cronje handled involved the kidnapping of Rena Pitsiladis, the daughter of businessman John Pitsiladis, in March 1999. A R2 million ransom had been demanded from her father, and she had been released eight hours after he paid up. The assets of the two men convicted of her kidnapping were seized.[27]

A criminal case involving fraud of about R5 million from the justice department in Umtata collapsed because the court found that confessions had been illegally 'extracted' from the accused by the police. However, the AFU was able to proceed and seize the R2 million that the police had found buried in the garden of the accused. The AFU were then able to prove, on the balance of probabilities, that the two men had stolen the money. The money was returned to the bank that was found to be the legal owner of the cash.[28]

In another case in KwaZulu-Natal, the property of alleged Durban drug kingpin Ronny Johnny Smith was seized in October 1999. Smith had been arrested in April 1999 after a drug bust in Middelburg, Mpumalanga, and was out on bail at the time. He was living the high life, flying around the world and spending wildly. In possession of five passports, he was known to both the FBI and the Drug Enforcement Agency in the USA as a suspected druglord, and had been watched by police for ten years. He was suspected of smuggling mandrax and cocaine from Swaziland to wholesalers in Durban and Johannesburg in luxury vehicles belonging to his family, and laundering the proceeds through a number of front companies in Swaziland.[29] He owned houses in Durban, a farm in Jamaica, bank accounts in Jersey, about 20 luxury cars, and assets of over R10 billion, but had no business interests in South Africa.[30]

It was his lavish lifestyle that was his downfall. While drug charges were hard to prove, things began to get tough when prosecutors questioned the movie-star lifestyle he and his family enjoyed. The AFU seized his luxury home on the Bluff in Durban, ten vehicles and an imported mobile home. Curators appointed by the AFU said they had found R400 000 belonging to Smith in a Durban attorney's trust account, a house belonging to Smith in La Mercy and several other luxury cars. These were auctioned off, and the proceeds of about R6 million deposited in the criminal assets recovery account.

Smith was rearrested in September 2000 following a joint sting operation by the Scorpions and the SAP, during which 84 000 mandrax tablets with a value of R4.2 million were confiscated. He faced further charges of drug dealing, corruption and conspiracy to murder – there were allegations that he planned to kill the prosecutor assigned to his Middelburg case.[31]

He was convicted of corruption in 2001 after pleading guilty and given a six-year sentence or R300 000 fine. He was never convicted of drug charges – the criminal charges were hard to prove – but he did not escape the clutches of asset forfeiture. They took everything they could find in South Africa.[32]

Bulelani recalls also a memorable case in which the AFU seized a tombstone, and several properties and vehicles. Frank Kutumba Kwezi and his wife, Dorcas Pitso, had defrauded hundreds of people in a R15-million pyramid scheme between 1996 and 1997 in Kimberley in the Northern Cape and Thohoyandou, Limpopo.[33]

The tombstone proved to be a sensitive matter and the cause of some debate among the team. Bulelani was opposed to the idea, saying that attaching a tombstone amounted to desecration of a final resting place.

> Willie adopted a hard line. He said that we must show that crime doesn't pay, even if you're dead. What finally persuaded me was when they told me that the family didn't want the tombstone either because they felt their mother would not rest easy knowing that her tombstone had been paid for from the proceeds of crime.

16.
The Scorpions

'Loved by the people, feared by criminals, respected by peers.'

It was 2 June 1999 and South Africa's second democratic national elections were taking place. Nelson Mandela was about to hand over the reins to Thabo Mbeki.

Bulelani believes in voting early, so he was among the first in the queue at his nearest polling station in Cape Town. He had just returned home when he received a call from Sydney Mufamadi asking him to come to a meeting at the deputy president's official residence.

When he arrived, there were a few people in attendance and Mbeki wasted no time in telling them of his experiences on the campaign trail: everywhere he went, people had complained about crime. 'We have to do something about this,' he said.

The country was indeed reeling under a wave of violent crime. Research by the Institute for Security Studies shows just how crime had escalated, starting in the mid-1980s but taking off dramatically in the 1990s. 'The expectation which many had in 1994 that crime – especially violent crime – would decrease has not materialised. Crime figures for 1999 indicate that the number of recorded crimes is at an all-time high. The increase in the overall number of recorded crimes, including the number of violent crimes, was greater between 1998 and 1999 than in any previous year after 1994.'[1]

And the dawn of democracy had brought an unwelcome visitor to South Africa's shores – organised crime. John Blaney, a former US state department official who was one of those who assisted in coordinating FBI assistance in training the Scorpions, describes how he remembers 'watching international crime figures literally moving into the best [neighbourhoods] in Pretoria during this era. International underworld connections were being established or strengthened.'[2]

Mbeki gave Bulelani details of the areas he had visited and what people had said. He emphasised the fact that he had told people he had heard them, and said the team should come up with proposals to include in his state of the nation address which he was to deliver at parliament in a few weeks' time.

The gathered group threw around a few preliminary ideas. A specialised unit of investigators and prosecutors under a single command was the final decision.

When Bulelani got back to the office, he convened a meeting with some of his closest advisors and a few individuals from outside the NPA. He told them about the conversation and they worked on a proposal which they sent to the president's office.

Mbeki was elected president on 16 June 1999 following the victory of the ANC in the 2 May 1999 elections. When he delivered his state of the nation address on 25 June 1999, he announced that 'a special and adequately staffed and equipped investigative unit will be established urgently, to deal with all national priority crime, including police corruption'.[3]

The Directorate of Special Operations was publicly launched by President Mbeki in Gugulethu outside Cape Town on 1 September 1999. It was at this September launch event that the unit first unveiled its red and black branding with the Scorpions logo.[4]

The nickname 'Scorpions', the brainchild of Steve Tshwete, came from the isiXhosa song that goes, '*Mna ndiyamoyika unomadukudwane...*' ('I am afraid of the scorpion ...'). And indeed, the black turbo-powered VW Golf GTIs with their distinctive red logos would soon become a welcome sight, or otherwise, depending on whether one was a suspect or an ordinary South African who wanted to see a more effective response to crime.

The Scorpions got straight to work, operating through investigating directorates while the legislation was being prepared. These directorates had considerable powers, including the power to summons, search and seize as required and within the confines of the law.[5]

One of the first and most important tasks was the recruitment and training of personnel. Shortly after the president's announcement in parliament, Bulelani was attending a police training conference in Durban when he met Dr Ruben Richards, a teacher from the Pretoria Technikon. Ruben had applied for the position of commissioner of police in the Western Cape but, after talking to Bulelani, was persuaded to take up the position of head of training for the Scorpions.

Training was one of the most urgent priorities, since the bulk of the new Scorpions were new recruits. This was a deliberate decision: the new agency would require a new mindset and a new set of skills. The focus was on building investigative capacity, and both Scotland Yard and the FBI would play important roles.

Entry requirements were high. 'To ensure that the DSO succeeds, we have to ensure that the DSO recruits the best and most talented corps of personnel available. Initial entrants will therefore be graduates or highly qualified personnel in a number of technical areas and at senior level. Preference will be given to the recruitment of people with experience and high levels of technical skill,' Penuell Maduna explained.[6]

Candidates not only had to have a university degree in a field such as computer science, accounting, law or psychology, but also had to pass a battery of psychological and physical tests. They had to be under 34 years of age, undergo drug testing and polygraph testing, have no previous convictions, and show demonstrable support for democratic values and ideals. From an initial 6 000 applicants who responded to a nationwide advertising campaign for Scorpions positions, only 400 made it onto the shortlist and 50 were selected.[7]

In order to attract the best, the Scorpions would need to pay higher salaries than was the norm for new recruits. This would likely attract much criticism but, as Maduna explained, 'since the special investigators of the DSO will include chemists, forensic auditors and computer specialists, it would be short-sighted to compare the salaries they will earn to those of ordinary constables in the police service'.[8]

❑

Bulelani was watching CNN in the early hours one morning when he saw a US delegation visiting Israel. He suddenly saw a familiar face in the delegation – Richard Laing.

Bulelani had met Richard shortly after he assumed office. He'd introduced himself as an official from the department of justice in the USA, and said he was on a programme of assistance with the department of justice in South Africa. He had helped Bulelani in setting up his office.

Richard hadn't told Bulelani he was leaving the country on

other business, and now Bulelani was intrigued. Who exactly was Richard Laing?

On his return, Bulelani put the question to him, and Richard told Bulelani he was a trained FBI agent with considerable expertise in policing. He became the contact between the Scorpions and the US department of justice and provided valuable advice on organisational design for the Scorpions.

Laing recommended that Bulelani and his team visit the FBI Academy at Quantico to see how the FBI was structured, and made arrangements for the visit.

> I was suspicious at first, of course. You know how we are, suspicious of everything American. But then I thought, *He's FBI, not CIA.*
>
> I was impressed with what I saw at Quantico and decided that I would like my team to be trained there. I knew there would be lots of questions. But then, I thought, lots of people go to Harvard and Yale, and nobody has troubles with that, so why shouldn't the Scorpions be trained at Quantico?
>
> When we got back, I raised it with the president [Mbeki] and he agreed with me.

Ruben introduced Bulelani to Sir John Stevens, chief of Scotland Yard in the UK, and in October 2000 the NPA signed an agreement with him, formalising a partnership with Scotland Yard for the next three years.

The first group of 50 Scorpions who had made it through the selection process underwent a five-week induction camp in South Africa provided by the NPA and the SAPS, which included training on the constitution and the bill of rights, integrity and basic detective work. Instructors from Scotland Yard and the FBI observed recruits during this leg.

Next came international training, and the first group of Scorpions recruits left for Quantico in April 2000. The first to be trained were junior investigators, followed by senior investigators. The fact that they were trained by agencies like the FBI and at places like Scotland Yard boosted the morale of the new recruits, and they came back to South Africa in high spirits and determined to make their mark.

In total about 80 recruits were trained by the FBI and 100 by Scotland Yard.

❑

The Scorpions described themselves as a multidisciplinary agency investigating and prosecuting organised crime. The focus was on crimes of national impact that required the integration of intelligence, investigation and prosecution, supported by modern technology.[9]

They were often referred to as 'South Africa's FBI' but, as Lungisa Dyosi points out, the Scorpions took the FBI approach one step further. 'In the FBI, everyone is an investigator. There may be people who trained as lawyers, but in the FBI they function as agents or investigators. Once they complete an investigation, they hand the matter over to the attorney-general for prosecution.

'In the Scorpions we had investigators, who may or may not have had legal qualifications, but we also had lawyers, who retained their positions as prosecutors. We retained the two professions, co-located in one unit, and, of course, we had analysts as well, supporting the work of investigators.

'There were two kinds of prosecutors in the Scorpions. One

prosecutor would always keep their distance from the investigation to avoid becoming a witness in their own case. They would sit with the team to assess the situation and give guidance but would not become involved in the actual investigation as they would ultimately have to take the decision whether to prosecute or not.'[10]

One of the best explanations of the Scorpion's 'troika' methodology is found in Judge Sisi Khampepe's report following the completion of her inquiry into the mandate and location of the Scorpions in 2006. Khampepe provided a detailed analysis of the approach and pointed out that while investigators didn't have the necessary legal understanding to know what evidence was required, the multidisciplinary approach allowed prosecutors to guide investigators from the start of the process. 'The troika principle uses the skills of a prosecutor in directing the investigation, and uses the skills of the analyst in interpreting the information that is revealed by the investigation, and the skill of an investigator to collate the evidence for a successful prosecution.'[11]

Analysts were the link between investigation and prosecution, and were responsible for operational analysis of crime information and ensuring a constant supply of operational and overt information to Scorpion investigations. They played an important role in directing the work of the unit and were recruited from law enforcement, intelligence, and academic and professional backgrounds.

The crime-analysis division was led by Dr Khosi Msimang, who passed away in December 2000, just as the Scorpions were taking off. Indeed, it was the recruitment of senior individuals such as Msimang and Pete Richer from the ranks of NIA, that bought the Scorpions much-needed legitimacy in the eyes of the intelligence community. Before this, when the structure and location of the new crime-fighting organisation were still being debated, the NIA were vying for leadership by insisting on a methodology of 'intelligence-led, prosecution-driven investigations'. After much negotiation and discussions, the agreement was 'intelligence-driven, prosecution-led investigations'.

Lungisa recalls that one of the turning points was an address that Bulelani gave to senior intelligence officers at NIA headquarters. It was during this address, he says, that the importance of prosecution-led investigations was finally driven home and accepted, when Bulelani spoke of the biggest heist in the country at the time, the SBV R31-million case in KwaZulu-Natal, in which SAPS investigators had made mistakes that could have been avoided had prosecutors been on hand to guide matters. SBV was a security company transporting large amounts of cash for banks.

Investigators had got a warrant from the judge to tap the phones of the accused. This was a breakthrough in their investigation that led to arrests and people being charged. However, in the application, one of the detectives didn't make a full disclosure. He had hidden some facts. So the defence was able to use the old legal principle of 'fruits of the poison tree' to get this evidence excluded from the trial, and some of the accused were released.

'Now, if a prosecutor had been part of the process, they could have guided the drafting of the affidavit, fully appreciating the consequences of not disclosing all the necessary facts,' notes Lungisa.[12]

The Scorpions also set up an operational support division which was responsible for planning all operations and providing tactical support, crime-scene management and surveillance.

The Scorpions never had a staff complement of more than 500. At the time it was disbanded in 2008, there were just over 460 people, roughly the same number as in 2001 – 320 investigators, five forensic accountants, 55 lawyers and 86 administrative personnel. Of these, 60 percent and more were investigators, 10 percent were lawyers and 43 percent were tasked with operational aspects.[13] More than a quarter of the Scorpions were under the age of 30.[14]

It had not been easy to achieve representivity at a senior level, recruiting as they did at this level from the ranks of former SAP officers, but it was achievable when it came to new recruits: in 2003, nearly 70 percent were black, with black females representing 23 percent of the staff complement (although achieving enough female representivity remained a challenge). One researcher commented that it was clear that 'the DSO consists of many talented individuals keen to make a difference and not afraid to speak their minds; any complaints ... tended to revolve around frustration at not being able to do more in their positions in the DSO'.[15]

It was also important that the unit established the criteria that would guide its selection of cases. At one of the first briefings to parliament, in November 1999, Bulelani explained that the criteria that would guide the Scorpions would include the level of seriousness of the crime and the harm it caused at an individual and societal level; whether the case involved a high level of violence; the degree of organisation involved and whether the crime was part of an ongoing criminal enterprise; and the extent to which the case required a multidisciplinary approach in order that it be effectively solved.[16]

By 2001, the focus areas had been identified: drug trafficking, organised violence, urban terror and street gangs, precious-metal smuggling, human trafficking, vehicle theft and hijacking syndicates, serious economic crime, and organised public corruption.

❑

One of the most complicated investigations undertaken by the Scorpions was Operation Guanxi,[17] targeting Chinese organised crime. Chinese syndicates were considered to be among the most difficult crime groups to tackle, and this was a large operation that was still under way when Bulelani left in 2004. Its focus included drugs, human trafficking and money-laundering.

The Scorpions worked with a number of role-players including the SAPS, asset-forfeiture specialists, the South African Revenue Service (Sars), intelligence agencies, the department of trade and industry, the marine and coastal management branch of the department of environmental affairs, the International Organisation for Migration, and the financial-services sector. The Drug Enforcement Agency in the USA, UK and Australian drug-liaison officers, and the Hong Kong and Namibian police were also involved.

The first goal was scored in August 2000 when the Guanxi team seized a container containing 1.9 million mandrax tablets[18] with a street value of more than R200 million at the City Deep container depot in Johannesburg.[19] This operation resulted in 66 arrests. Close to R2 million in cash was seized, along with 800 cases of counterfeit cigarettes with a street value of over R48 million. The Scorpions also confiscated 180 boxes containing dried perlemoen weighing 1 030 kg.[20]

The City Deep bust was outdone by another in July 2003

when the Scorpions arrested five Chinese men and seized 4.2 tonnes of pure methaqualone, 100 million cocaine tablets and a bag of compressed dagga from houses in Randburg in Johannesburg – the biggest drug bust in South Africa at the time.[21]

This was followed by an operation in which a container was seized in Durban harbour containing six tonnes of methaqualone powder – which, compressed, would have yielded 18 million mandrax tablets with a street value of about R1 billion – shipped out of China and destined for Mozambique. In a statement to the press, Bulelani noted, 'I've been informed by agents of the United States Drug Enforcement Agency that this is the biggest haul in the world.'[22]

Perlemoen poaching along South Africa's West coast was another key focus of the investigation of Chinese organised crime. The trade was connected to drugs, guns and gangs. Chinese triads arrived in 1994 to supply perlemoen to black markets in China, Taiwan, Japan and Korea. Local residents described how, almost overnight, small towns were suddenly awash with cash, drugs, fast cars, speedboats and scuba gear, and how gang wars soon became the order of the day as locals rushed to satisfy the triads' demands and denuded the sea floor.[23]

An undercover Scorpions investigator infiltrated the group surrounding the so-called 'perlemoen poaching godmother' of Gansbaai, Elizabeth Marx,[24] and in 2003 Marx and her syndicate members forfeited R16 million in assets to the state, including houses, boats, businesses and a bank account containing more than R430 000.[25] Later that year another Scorpions sting resulted in Marx's arrest along with all 54 members of her syndicate, of whom 41 pleaded guilty.

The Scorpions also moved against a company called

Hout Bay Fishing Industries, which had engaged in what was described as 'an elaborate scheme to illegally harvest' large quantities of crayfish – rock lobsters – 'for export to the United States in violation of both South African and US law'.[26] The resulting forfeiture of R39 million was the biggest in South African asset-forfeiture history at the time.

During the Hout Bay investigation, the team discovered that another company, SA Hake Fishing, had entered into a joint venture with Hout Bay Fishing in overharvesting hake, with the profits shared equally between the two companies. The AFU attached an SA Hake Fishing boat worth an estimated R6 million, together with its gear, equipment and stores,[27] and the company's director was sentenced and paid a fine.[28]

In another case in Mossel Bay, the Scorpions were involved in an investigation of the overharvesting of pelagic fish running into some 3 000 tonnes. Eight companies and 21 individuals were targeted, and the documentation seized during the various searches filled a very large strongroom. The team filed documents that supported 1 236 incidents of poaching and 42 arrests followed.

❑

Project Yield was another investigation focusing on South Africa's natural resources. South Africa has 90 percent of the world's platinum-group reserves, and by the late 1990s the industry was a target for the illicit gold and platinum market. The Scorpions were asked by one of South Africa's largest mining companies to take over an SAPS investigation – and with good reason, as it would turn out, as investigations showed that police corruption was part of the problem. The UK National Crime Squad assisted in unravelling and deciphering commercial transactions and illegal exports, and cooperated in operational planning on arrests, searches and seizures. The investigation was still under way at the time the Scorpions were disbanded in 2008.[29]

One of the most controversial and complex financial investigations taken on by the Scorpions was the Dave King matter. King was alleged to have pocketed a billion rand by selling his shares as sole director of a listed company and channelling the money overseas without Reserve Bank permission.

The UK Central Authority cooperated in the investigation and King was arrested in 2002, facing over 300 counts of fraud, tax evasion, contravening exchange-control regulations, money-laundering and racketeering. The docket consisted of more than 200 000 pages, including more than 21 000 emails, and there were about 270 lever-arch files of additional documents.

Like many accused of such crimes, King had deep pockets and ended up fighting in the courts for more than a decade. He finally pleaded guilty to lesser charges and ended up paying R3.2 million in fines to the state and R8.75 million into the criminal assets recovery account. Sars ultimately received R700 million;[30] the legal fees King and Sars accumulated were said to be in the region of R400 million.[31]

In what was regarded as a quick win, the Scorpions wrapped up an investigation into tender fraud at the giant oil and gas company Sasol in six months. The matter involved a contract for hauling coal and magnetite and renting front-end loaders, awarded to Coal Trans, one of the biggest tipper contract companies in the country at the time. The investigation ended in a plea agreement with the owner of Coal Trans, Pieter Buys, who agreed to pay R20 million into the criminal assets recovery account – the biggest amount paid into it at the time – and received an eight-year sentence, suspended for five years.[32]

LeisureNet was another of the big financial cases the Scorpions took on, involving charges of fraud and insider trading. The company, which owned the Health & Racquet Club franchise, Planet Hollywood restaurant and the Imax theatre at the Victoria & Alfred Waterfront in Cape Town, collapsed in 2000 in what was described at the liquidation proceedings as the largest corporate collapse in South Africa at the time. The two CEOs had benefitted to the amount of about R6 million each from a transaction they had induced LeisureNet to enter, and were living extremely lavish lifestyles.[33]

Three Sars officials joined the Scorpions investigating team; the Scorpions also developed good relations with the Serious Fraud Office in London, which indicated for the first time that it was prepared to assist in matters involving the contravention of tax laws and exchange-control regulations linked to allegations of fraud.[34]

This case is another that demonstrates how long it can take to deliver justice when dealing with organised crime and those with deep pockets: the pair were arrested in 2002; they were convicted in 2007, and only started serving their time in 2011 when the Supreme Court finally dismissed their appeals.[35]

While most of the Scorpions' cases were led by senior investigators, junior investigators proved their mettle in the GEMS case. GEMS was a microlender – an organisation that lent money, usually at a high interest rate, to people who were excluded from the traditional banking system – which had acquired business from municipal employees across the country in a corrupt manner by paying influential members of the South African Municipal Workers' Union. The company was fined R5 million and directed to pay R60 million to the families of the victims of their corrupt venture. The operation was the work of junior investigators assisted by an advocate and an external auditing firm.[36]

❑

Corporate-identity hijacking and website-spoofing were also among the crimes the Scorpions took on. Key institutions like the Reserve Bank were being targeted by corporate-identity hijackers as part of the '419' racketeering investigation, a reference to Section 419 of the Nigerian criminal code prohibiting the use of false letters to solicit funds.

In 2002, 18 Nigerian nationals were convicted of racketeering and money-laundering in the 419 investigations. The operation disrupted seven syndicates operating in South Africa, Europe and North America, and assets to the value of R8.9 million were confiscated.[37]

The Scorpions were approached in 2001 by the minister of finance, Trevor Manuel, to investigate a case in which a company in Johannesburg was using the South African coat of arms to make false presentations in the US to solicit funds by way of advance fees. The guilty parties were arrested, convicted and sentenced.

Gang warfare, drugs and gun-running were another of the areas that the Scorpions tackled. One of the most dominant gangs in the Cape Town area was the Sexy Boys, known for drug-running and demanding a 'tax' on anyone passing through their territory. Sexy Boy leaders Jerome and Michael Booysen had started off with a taxi business in the early 1990s but were soon involved in a conflict with the 28s gang over protection money; in turn, the brothers demanded protection money from the 28s, leading to an all-out war that went on for decades.[38] By the late 1990s rival gang leaders and members, and innocent bystanders, were being killed every week in the gang's area of operations.

The SAPS had initiated a Sexy Boys project, and the Scorpions consolidated all the Sexy Boys cases, then dealt with individual cases. Working with the SAPS, the Scorpions succeeded in getting three gang leaders convicted, including Michael Booysen and two of his lieutenants; all received life sentences. Two other top gang members and a Sexy Boys hitman were also put away.

The Scorpions were also the first in law enforcement in South Africa to take on racketeering cases, making use of the provisions of the Prevention of Organised Crime Act, which defines racketeering as the 'planned, ongoing, continuous or repeated participation' in crimes that include rape, murder, kidnapping, public violence, robbery and fraud, and crimes related to drugs, wildlife trafficking and contraventions of the Arms and Ammunition Act.[39]

The Scorpions took on their first racketeering prosecution in the case of the 'Ladysmith Mafia' in 2002. They did not succeed with a conviction but Patrick and Peter Green, and Nkosinathi Gabela, leaders of this criminal enterprise, were found guilty on alternative charges of drug dealing, murder and attempted murder, and given life sentences.[40]

This case led to further investigations, and the SAPS and the Scorpions worked together in the so-called Indigo case in KwaZulu-Natal; and this time they succeeded with the first racketeering conviction recorded in legal history in South Africa. A joint sting operation was conducted with the SAPS, and three people were arrested and ultimately sentenced to ten years' imprisonment each. Large amounts of drugs were confiscated and assets to the value of R500 000 were forfeited to the state.[41]

After this, the Scorpions stepped up the pace with racketeering charges and in 2005 took on 15 racketeering prosecutions, resulting in 23 convictions.[42]

Another case that grabbed public attention was 'Malatsigate', which involved the conviction of Count Ricardo Agusta, an Italian billionaire and real-estate developer, for corruption in October 2003 after he admitted to paying Western Cape premier Pieter Marais and MEC David Malatsi to fast-track a golf-estate development in Plettenberg Bay. It was the first conviction of a multinational on corruption charges in South Africa.

Agusta was connected to yet another controversial figure, Italian mafia boss Vito Palazzolo, who was arrested by the Scorpions in November 1999 based on fraudulent information he had provided to the department of information for his South African residency permit. Palazzolo had been convicted in absentia in Italy of money-laundering and drug trafficking, and the FBI regarded him as one of the top seven members of the Sicilian mafia group Cosa Nostra.

Palazzolo was given Ciskei 'citizenship' and appointed political advisor and ambassador plenipotentiary by the head of the 'republic', Oupa Gqozo, in 1990. By 1994 Palazzolo had gained South African citizenship based on this Ciskeian citizenship.[43] While much of the available information about Palazzolo related to this citizenship, he was suspected to be one of the figures in international organised crime who were playing a role among gangs in the illegal drug trade in South Africa; among those he was reportedly linked to was Rashied Staggie of the Hard Livings gang.[44]

> It was clear that it was going to be difficult to prosecute Palazzolo in South Africa. The priority was to get him out

of the country and work with the Italians, who wanted him to serve time there.

The law finally caught up with Palazzolo in 2012, when he was arrested at Bangkok's international airport in Thailand, still using a South African passport.[45] He was extradited to Italy to serve the nine-year sentence handed down years before in his absence.

Another investigation that got going during Bulelani's time was the 'Travelgate' matter, involving the abuse of parliamentary travel vouchers by ANC and Democratic Alliance (DA) MPs. The investigation was with the SAPS and going nowhere, until it was taken over by the Scorpions in June 2004. In March 2005 (after Bulelani's time) seven travel agents and 23 MPs and former MPs were arrested on fraud charges.

There would be those who would later question the conflicts of interests in parliament of some of those who had been found guilty of fraud as a result of the Scorpions' work in the Travelgate investigation, when they decided the fate of the unit as its disbanding was voted on in 2008. In his book *My Second Initiation*, Bulelani's successor Vusi Pikoli says he was subjected to considerable pressure during the case by 'ANC comrades and cabinet ministers'. 'Looking back now, the interference and pressure I experienced was a sign of the rot beginning to set in. It went completely against the values of our struggle for national liberation, which is exactly why I could not compromise on the issue.'[46]

In another case involving corruption, the Scorpions investigated fraud at the Road Accident Fund, which covers claims for injuries or deaths from vehicle crashes. Scorpions junior analysts played a key role, using specialised software to scan a huge number of documents. Dates and times of appointments, accident dates and other details were cross-referenced by the software in order to pinpoint improbabilities and likely fraud that could be investigated. 'Without an analyst skilled in such software, huge volumes of data are simply impenetrable by an ordinary investigator,' a subsequent report pointed out.[47]

The Scorpions succeeded in obtaining convictions for fraud involving doctors, accountants and lawyers, all suspected of belonging to a syndicate that had defrauded the fund of millions.[48] They were convicted and sentenced in 2004.

In a case involving another state institution, the Land Bank, convictions and sentences up to 15 years followed an investigation into fraudulent loan applications and corrupt payments and bribes by syndicates and bank officials. When the Scorpions began looking into it, it was estimated that the value of fraudulent transactions was R3.8 million; by the end of the investigation this had increased to R100 million.[49]

❑

In 2002, the Scorpions finalised 180 major convictions and 190 investigations. They achieved a conviction rate of 86 percent, although provinces like Gauteng and the Eastern Cape had much higher conviction rates than the national, of 98 percent and 97 percent respectively.[50]

In 2003 their conviction rate went up to 94 percent. They finalised another 189 major prosecutions and 205 investigations. In 2004, the conviction rate was still an impressive 88 percent, and they finalised 234 major prosecutions and 325 investigations.[51] Between 2004 and 2007, more than 900 investigations were finalised and there were 691 prosecutions, with an average conviction rate of 85 percent.

There were those, particularly in the SAPS, who would

accuse the Scorpions of achieving these figures by 'cherry-picking' what cases they took on. But the Scorpions were never intended to 'compete' with the SAPS or any other law-enforcement agency, a fact that Judge Khampepe went to some lengths to point out in her final report. The Scorpions were mandated to deal with particular crimes, and their work by its very nature involved selective investigation and prosecution. 'For example, consider what might have occurred had the [Scorpions] in the Western Cape ignored the problem of the numerous bombs exploding over Cape Town during the 1998-2000 period, but chosen instead to prosecute 200 fraudsters rather than 20 bombers?'[52]

Comments were made at various meetings in parliament that the Scorpions were being treated as the 'Rolls-Royces' of law enforcement, and could pick and choose their cases because of the resources allocated to them. Chair of the justice committee Johnny de Lange responded to one such criticism at a committee meeting by saying that 'specialised units inevitably take the best cases and have the best lawyers. It would be bad if they did not have the high success rate [that] they [do] have ... This is true all over the world.'[53]

An Institute for Security Studies report on the performance of the various NPA units in 2001 showed how much the Scorpions had achieved as far as public opinion was concerned in just three years. They had outperformed other NPA units by far, achieving, in the eyes of the public, an effectiveness rating of 84 percent against the AFU's 64 percent and the prosecution service's 47 percent.[54] The Specialised Commercial Crimes Unit, one of the best-performing units in the NPA, with conviction rates equal to those of the Scorpions, scored only 49 percent in the eye of public opinion. Interestingly, the same study showed that the public recognised the name 'Scorpions', giving it a rating of 84 percent, while the more formal 'Directorate of Special Operations' got a rating of 58 percent, demonstrating the power of the brand.

'The Scorpions became almost mystical,' a paper reported. 'The morale of a frightened, victimised public of all ethnicities rose. The criminal world was genuinely afraid of the Scorpions. There was certainly a significant criminal-deterrence effect associated with the Scorpions across the board, but especially pronounced on high-end crime. While early ANC-led governments were already more stable than most post-conflict regimes, their legitimacy nevertheless strengthened as they demonstrated through the Scorpions the will and a means to fight a terrifying crime wave.'[55]

But in the end it mattered little how the Scorpions fared in the court of public opinion. As their success grew, so did resistance in the corridors of power.

They were stepping on too many toes.

PART V
The Final Straw

PART 1

17.
A whispering campaign

'I will not be chased away by criminals masquerading as comrades, no matter how well connected or rich they might be.'

In early 2003 the NPA were at a crucial stage of their investigation into the arms deal and what they believed was a generally corrupt relationship between Schabir Shaik and then Deputy President Jacob Zuma. And that's when damaging gossip began circulating about Bulelani.

There were rumours, stories and emails. Threats were made, usually on a Saturday, that stories would appear in the Sunday newspapers. Bulelani had impregnated a 12-year-old girl, one article said; he had US$10 million in a Swiss bank account, and Cyril Ramaphosa and Saki Macozoma had paid off the girl's family not to go public with the allegations. Another alleged that Bulelani would be resigning as NDPP to join the mining giant De Beers in exchange for concessions obtained from his wife Phumzile Mlambo-Ngcuka, then minister of minerals and energy.[1]

Schabir Shaik issued a statement to the *Sunday Times* in December 2002 threatening that 'one day I am going to talk and Bulelani will run back to his hole in the Eastern Cape.'[2]

In July 2003 the 'dirty tricks' campaign against Bulelani was stepped up as the probe into corruption in the multibillion-rand arms deal gained momentum, and two emailed pages of allegations against him were sent to editors across the country. The *Weekend Argus* declared that it was 'aware of highly defamatory false rumours about Ngcuka, apparently emanating from Durban, which have on investigation been found to be baseless and unpublishable'.³

> It was a whispering campaign – nothing on the surface but very, very extensive. Their strategy was simple: throw as much dirt as you can and hope some of it sticks.

Bulelani made it clear he would not be deterred by those he described as 'comrade criminals', and vowed not to be put off by 'criminals masquerading as comrades'. 'We are not Scorpions for nothing,' he told the media when the *Sunday World* published the De Beers story.⁴

While Bulelani didn't say who he was referring to, one of the people who was under the spotlight at the time was Brett Kebble, who the Scorpions were investigating for share-price manipulation, fraud and tax evasion (for which both Kebble and his father were eventually charged⁵).

Kebble was a controversial figure who had become a powerful mining magnate by the age of 31. He had a network of contacts in the ANC, including highly placed individuals in the ANC Youth League. He had brought the Youth League into several empowerment deals in mining, property development, fishing and agriculture through the Youth League's company Lembede Investment Holdings.

Given Kebble's political ties, it was no surprise that many in the ANC came forward to lobby Bulelani on his behalf.

'*Umlungu wethu*,' they said. 'He's our white man.' They

wanted me to leave him alone. I told them it could not be done.

Kebble then played 'the Zuma card' and pulled together a fantastical smear campaign alleging that Bulelani was part of a network involving the CIA, mining entrepreneur Mzi Khumalo (who happened to be one of Kebble's business rivals and who was suing Kebble at the time), Saki Macozoma, Penuell Maduna, Phumzile Mlambo-Ngcuka and Thabo Mbeki that was designed to ensure that Macozoma succeeded Mbeki as president of the ANC.

Writer Rian Malan concluded that Kebble's motives were 'purely selfish': if he could show that Zuma was the victim of a malicious politically based smear campaign, he (Kebble) might also be able to discredit the charges of fraud and share-price manipulation he faced as part of a power play within the ANC. 'Kebble thus became an outspoken Zuma supporter, haranguing journalists about the Scorpions' "sinister machinations" and financing ANC rebels who shared that view.'[6]

At about this time several media personalities emerged on the scene. One of these, David Barritt, a public-relations consultant, had assisted Bulelani when the Scorpions had been launched five years earlier, in 1998. Now, in 2003, Bulelani says, Barritt approached him and told him that he had been offered employment by Kebble and asked whether he had any objections to him taking up the offer.

Bulelani was, of course, aware of the investigation into Kebble's business affairs but told Barritt that he should go ahead and work with Kebble if that was what he wanted to do.

The smear campaign to discredit Bulelani picked up pace. In one of several affidavits or statements that came to light during the trial of national police commissioner Jackie Selebi,

THE STING IN THE TALE: BULELANI NGCUKA

Glenn Agliotti claimed that Kebble and his business partner, John Stratton, had initiated a project to get Maduna and Ngcuka 'out of office' and that one of the strategies involved a newspaper campaign 'put together by Willem Heath and Dave Barret [sic]'.[7]

Agliotti said he was told by Stratton that 'one of the Shaik brothers'[8] had been paid R100 000 to 'facilitate' a woman to come forward and expose that she was underage at the time that she had been made pregnant by Ngcuka; he was 'present when Stratton phoned Mo Schaik [sic] and discussed it with him', Agliotti stated.[9]

David Gleason was another media personality associated with the campaign against Bulelani: a columnist for *Business Day*, he started writing regular pieces attacking Bulelani. Gleason was described at the time of his death in 2014 as 'the paid voice of Brett Kebble'[10] and 'the unchallenged leader of the pro-Kebble media pack'.[11]

'At this time the arms-deal investigation was coming to a head and two issues were still outstanding – Schabir Shaik's testimony, and the deputy president's answers to the 35 questions put to him by the Scorpions. We had come to the decision that once these two outstanding issues were settled, we would then close the investigation and take decisions on whether or not to institute criminal prosecutions,' Bulelani said.[12]

Scorpions' spokesperson Sipho Ngwema said that most of the questions related to Zuma's relationship with Shaik and Shaik's company Nkobi Holdings. Other information asked of Zuma related to financial benefits he had received from various sources, including former president Nelson Mandela, his debts, and all expenses he'd paid on behalf of the ANC since 1994. 'Zuma has not been asked to write an affidavit but has been invited to answer the questions in writing. His diaries, official and private travel plans and itineraries since 1995 have also been asked for,' an article at the time reported.[13]

At the same time, Bulelani said, it was becoming clear that something had to be done about the disinformation campaign, which, by mid-2003, was peaking, with rumours, calls and messages constantly being received by members of the NPA that he was going to be arrested for 'a whole range of offences'. The *Sunday World* article claiming that he was leaving the NPA to join the De Beers mining company had 'unsettled the National Prosecuting Authority and dampened the morale of many members of the organisation,' he later told a commission of inquiry run by retired chief justice Joos Hefer, and 'a lot of questions remained unanswered in the minds of the organisation'. He noted, 'Some members started believing that where there was smoke, there was fire. The result was that in every meeting of the NPA, the leadership had to give a response to the allegation carried in the article of the *Sunday World*.[14]

'The leadership of the NPA was beginning to suffer from a form of psychological torture of not knowing who is going to say what, when and about who. We decided to stop the smear campaign by not dealing with individual journalists but rather to call an off-the-record briefing with the editors and/or senior journalists of leading newspapers.' Bulelani wanted to clarify the 'many half-truths, distortions, fabrications and outright lies' that had been circulated during the campaign.[15]

When information is provided to the media off the record, the understanding is that nothing that is said can be used in any way, shape or form. At the Hefer Commission, Bulelani defended off-the-record briefings as 'very common practice' by senior civil servants, politicians and leaders in the business community to explain the background and context of a particular matter to journalists. In this case, the NPA had 'been subjected to a concerted misinformation campaign, joined by a whole range of otherwise disparate bedfellows, their only common interest being their desire to discredit our organisation,' he said, and 'it was important to give the background and context in which these allegations were being made. With this background, we asked the journalists to make a distinction between a source and a disinformation agent.'[16]

The essence, he says, of what he told the editors who attended the briefing was:

> These are all the cases we're dealing with and this is my position, and this is why you're seeing this vicious attack, not just on the NPA, but on me.
>
> If you believe that what I'm doing is wrong, then say so. And if you believe that I have this child, that I have all this money, then go ahead and publish those things and denounce me. If you think I'm abusing this office for political objectives, then say so. However, if in your investigations you find that all these things are false, then expose your sources.
>
> Now, I never believed or expected them to tell me who their sources were. I thought it was important, however, that they had the context and knew what we were dealing with.

The majority of those present at the briefing responded positively, with most writing favourable editorials after the meeting in support of the NPA, but the onslaught continued.

❑

A WHISPERING CAMPAIGN

The arrogance of Brett Kebble's legal team, emboldened no doubt by their proximity to political power, was demonstrated on the day Kebble was due to face charges in court.

> My team was told by Kebble's lawyers to go and see me in my office to discuss the withdrawal of the case. I was told the whole team was there.
>
> I called Willem [van der Linde, the leader of the prosecution team handling Kebble's case on behalf of the NPA]. I refused to see them. I told him that if I wanted to see him, I would call him directly. You can't be told by Brett Kebble's lawyers to come and see the National Director of Public Prosecutions!
>
> I had heard that Kebble's daughter had been injured in an accident so I told them to ask for a postponement. But otherwise the case would have proceeded.

Bulelani recalls a discussion he had with Van der Linde, in which the prosecutor told him he had consulted a friend in the judiciary and asked him what he thought an appropriate sentence would be for someone who faced the types of charges facing Kebble.

> The judge responded by saying that 'when someone hijacks a car, they normally get 15 years. What do you do when someone hijacks a company worth millions more than an ordinary car?'

So the stakes were high, and Kebble didn't give up – he asked to see Bulelani and again asked for the case to be withdrawn, and this was again refused.

But Kebble's case never did go to trial. The charges against him were withdrawn following his death in September 2005, when he was shot dead at 9 pm in his car on a quiet suburban road in Melrose, Johannesburg. He was alone in his vehicle. Three gunmen fired seven shots through the driver's window.

The official version is that it was an assisted suicide. Three figures associated with the criminal underworld received full indemnity on the murder charges in exchange for testifying for the state; Agliotti was the only person charged with the murder but he was eventually acquitted in 2010.

18.

Spies, lies and more lies

'Asoze ndijike – I will not turn back.'

Things came to a head with the *City Press* headline in September 2003 'Was Ngcuka a spy?' with the story identifying the NDPP as 'possibly, but not conclusively', Agent RS452.[1]

It was more than a question, though, because the article went on to state that documents said to have been sourced from an intelligence database and supporting this supposition had been leaked to the newspaper by a senior investigative journalist; a Lieutenant Karl Edwards of the then National Intelligence Service[2] had supposedly been Bulelani's handler.

His accusers were Riaz 'Moe' Shaik, an ANC intelligence operative during the underground days who had gone on to occupy senior positions in the new intelligence services after 1994, and Mac Maharaj, a struggle veteran who had spent 12 years on Robben Island with Nelson Mandela and who went on to serve in Mandela's first cabinet after 1994 as minister of transport. Both men had worked closely together in underground ANC structures before 1994; Maharaj had been the head of Operation Vula, the ANC's biggest underground operation since the 1960's.

Moe Shaik claimed that he had investigated Bulelani in the

late 1980s and reached the conclusion that 'there was a basis for suspecting Bulelani Ngcuka as being RS452'.[3] Just what this 'investigation' amounted to would emerge later in the commission of inquiry under retired chief justice Joos Hefer established by Mbeki to investigate Shaik and Maharaj's allegations.

All the records of the unit that had made this finding, Moe Shaik said, had been sent to the NIA in 1994 for safekeeping. (This was not true, as Shaik himself later admitted.) Claiming to have no records in his own possession, he had, he said, used 'a database of more than 880 suspected apartheid government spies' that he had in his possession to 'reconstruct' the original intelligence report. This he had handed to *Sunday Times* reporter Ranjeni Munusamy.[4]

Mac Maharaj himself said he had no independent information on the matter other than what he had been told by Shaik.

A director of FirstRand bank at the time, Maharaj was himself being investigated for contracts awarded to Schabir Shaik's company by the department of transport during his time as minister of transport. A few months earlier, in February 2003, the *Sunday Times* had published information claiming that Maharaj and his wife had received gifts and payments of more than R500 000 from Schabir Shaik, including a trip to Disneyland. These payments had reportedly been made between 1997 and 1999, while Maharaj was minister of transport, when a R2.5-billion tender for toll roads and credit-card-style driver's licences was awarded to a consortium in which Shaik held shares.[5]

Maharaj resigned from FirstRand once it became known that the Scorpions were investigating him, and FirstRand conducted its own investigation. The bank never published its findings but said 'the team did not find any evidence in the available information that Mr Maharaj intervened with the process or influenced the awards of [the tenders and contracts].' The bank announced at the same time that they had accepted Maharaj's resignation.[6]

> I was shocked that someone like Mac would behave as he did. But in the end, it did not help him to attack me. Attacking me would not make the allegations against him go way.

It's worth noting that a month before *City Press* published the spy allegations, the newspaper had been running articles that were, in fact, favourable to Bulelani. For example, on 27 July 2003 *City Press* editor Vusi Mona wrote, 'For some time now the media has heard all sorts of damaging rumours about Ngcuka. That we have not published these proves a level of maturity by the SA media.' He went on to say, 'If some of us don't like [Bulelani's] decisions, tough luck ... Until it can be proven that he is prone to poor judgement in the execution of his work or that he is using his office to pursue personal agendas, Ngcuka should be left alone.'[7]

This was followed a month later by another piece noting that the paper was 'recently treated to very damaging rumours, through an anonymous email, about the head of the National Prosecuting Authority, Bulelani Ngcuka'. 'I have been exposed to the most vitriolic foul-mouthing against black leaders,' Mona wrote. 'Almost every week I have to make serious decisions about such stories, their credibility and the motives of the sources who bring them to our attention. ... The only difference between the assassinations in the taxi industry and those in business and politics is that the latter are carried out by slightly more sophisticated people. And so it is not body bags we end up with but destroyed reputations and assassinated characters. But is it really necessary?'[8]

Ironically, it was Mona himself who became the assassin when he published the allegations about Bulelani being an apartheid spy.

❑

On the day the spy allegations were published by *City Press*, Bulelani was called by his close friend Ntobeko Maqubela, against whom he had refused to give evidence in 1981, and his co-accused in that case, Litha Jolobe. They told him that they had been contacted by individuals from within the NIA who wanted information and wanted Patrick to 'cooperate' with them in building a case against Bulelani. Patrick told Bulelani that he had told them there was nothing to find and had dismissed them.

It appeared, however, that it was not only the intelligence agencies that were involved in attempting to dig up dirt on Bulelani. He also received information from colleagues in the SAPS that national commissioner Jackie Selebi had instructed his commissioners to send all intelligence files to head office.

What Selebi hadn't counted on was the fact that the Scorpions enjoyed good relations with the SAPS, and that Bulelani already knew what Selebi was up to.

> Some of the commissioners called me. 'We're looking to see if we can find anything about you,' is what they told me. I told them to go ahead and share the information with me if they found anything.
>
> The other thing is that most of those files the police were looking for were already with the NPA.

Also on the day *City Press* published the damning accusations, Bulelani's friend from university days, Dumisani Tabata, who was still in the Eastern Cape, immediately drove to Middledrift to speak to Bulelani's mother, who he knew would be shocked by the reports. He told her, of course, that the allegations were false and that they would expose them as lies.

'She said, "*Bade banenumbere* [they even had a number]",' Dumisani recalls;[9] she was referring to the elaborate nature of the lie. 'It was quite a shock to his family. It was a mixture of anger and disbelief that they would try to bring this kind of shame to their family, and on Bulelani, who is the shining light in that family.'

And there were people who began to have creeping doubts, says Dumisani. 'There is an automatic veneration of people who come from MK. There is a tendency not to question what they say, so when people like Moe and Mac say such things, people begin to think that there's something there. And, of course, the apartheid state was powerful. They were able to turn people. It's part of the reason why they succeeded for as long as they did. So some people began to doubt. Others, of course, seem to celebrate when those in high office are knocked off their pedestals.'[10]

Bulelani says Dumisani's visit was reassuring for his family, and it was comforting for his mother to know that in the midst of all these troubles, his friends were there for him.

> The appearance of a close friend was a relief to them. This was the norm throughout the country – the outpouring of love and support. Of course, people were upset and people were crying in the corridors at the NPA, but the support was solid. That's what gave me a lot of strength.

Thabo Mbeki called the Ngcuka home in Johannesburg on the same day. Bulelani was not at home so he spoke to Phumzile, asking how her husband was doing. She said he was okay and was thinking of suing both Shaik and Maharaj. His response was that Bulelani should go ahead and sue them, and that if there was anything he needed, he should just ask. That was, says Bulelani, 'comforting'.

> In the meantime, work had to go on. We had received [word] that Alain Thétard was willing to come to the party. He wanted to talk to us but would only give a statement to me. We debated it a bit and agreed we should go. So on the Monday, [Advocate] Lynette [Davids], Lungisa and I flew to Paris and met with Thétard.
>
> After exchanging a few pleasantries, I started asking him some questions. 'Can you tell us about the circumstances in which you wrote the fax?'
>
> 'I can't remember.'
>
> 'Is this your handwriting?'
>
> He turned around and looked the other way, avoiding my eyes. 'I can't remember.'
>
> 'No, but you know your handwriting! How is it you can't remember your own handwriting?'
>
> 'I can't remember.'
>
> And that was it. Obviously, the fellow was evasive. I don't know what happened between the time we left South Africa and when we arrived in Paris, but something must have, because now he just couldn't remember anything!
>
> There was nothing we could do. I called Dumisani [who I had asked to look into possibly suing Shaik] from Paris and asked him whether we were making progress. I had told him to serve summons on both Maharaj and Moe. He said he had a suggestion to make and we should talk when I got back.

When we got back, this spy story was still in the news, of course, and we discussed it at the office. People felt that staff were bleeding, they were hurting. They needed to hear from me. So we agreed I would address the staff.

I was on my way to the office on the day I was going to address the staff when my mother's priest, Reverend Boyce, called me. He asked if I was driving. I said I was in the car but we could talk. He said no, I should stop the car.

So I stopped the car and he said, 'Let us pray.'

We prayed on the phone, and then he said when I get to the office I must read Psalm 35. I got to the office and asked for a Bible. I read it. 'Plead my cause, O Lord, with them that strive with me: fight against them that fight against me ... False witnesses did rise up; they laid to my charge things that I knew not .'

We decided that I would include it in my speech to the staff that day.

The message was well received and the staff were happy to hear that we were fighting back. But that weekend the *City Press* came out with an article with the headline 'Ngcuka turns to God'.[11]

Bulelani laughs.

They underestimated how religious South Africans are. People from all over the Eastern Cape visited my mother and prayed at her home. The women from the Eastern Cape arranged a prayer service at her home which was well attended. 'If you'd seen them all, *umntwana wam* [my child],' she told me, 'you'd have been proud of yourself. If you could see the people here, you will also see how big my funeral will be.'

THE STING IN THE TALE: BULELANI NGCUKA

There's a radio programme on *uMhlobo Wenene* that used to start at 12 in the evening called *12 Down*. People would call in and talk about all sorts of things. For days on end, that programme was devoted to me. My mother would call me and say, 'Please, just listen to what people say about you.'

I flew to Port Elizabeth on business shortly thereafter, and as I was going to collect my bags [from the airport conveyor belt], one of the cleaning ladies, an old woman, walked over to me. She grabbed me by the arm and slapped me on the wrist. 'You silly child, how dare you do this to me! Look at my knees. My knees are scratched from praying for you!'

I didn't know her. She was just an ordinary woman, a cleaner at the airport, praying for me. That touched me. That was the norm throughout the country.

I agreed to appear on SABC TV and was interviewed by Redi Tlhabi. She didn't like the [prepared set of] questions she had been given to ask me, and as she was asking me the questions, she kept saying to herself, 'But this is nonsense. I'm not going to ask these questions.' However, the people were phoning in to the show and were very positive.

Now, I had worked in parliament with Redi's aunt, Winkie Direko, who was then premier of the Free State. She called me after the show. 'I told that daughter of mine she must leave you alone.'

'No, she is just doing her job.'

'Nonsense, I told her she must leave you alone!'

George Fivaz called me and said, 'No, Bulie. This is rubbish. I had a list of everyone who was a spy and you certainly were not one of them. I'm willing to go on record.' Which he did.

Jan Henning also wanted to help. He had done a lot of the political trials in the past and was very close to some of the former security police. He contacted one of the old security guys and arranged that we meet. This fellow said he was worried.

'I can see this steam engine running away. It's going to cause a big collision. I don't know who's going to stop it. I'm worried about what's happening. I can tell you that you never were a spy.'

'I know that!'

'I can also tell you that Moe was never a spy. I worked with him during the transition. This thing is false and it's bad for our country. I don't like it but you're fighting among yourselves now as the ANC.'

The media, too, on the whole were very responsible. Even though the story was a juicy one, they dealt with it responsibly and credit is due to how we had dealt with them as an organisation. We had always dealt with the media with integrity and Sipho [Ngwema] was a great part of that. We'd always been frank and open.

On the same day that the *City Press* claimed that Bulelani had 'turned to God', *Sunday Times* editor Mathatha Tsedu published an editorial defending the paper's decision not to publish the spy allegations. He said that he had set conditions before the story could be published, including that the newspaper be given all the information so that they could see on what basis the conclusions had been reached in the initial investigation and could carry out their own investigation. If *Sunday Times* journalists then agreed with the conclusions reached about Ngcuka, they would go ahead and publish.[12]

THE STING IN THE TALE: BULELANI NGCUKA

When the *Sunday Times* had refused to run the story, the newspaper's political reporter, Ranjeni Munusamy, had passed it on to rival *City Press*.

❏

'I couldn't believe it,' says Madeleine Fullard, recalling her reaction in September 2003 when, sitting in the USA, she switched on her laptop and looked at the South African news, and there was the allegation that Bulelani Ngcuka was Agent RS452.

Madeleine, who now heads the Missing Persons Task Team at the NPA but at the time was a researcher at the TRC, says, 'There was only one source that I knew the identity of, and it was Agent RS452. I knew exactly who Agent RS542 was, and I had some documents back in South Africa that could prove it. So I phoned Willie Hofmeyr and said, "Willie, you are not going to believe this, but I can give you documents that will prove who Agent RS452 was."'[13]

Some time before, Madeleine had been contracted to dig up information about the Motherwell Four bombing,[14] one of the cases that had been referred to the NPA from the TRC. When she was informed that a box of old security-police documents had been found in a building in Pretoria, she was asked to go through them, specifically looking for information that there were sources in Port Elizabeth feeding information to the ANC. 'We were super thrilled. What could be more exciting than going through old security-police documents?'[15]

She and a colleague went there, 'and, sure enough, there in the basement of this building was a random collection of files. Some were files on individuals, as well as telex reports, source reports. The individual files were quite random. It was almost as if this box of documents had just been forgotten when they were loading documents on trucks to be destroyed. There was no rhyme or reason or connection between the documents.

'We started going through them, sorting them, and making an assessment of what was there. Any time we came across a source report from someone who was clearly in the Eastern Cape, we would pay particular attention to it. We were not supposed to copy things, but we did. I recall very distinctly looking with interest at one particular source. The thing with those source documents is that if you've got enough of them, you can eventually work out who the source is, because the source includes themselves when recording who is at a particular meeting. After a while, I realised that this particular source, RS452, was Vanessa Brereton.'[16]

Brereton had worked as a human-rights lawyer, taking on high-profile cases under the apartheid regime, and when the ANC was unbanned in 1990, she was unanimously elected as the treasurer for the Port Elizabeth branch. She admitted in October 2003 that she had been a spy.

> Once we knew Madeleine had the files, I was relieved because my biggest fear was that these people [his accusers, including Moe Shaik and Mac Maharaj] would somehow concoct files and information. So we knew who Agent RS452 was even before they knew.

❏

When Bulelani and his delegation returned from Paris, he and Dumisani met to decide whether to go ahead and sue Moe Shaik and Mac Maharaj.

THE STING IN THE TALE: BULELANI NGCUKA

'You know what Bul is like,' Dumisani says. 'At first he was very angry and wanted to know why I didn't want to sue these guys. I told him that if we were lucky, we would be in court in a year or two. In the meantime, the propaganda would be sustained and the NPA would continue to be trashed. Maybe at the end of the process, in a few years' time, they would withdraw on the steps of the court and apologise. So I asked him, "Do you believe that you still have the president's confidence?"

'He said yes.

'"Well, then," I said, "let's expose these guys. When Siphiwe Nyanda and others were accused of plotting a coup, Madiba appointed a commission of inquiry and the matter was dealt with immediately.[17] So if you believe that you have the president's confidence, he must act immediately and appoint a commission of inquiry. This thing goes to the heart of the NPA. You can't have people thinking that an institution like the NPA is headed by someone who was an apartheid spy. Let's deal with it now."'[18]

> On the same day Smuts [Ngonyama, head of the ANC presidency] called me and said, 'Gqunu,[19] why don't you ask the president to forgive you? He's a very forgiving man. We've forgiven these apartheid spies and everyone else.'
>
> I said, 'There's nothing to forgive. I can't do that. There's no truth to these allegations.'
>
> Then I thought, if a person like Smuts thinks like this, it's more serious than I thought. It's very important that we act, and act quickly. So we went to see the president.

'The president was reluctant at first but then agreed and appointed the Hefer Commission,' says Dumisani. 'I believe that in this way we caught Shaik and Maharaj unawares. They thought they would still have time to run with their propaganda campaign.'[20]

> I thought it would be good to have someone like Dikgang Moseneke, with struggle credentials and who understands what it means to be called an apartheid spy, to head up the commission. The president agreed.
>
> There was an ANC NEC meeting that weekend. [Mbeki] went there and they raised [the spy allegations]. He said, 'No, I'm not discussing it with you. I have a plan but I'm not telling you. You leak.'
>
> He approached Arthur [Chaskalson], who was the chief justice, who said he couldn't appoint a sitting judge. Arthur said there's a retired judge by the name of Joos Hefer. He said he was a fair man. He knew him and would speak to him. Mbeki agreed.
>
> And that's how the Hefer Commission came about.

19.

The Hefer Commission

'I am not here to clear my name.
I am not here to prove my innocence.
There is no need for that.'

The formal surroundings of a courtroom could not be further removed from the shadowy world of the ANC's time of exile and underground struggle in the 1980s. However, this is the world that Judge Josephus 'Joos' Hefer found himself entering on 22 October 2003 when he opened the proceedings of the Hefer Commission – what became known to many South Africans as 'The Mac and Moe Show': the two main witnesses before the commission were, of course, Bulelani's accusers, Moe Shaik and Mac Maharaj.

Hefer's terms of reference were to 'inquire into, make findings and report on the allegations by Messrs Maharaj and Shaik that the National Director of Public Prosecutions was an agent of the security services of the pre-1994 government under code name RS452 or any other code name and, as a result thereof, improperly and in violation of the law, took advantage of or misused the prosecuting authority and, in particular, abused, advanced, promoted, prejudiced or undermined the rights and/or interests of any person or organisation.'[1]

The challenge that lay before 'Mac and Moe' was to provide

some proof of their damning allegations against one of the country's top law enforcers. If they had hoped for any assistance from the intelligence services, they were soon to find they were on their own.

Veteran human-rights lawyer George Bizos had approached Bulelani before the commission got under way, and told him he had been asked to represent Maharaj. He had refused. He had never done this with any client before, he said, but he'd felt compelled to do so in this case as an expression of his indignation.

Shaik and Maharaj were convinced that the Scorpions' investigations of first Chippy and Schabir Shaik, then Jacob Zuma and Maharaj himself, revealed a pattern that they believed spoke for itself. In their view, Bulelani was using his position to 'get even' and act against those who knew of his alleged collaboration with the apartheid police.

Maharaj's main concern at the commission was the complaint about alleged abuse of power, and this was what he spent most of his time talking about when he gave evidence. He said that information about the Scorpions' investigation into contracts awarded while he was still minister of transport had been leaked to the media, and that Bulelani was either directly responsible for or had condoned this, which had led to Maharaj and his wife being vilified in the public eye.[2]

Bulelani has never denied that the leaks to the media, including those concerning Maharaj and his wife, could have emanated from the NPA or the Scorpions. In January 2004, in fact, he conceded that 'a possibility still exists that a culprit or culprits could be among our ranks'. But, he added, 'That, to me, would be completely unacceptable. We are in the process of tightening systems within the organisation in a bid to ensure that we limit the chances of classified information leaving our organisation and landing in the wrong hands or ears. Furthermore, we shall ensure that any employee who flouts the relevant rules and regulations is severely dealt with, in accordance with the law.'[3]

On the issue of abuse of power, Bulelani told the commission, 'I have personally been the subject of the arbitrary and draconian abuse of power, such as detention without trial ... I know what it means to be detained without trial, to be denied access to legal representation, to be denied access to the ones we love. I know very well what it means to be on the receiving end of the abuse of state power.

'The power to institute criminal proceedings on behalf of the state is one that needs to be exercised with great care and discretion. I am acutely aware of the fact that the institution of a criminal investigation and prosecution can impact adversely on the lives and reputations of those who are investigated and/or charged.

'I am deeply respectful of the office I hold and the responsibilities entrusted to me by virtue of that office. I deny that I have abused the powers in my office.

'That said, there appear to be some in our country who hold the view that the criminal investigation or prosecution of any senior or respected member of the African National Congress constitutes an abuse in and of itself. To those I say today, the view you hold is not only unfortunate, it is uninformed. It is a betrayal of everything we fought so hard to achieve.

'The values of the ANC that I know, the values that I was socialised into, are those of the highest ethical standards. They dictate justice and common decency in the way we conduct our lives. That is why I have always respected them and why I always will. These are the same values that now underpin the constitution and that serve as a lodestar for all South Africans. It is precisely those values that dictate that we are all equal before the law. That no-one is above the law. That where you err, you shall be treated like anyone else.

'I took an oath of office, a covenant with the people of South Africa, that I would help create an institution that would play a central part in the uprooting of criminality in our society. I have been faithful to that oath and will continue to do so until I leave office.'[4]

Judge Hefer was unable to make a finding about the leaks – he could not say that Bulelani had condoned the leaks – but he expressed his strong disapproval. He said that it was 'highly likely that the guilty party was within Mr Ngcuka's office and we have it from Mr Ngcuka himself that he or she could not be traced. Such a state of affairs cannot be tolerated.'[5]

When it came to Maharaj's evidence on the question of whether Bulelani was an apartheid spy, Hefer said, 'Mr Maharaj's evidence provides a useful broad outline of what happened during 1989. At that time he was head of Operation Vula, which had been devised with the aim of infiltrating senior members of the ANC into South Africa in order to coordinate operations in this country. His orders included liaising closely with Mr Shaik to ensure that Operation Vula would not be compromised.

'Mr Maharaj came to know of Mr Ngcuka when he wanted to know whether he could safely make contact with Nadel and Shaik advised him not to do so as he thought that there was a government agent in Nadel and that he suspected Bulelani Ngcuka. To substantiate his suspicion, Shaik first produced documents procured from security branch files; but he was only able to persuade Mr Maharaj later by pointing out suspicious features of Mr Ngcuka's passport and identification documents as well.

'In his evidence, Mr Maharaj conceded that he has no independent knowledge of the facts on which Mr Shaik's suspicion was based. Although, as he repeatedly said, he has no expertise in intelligence matters, he supported the conclusion at the time and still believes that it was correct. But it is quite clear that he is entirely reliant on the validity of Mr Shaik's inferences and the adequacy of the latter's reasoning. For this reason, he conceded in cross-examination that he does not really know whether Mr Ngcuka was an apartheid spy or not.'[6]

This was an important concession by Maharaj during three days of cross-examination by advocate Boyce (Marumo) Moerane, who was acting for Bulelani. 'I do not know if Bulelani Ngcuka was an apartheid spy,' Maharaj told the commission.

Moerane, smiling, responded, 'Thank you, thank you. Now the whole of South Africa knows that Mr Mac Maharaj does not know whether or not Mr Ngcuka was a spy.'[7]

❏

Moe Shaik did not fare much better when it came to his turn on the witness stand. Trying to explain the motives behind his behaviour, he said that Bulelani's decision to announce that a prima facie case existed against Zuma despite the fact that he was not being charged, meant that Zuma was 'forever branded as corrupt'. 'From that day to this, the deputy president has tried to clear his name. Like Jesus Christ, he was to discover how cruel and devious Pontius Pilate was. At the sight of my comrade, commander and friend carrying his cross to that place where he was to be crucified, I could endure his pain no longer. I refused to stay silent and be a curious onlooker at this spectacle.'[8]

Shaik was at pains to explain that he had done the honourable thing speaking out, not to conduct a 'smear campaign' but

THE HEFER COMMISSION

to tell 'the truth'. He had, he said, sent a file to the ANC's headquarters in Lusaka in 1989 in which he had set out his reasons for believing that Bulelani was an apartheid spy. While this report was no longer in his possession, he had, he said, kept a database of more than 880 suspected apartheid spies, and he still had this. He said that he regarded the information on the database as belonging to the ANC, and that only when they instructed him to hand it over would he do so.[9] He told the commission that it was this database he had used in December 2002 to 'reconstruct' the file, concluding that Bulelani had 'most probably' been an apartheid spy.[10]

Dumisani Tabata saw this file. 'I remember when we received a copy of the RS452 file. It was sent to us to prepare for the commission. I went to the airport to fetch it myself and I read it in the car. I couldn't believe it. I phoned the guys and told them it was complete trash. That's how bad it was. I understand raw intelligence but the quantum leaps that were made to reach the conclusion that one wants are scary. It's also scary that archival material like intelligence files [was] kept by individuals like Moe to use as he saw fit.'[11]

And, indeed, Judge Hefer made short work of Shaik's investigation methods, noting that at the time 'he was a young man in his mid-twenties with little experience of counterintelligence work'. The judge concluded, 'In the absence of any direct evidence of Mr Ngcuka's duplicity, Mr Shaik had to rely upon inferences which he drew from documents stolen from security branch files and from peculiarities pertaining to Mr Ngcuka's passport and identity documents. He repeatedly stressed in his evidence that, in the event of one of his inferences or assumptions being shown to have been fallacious, he was prepared to concede the fallacy of his conclusion too.'[12]

THE STING IN THE TALE: BULELANI NGCUKA

Regarding the file Shaik said he had sent to the ANC's headquarters in Lusaka in 1989, it was not clear from his submission whether this file was now in the hands of the country's new intelligence agencies, but as Hefer found out when he approached the NIA, SAPS crime intelligence and military intelligence, they were not willing to come to the party. George Bizos had been hired to represent the intelligence agencies at the hearings, and their position was unambiguous: legislation prohibited intelligence agencies from disclosing any classified and/or confidential information.

Hefer then wrote to Frank Chikane, director-general (DG) in the presidency, asking him to examine a 'personnel list' containing the names of intelligence agents which had apparently been handed to President Mandela in 1994.[13] Chikane's response made it clear that the ball was in Shaik and Maharaj's court. He pointed out that the list Hefer was referring to was of staff members, and that Bulelani was not a staff member of the intelligence services. Further, he noted that with respect to agents and sources, 'the president has unfettered access to all information in the possession of the state intelligence and security structures. These structures have made no allegations that bear on the matters being considered by the commission. The allegations that form the basis of the appointment of the commission relate to information held by persons outside the state security structures.' (Hefer later called these allegations 'ill-conceived and entirely unsubstantiated'.)[14]

Bulelani himself was not concerned about what information would emerge from old intelligence files. He recalls a conversation with Vusi Mavimbela, DG of intelligence at the time, saying that if the intelligence services indeed had information that he had been a spy, they should say so.

THE HEFER COMMISSION

'Come on, DG. If I was a spy, then say so openly. Tell them I was a spy.'

'No, no, *umtshutshisi* [prosecutor]. It's very complicated. We can't open this door.'

In his memoirs, Mavimbela refers to this exchange but he recalls a somewhat angrier Bulelani, who demanded to know why the NIA wouldn't release whatever information they had on him, saying that by not doing so, they were perpetuating the lies about him being a spy.

Mavimbela says he understood Bulelani's anger and sympathised. 'Both of us knew that a number of good comrades and cadres were victimised – indeed, some died – simply because someone erroneously thought that they were apartheid spies.'[15]

Judge Hefer pointed out the obvious. 'Of course, the first problem which Mr Shaik had to face in his evidence was that, contrary to his 1989 conclusion, it is common knowledge now that Mr Ngcuka could not have been RS452. Ms Brereton's revelation that this was, in fact, her code number has obviously left Mr Shaik in a quandary. ... Instead of conceding that he made a mistake, Mr Shaik has come up with a new theory. It has recently come to his knowledge, he says, that the security branch and the NIS resorted to what is known in the intelligence community as "false flag" or "stratcom" operations, by means of which information supplied by one source was attributed to another source. What he suggests is that the information attributed in the two reports to RS452 did, in fact, not come from Ms Brereton, but from Mr Ngcuka.'[16]

Hefer was having none of Shaik's new theory of 'false flagging': not only was it an 'afterthought', he said, applied 14 years after the event, but Shaik could provide no evidence to back up his new theories. 'Had there been any evidence that the information in question could not have been supplied by Ms Brereton, the position might have been different. But there is none.'¹⁷

Hefer rejected also the suspicions that Shaik had about Bulelani's passport and identity documents, and said that had he asked, the explanations now provided would have been available to him too. 'I do not intend dealing with all the points [that dispelled any suspicion relating to these documents], and merely mention two of them by way of example. First, there is the fact that a passport was issued to Mr Ngcuka during December 1981 with apparently unseemly haste [but] ... this was by no means unusual.' As for the fact that Bulelani had multiple identity numbers, 'Suffice it to say that I have been convinced beyond any measure of doubt that the sinister inferences for which Mr Shaik contended, in respect both of the passport and of the identity documents, are not justified,' Hefer said.¹⁸

'For these reasons I have come to the conclusion that the 1989 investigation was fatally flawed by unwarranted assumptions and unjustifiable inferences, and by the blatant failure to examine available avenues of inquiry.'¹⁹

As for Vusi Mona, the editor of *City Press*, whose publication of the 'apartheid spy' article had started all the trouble, it emerged that his reasons for doing so were perhaps more personal than political. The evidence leader suggested that 'Mona's true motives for divulging the off-the-record briefing had more to do with concerns that he himself was being investigated by the Scorpions and by the pressures of third parties'.²⁰

Mona began his testimony by apologising 'unreservedly to Ngcuka, his family and to the National Directorate of Public Prosecutions for the pain the story caused. I still regard Ngcuka as a man who can do his work.'²¹

But this did not save him. At the end of his testimony, Hefer concluded that Mona's 'credibility had been reduced to nil'.[22]

City Press later made it clear that the information Ranjeni Munusamy had given to them was 'devoid of truth, contrived and misleading'.[23] Acting editor Wally Mbhele issued a front-page apology to Bulelani, saying evidence before the commission had 'left little doubt that there is no credible substance to reports suggesting that he was or could have been an apartheid spy'.[24]

❏

Judge Hefer concluded that not only had he found nothing showing, as a matter of probability, that Bulelani had been an apartheid spy, but that the probabilities in fact favoured the very opposite. Citing the number of times Bulelani had been detained, his arrest and imprisonment, and his treatment during his time in prison, the judge noted that this 'is certainly not the kind of treatment meted out to government agents. And his experiences in jail while serving his sentence for his refusal to testify against Mr Maqubela speak volumes in similar vein.

'He was isolated from his fellow prisoners because the prison authorities considered him to be too militant and far too ideological. Thus when Mr PW Botha had made an offer to release Mr Mandela on condition that the ANC renounces violence, and Mr Ngcuka had joined other prisoners in expressing their dissidence, the prison authorities justified his isolation by insisting that he would probably influence other prisoners to reject the offer. I simply cannot believe as a matter of probability that he would have been treated in this way if he had been a government agent at the time; nor that he would have been amenable to become one after his ordeal.'[25]

Hefer pointed out the personal cost Bulelani had had to bear. 'When he was detained the first time during 1981, he was on the point of marrying his present wife. Of course, nothing came of the intended marriage. It had to wait for several years. While in jail, letters from his fiancée were intercepted and not delivered to him. She was refused permission to visit him because she was not regarded as a member of his family. And when he applied for permission to marry her, it was refused.'[26]

❏

Dumisani Tabata says that both Moe Shaik and Mac Maharaj underestimated Bulelani. 'By the time we went to the Hefer Commission, we knew, of course, that RS452 was someone else. Then they came with all sorts of other allegations, such as that the apartheid state had paid for Bulelani's studies at Fort Hare and that he was given privileges in prison that had not applied to others.

'I went to Fort Hare and found his files there. I don't think they thought that files from the 1970s would talk back to them. Paper does not lie. We had evidence of his bursary and what his family had contributed.

'I also went to the national archives and found his prison files. There I found that famous letter from Phumzile which he had never received.

'In the end, all their lies just didn't stack up.'[27]

Dumisani recalls also the attitude of disdain Shaik and Maharaj displayed when the Hefer Commission got under way. 'They were very arrogant. Remember, they had the media on their side. People like Ranjeni Munusamy had given them a lot of publicity and it was like they were walking on air. It was like they expected that one must accept that you can be trashed by them because they were former intelligence agents of the ANC and we must take their word for it. They were angry that we were questioning them.'[28]

In his statement to the Hefer Commission, Bulelani said that 'after the publication in the *City Press* that I had been an apartheid spy, my wife issued a statement in which she said, "My husband was not a spy." A week later my mother did the same, and issued a statement which said, "My son was not a spy."

'My wife stated that we were not going to embark on a crusade to clear my name, and that we were rather going to continue with the execution of the responsibilities entrusted to us by the people of this country.'[29]

He recounted his years of service in the ANC and said that not a single member of the ANC, out of all those he had worked with, had ever suggested he had sold them out. 'The reason I am here,' he told the Hefer Commission, 'is to defend an institution established by the constitution, the institution of which I am a member, the National Prosecuting Authority. It is an organisation which strives to make a reality of the principles of freedom and justice to which we dedicated our lives. It is an organisation of which I am very proud.

'It is our organisation's duty to prosecute and investigate crime in such a manner that treats all persons not only with justice and respect, but with equality. Anyone who violates the laws of this land will be investigated and where necessary prosecuted – regardless of who they are, regardless of their colour, their gender, their religious beliefs, their status in life, regardless of whether they live in a poor township or a wealthy suburb, regardless of the office or position they hold, regardless of their past contribution to our liberation struggle.

'No-one is above the law, no matter how wealthy or powerful

they might be. This is a sacred constitutional principle. It is precisely because the National Prosecuting Authority has upheld this principle that it has come under very serious and sustained attack during the past six months.

'I am here because I lead that organisation. If I were not the National Director of Public Prosecutions, none of those who have sought to defame and discredit me would have shown the slightest interest in digging up and delving into my personal history and my private life. It is a mere accident of history that this person whom they have sought to discredit happens to be me.

'I am here today because the organisation I have been tasked to lead has performed its functions without fear, favour and without prejudice. ... I am here to make it clear that we shall not be intimidated by those who have sought to discredit us in an attempt to derail and discredit our investigations in order to protect their own vested interests.

'When I was persuaded to take this job, I was aware of its dangers. I was aware that it would change my life forever. I knew that if I did my job well, without fear or favour, there would be some in our society who would come to bay for my blood. I knew that they would try and bribe, intimidate and blackmail me, and even try to kill me.

'I was prepared for all that, to make my contribution to a South Africa that is free of criminals, criminality and corruption. It never occurred to me that I would find myself defending the reputation and the effectiveness of the institution I have been privileged to help create, from individuals who have been my comrades and leaders. I never thought that I would have cause to investigate or prosecute any senior member of the movement that has created the political and moral order that we have in South Africa today.

'I want to state it clearly and unequivocally that *asoze ndijike* – I will not turn back. The people of this country have paid a very high price for our constitutional democracy to be based on the principles of equality and justice. We dare not sacrifice those principles to benefit the few among us who wish to abuse their past contribution to the attainment of freedom as a licence for their own contribution and greed.

'I am not going to run back home and creep into the hole that I came from, as has been suggested. I will stand firm with the multitudes of our leaders who stand for the truth, and the millions of decent South Africans who say with me *asijiki*. We shall not turn back.'[30]

❏

Judge Hefer handed his report to Thabo Mbeki in January 2004.

In the next issue of the ANC's newsletter, *ANC Today*,[31] Mbeki said that the ANC had known of the allegations against Bulelani before they returned from exile and, he clarified, 'We never took any action to isolate him or otherwise break his links with the movement. When we returned, we did nothing to exclude him from our ranks or stop him assuming senior positions both within the movement and, later, the state institutions.

'We sat in the national cabinet and accepted the recommendation of the then minister of justice, Dullah Omar, a highly respected leader of our people, that Bulelani Ngcuka should be appointed our National Director of Public Prosecutions.

'He would exercise powers we had described in a law that we, the constitutionally mandated national executive authority of the Republic, had drafted and approved for submission to parliament as the constitutionally mandated national executive authority of the Republic.

'If the leadership of our movement had allowed all these things to happen, all the time knowing that it was wilfully permitting a known secret agent of the forces against which we had waged a protracted and relentless struggle, to place himself in positions of power, that leadership itself would have been guilty of a great deal more than a dereliction of duty.

'It would not have been able to answer the charge that it had acted as an accomplice to the preparation of conditions for the defeat of the very revolution for whose victory it had called on the masses of our people to be ready to sacrifice their lives. Its actions would not have been less than treasonable.

'The fact, however, is that this leadership was certain that it had never been presented with such convincing evidence as would have required it to act against the person accused, in defence of the revolution.

'Indeed, in all instances that I know, when we had convincing evidence of sponsored and conscious betrayal of the revolution, we acted as justified by the case in question and as circumstances would allow in terms of our movement's code of behaviour.

'We appointed the Hefer Judicial Commission of Inquiry because we had no information that created any basis on which we could conclude that either the National Directorate or the Scorpions had been transformed into a base of counter-revolution. At the same time, given the gravity of the charge, we had to ensure that we do not allow the situation to persist according to which things should continue to be said that served to discredit the institution or the office of the National Director or the person holding the office.'[32]

The 'Ngcuka Affair', Mbeki said, 'must teach all of us the

THE HEFER COMMISSION

important lesson that all of us must stop speculating about non-existent lists of apartheid spies. None of us should ever again seek to win whatever battles we are waging by labelling others as having been apartheid spies.'[33]

❏

In January 2004, Moe Shaik wrote a letter to Kgalema Motlanthe, then secretary-general of the ANC, in which he acknowledged the 'mistakes in the assumptions and analysis made in respect of the counter-intelligence investigation ... into Cde Bulelani Ngcuka' and offered his 'sincere apologies to Cde Bulelani Ngcuka and his family for the pain and hurt that this ordeal has caused and trust that he would take comfort in the findings of the Commission.'[34,35]

20.
Time to go

'Already in 2003 I felt like I had become a political football, and that it was time for me to go. Now it was worse.'

'I have addressed the NPA staff this morning and told them we must soldier on and do what the South African people expect us to do.'[1]

It was 22 January 2004, and Bulelani was addressing the Johannesburg Press Club in the wake of the Hefer Commission, and telling the audience about the terrible fallout of the attacks on him which, he said, had 'cascaded down to my staff, whose contribution to the NPA I treasure above all else'.

'The pain and suffering I saw on the faces of my staff – ordinary employees of the NPA – has left an indelible mark in my heart. There were times when people were not even sure if working for the NPA was a good thing or not. You must remember that the people who made allegations against me were people who were either investigated by my staff, or had their friends or relatives investigated by the NPA.'[2]

Turning to the issue of press reports that he 'would consult my family and friends on whether or not I should continue serving the nation in the capacity of National Director of Public Prosecutions', he said they were accurate. 'Events prior to and during the Hefer Commission caused my family untold suffering. If I continue with this job, these people whom I care for so much may still suffer more. If I continue as head of the NPA, I will still have to take decisions – sometimes difficult and painful – with even worse consequences for myself.'[3]

But, he told those gathered, he would not give in. Having considered his position and his future 'as a person, a husband, a father, a son, a brother, a friend and a patriot', he had decided that there were a lot of knots he still had to untie as South Africa's head of prosecutions. 'Despite personal suffering and peril, I am now more determined than ever to carry on with my job. It cannot be in South Africa's interests for me to give up the fight now.'[4]

The following month, when he addressed the NPA national conference, he assured delegates, 'There should not be any doubt in our minds that as an organisation we emerged a lot stronger after the Hefer Commission.' Still upbeat about his decision to stick it out as head of the NPA, he reasserted, 'I am not quitting. I am here to stay.'[5]

But it was not to be.

❏

In June 2004 public protector Lawrence Mushwana issued a report stating that Bulelani had abused his powers when he had announced in August the previous year that, although he was not prosecuting Zuma, a prima facie case of corruption nevertheless existed against the then deputy president.

Within a couple of months of Bulelani's original announcement, Zuma had lodged a complaint with the public protector not only about the 'prima facie' statement but contending also, among other things, that 'the investigation was conducted in bad faith and with the only intention to humiliate' him. He complained that the prosecuting authority had not properly informed him of the investigation and that detailed confidential information about the investigation was leaked to the media.[6]

The key issue was whether the pronouncement of a prima facie case had violated Zuma's human rights, and Mushwana found that the announcement 'unjustifiably infringed upon Mr Zuma's constitutional right to human dignity and caused him to be improperly prejudiced'.[7]

Bulelani points out that during Mushwana's investigation, he and his deputies, Willie Hofmeyr, Silas Ramaite and Leonard McCarthy, had met with the public protector. After the meeting Bulelani had sent a note to Mushwana confirming the content of their discussions.

> Mushwana said he agreed with us [that the matter was beyond his jurisdiction]. It was a preliminary discussion and he said he would be in touch.
>
> Then we got information that he was about to release a report with adverse findings, and that he was spending a lot of time at Zuma's residence. I called him and he said I shouldn't worry; he would talk to us before doing anything.
>
> On Friday 28 May 2004, I was in George, attending a funeral. I was told a story had appeared in the *Mail & Guardian*. Mushwana had released his report. My first thought was that he had succumbed to political pressure.
>
> I couldn't read the article until I was on the flight back on Saturday, and then I got angry. He said I had violated Zuma's human rights.
>
> I was asked by the SABC to do an interview on the same day. I tried to phone the president to alert him. I couldn't

find him, so I spoke to Mojanku [Gumbi, President Mbeki's legal advisor at the time] and told her about the interview I was going to have. I told her, 'I hope the president won't be angry but what Mushwana has done is unacceptable. I'm going to hit back.'

I put the phone down and proceeded with the interview.

Bulelani and Penuell Maduna, who accompanied Bulelani in his capacity as minister of justice, pulled no punches in their interview with the SABC. Maduna said that Mushwana's report was 'junk and a joke', while Bulelani said it was 'disappointing' that someone in the position of a public protector 'could produce such garbage'.[8]

'Mushwana had not seen a single document we had in our possession,' Bulelani continued. 'And yet he has the audacity to pronounce that we were wrong to say there was prima facie evidence against the deputy president.'[9]

Bulelani and Maduna's fury was evident in a joint statement they released at the time, in which they questioned Mushwana's integrity. 'Mushwana has sadly shown his hand in participating in an orchestrated campaign bent on discrediting the NPA. Like his bedfellows have experienced in the past, he will not succeed. This is indeed a sad moment for the public service, where one organ of state can cast unwarranted aspersions on a pillar of the rule of law, because of sinister bias.'[10]

> The following day Phumzile phoned me and told me I had lost the moral high ground. Dumisani called me. [Marumo] Moerane called me. And finally Bishop [Malusi] Mpumlwana [of the Ethiopian Episcopal Church] called me and also told me I had lost the plot.
>
> I knew I had to do something.

THE STING IN THE TALE: BULELANI NGCUKA

> It is at times like this that you experience the love of a mother. Her reaction was, 'You must fight back.'
>
> She and I were on the same page but, of course, I knew had to apologise.

The ANC held a meeting of its national working committee on the Monday, after which spokesperson Smuts Ngonyama berated Bulelani, Maduna and Mushwana for having made 'ill-considered' statements about each other, and 'called on all involved to act in a manner befitting their position, and to exercise due respect for these important institutions of state'.[11]

Addressing the Institute of Directors in Cape Town a few days later, Bulelani made it clear that he was apologising to the country and not to the public protector. 'I wanted to start off by apologising to you, and through you to the people of South Africa, that I shouldn't have done that. It was wrong of me ... I let you down ... because I allowed myself to behave in the same manner as our detractors.'[12]

But he wasn't standing down. 'Having said that, I want to make it equally clear – I'm going to fight that report because that report is fatally flawed. We are going to smash it to smithereens, but we'll do it correctly. When we go to parliament, we will show how flawed it is.'[13]

Penuell Maduna did send an apology to Lawrence Mushwana by SMS which read, 'Accept my own personal apology for the intemperate language Ngcuka and I used last weekend.'[14]

❏

With such a stormy beginning, it was clear that further clashes could be expected when the public protector's report was discussed in parliament.

Jacob Zuma as deputy president was the leader of government business, and he chaired the meeting that set up the ad hoc committee, chaired by Ismail Vadi, to consider the report.

The NPA had prepared its own response to the public protector's report and was ready to argue its case.

Bulelani says he was now approached by Brigitte Mabandla, who had succeeded Penuell Maduna as minister of justice, who told him that ANC secretary-general Kgalema Motlanthe had appointed advocate Seth Nthai to mediate between the two parties and see if a joint statement could be presented to parliament. Willie Hofmeyr was appointed to represent the NPA, and discussions ensued.

A joint statement was agreed on, which would have seen the committee 'taking note' of the report and its findings but not adopting it since the matter was sub judice, meaning that it was under judicial consideration and therefore prohibited from public discussion elsewhere. This was seen to be a 'politically neutral' position that was acceptable to all.

> So we were all happy. The statement was agreed to and was sent to the chief whip in parliament.
>
> The opposition wanted me to appear in parliament, and the media were asking questions. I replied saying I had faith in parliament and that there was no need for me to appear, that they could handle the matter on their own. I didn't want to push this thing of appearing before the committee. I was once a member of parliament myself and I knew they would do the right thing.
>
> Then we heard that the committee was going through the public protector's report line by line. No evidence was being heard. At one point, the opposition again asked why I was not there to answer to Mushwana's findings. An ANC

THE STING IN THE TALE: BULELANI NGCUKA

> MP replied that I had not given Zuma a chance to reply and that I therefore didn't deserve a right of reply either.
>
> At that stage I was not concerned. I was under the impression that we had reached an agreement and that this would be conveyed to the chair of the committee.

But by Thursday 24 June 2004, Bulelani realised that the joint statement had not, in fact, reached parliament. Parliament was about to adjourn for its mid-year break, so the report had to be adopted on Friday, the following day, in the national assembly.

A furious Bulelani called Nthai.

> I am not going to allow this and will be going to court to interdict parliament from adopting that report.

Nthai apologised, says Bulelani. He had given his word to negotiate a mutually acceptable position, he told Bulelani, but the ANC had failed to honour it. He said he would speak to the ANC and revert to Bulelani.

In the meantime, says Bulelani, Mohammed Bhabha, who had worked closely with Bulelani in the NCOP, approached committee chair Vadi, who said he knew nothing of the joint statement that the NPA and the public protector had agreed to submit to the committee.

> At 2 the next morning my phone rang and it was Thenjiwe [Mtintso, deputy secretary-general of the ANC]. 'I hear you are taking us to court. I have been asked to talk to you to say, don't do what you want to do,' she told me. 'The reason I am talking to you is because I'm your friend. And what I've been told to tell you is this. When we appointed you as the national director, we did not make a mistake. We have made many mistakes and what we're

going to do tomorrow is another mistake. It doesn't mean when we make mistakes, you must be angry with us, because there are good things we have done too. The resolution [by parliament, to adopt Mushwana's report] will be adopted tomorrow and please don't take us to court. That's what I've been told to say to you. We've made a number of mistakes as the ANC but we didn't make a mistake when we appointed you.'

'Don't worry,' I told her. 'The day I take the ANC to court is the day I give up on the ANC, and at this stage I'm not ready to do that. But I am very disappointed.'

The report was adopted, censuring me for making the statement about a prima facie case of corruption, and stating that the NPA and the public protector must find ways of working together. It was meaningless in the bigger scheme of things but I was disappointed.

The committee's report was described in the media as a 'mild rebuke' of the NPA head by the national assembly, and Vadi himself said it was 'not punitive but remedial'.[15]

However, the fact remained that parliament had adopted a report that said that the NPA had, in the course of its duties, infringed Zuma's constitutional rights.

> The public protector's report was wrong. You cannot say that I violated someone's rights when I was acting within the scope of my duties. Prosecution by its very nature affects people's rights. The matter was sub judice and should have been left there.

At this point, Bulelani says, he decided it was time for someone else to take over and lead the institution he had built from scratch, that he'd defended and for which he'd sacrificed so much. He had managed the pressures that came with the job of national director for six years but this last encounter had proven too much.

> I decided I had to leave. It was difficult, and many painful discussions took place with colleagues and friends, including, of course, with you [the author, at the time CEO of the NPA and the Scorpions], Dipuo [Mvelase, head of the NPA's integrity management unit] and others at the NPA.
>
> I started talking to the president about when I would leave. He was worried about what would happen to me and asked if I needed assistance in finding employment. I told him I didn't need assistance and that I still had a legal qualification and could practise. So once I knew I had the president's approval, I prepared a memo and sent it to his office.
>
> I decided I had to let the staff of the NPA know that I had decided to leave before they read it in the newspapers or heard about it in the corridors. At that stage only top management knew I was leaving.
>
> I held a meeting first with all of the DPPs. It was an emotional meeting, very emotional. Some people were crying. It was a very difficult time.
>
> Then I convened a meeting of all the employees at [NPA headquarters in Pretoria]. I told them that I had to leave for the sake of the organisation. I had become a target. I told them it was important for me to move on so that the organisation would survive. I ended the meeting by saying, 'God bless you all'.

Next, Bulelani undertook a farewell tour of the NPA's offices around the country.

TIME TO GO

Once again, this was a very touching experience. I received wonderful presents. My clan name is *Tshayingwe* [he who kills the leopard] and I received gifts of leopard and lion ornaments. It was very touching, the outpouring of love and affection.

The final gift I received was a big book with messages from all NPA employees. This remains my greatest treasure today and something I will pass on to my grandchildren.

After I had announced I was leaving, I felt relieved. This thing had taken its toll on me and my family. My mother's health had suffered. She was in hospital when my resignation was announced. I visited her that evening and we watched the news together as they said I was leaving the NPA. She was so happy because she knew what it had cost me.

She never recovered. She died on 22 September 2004.

Losing his mother a few weeks after he left the NPA was perhaps the bitterest pill for Bulelani to swallow after all that he and his family had endured. Kholosa had been his rock since his early days and had continuously urged him to pursue his dreams of studying and practising law.

Bulelani's last day in the office was Monday 31 August 2004. He laughs as he relates what happened the evening before.

> When I'm home in the evening, I usually switch my phone off. That evening I forgot, and the phone rang at midnight.
>
> It was one of my friends. He was drunk and was calling from Cape Town. 'Hey, boss, this has never happened to me, even during apartheid. They're just jealous of me because I'm driving a nice car, a Maserati, and they don't have one. Tell them to let me go. How dare they do this!'

It was an irresponsible young friend who had had too much to drink and had been pulled over by the police. Now he wanted me to intervene on his behalf.

The officer came on the line. The poor fellow was so apologetic. 'I'm so sorry, sir. We're not harassing him, sir, I promise you, sir. We just want him to sleep, sir. He can't drive like this, sir.'

I told him, 'There's no need to apologise, officer. You have done nothing wrong. Please, do me a favour. Just lock the chap up.'

'What? Are you sure, sir?'

'Yes, I'm sure. Lock him up.'

I was so annoyed. Throughout my time in the NPA I had boasted that I had never been placed in a position where I was in conflict and been asked to intervene in any matter in favour of a friend or family member. And on my very last day, this had to happen.

My final act as national director was to tell this officer to lock this chap up.

❏

The memo that Bulelani had sent to President Mbeki in July 2004 explaining his decision to leave the NPA was leaked, and the story appeared in the *Sunday Times* the next day. The newspaper described Bulelani as 'the latest victim of the political fallout from the Scorpions' investigations of alleged corruption by Deputy President Jacob Zuma.'[16]

The same opposition parties that had labelled him a party flunky at the time of his appointment now had nothing but praise for him. Patricia de Lille of the Independent Democrats described his resignation as 'a sad day for corruption busting in our country'. 'Instead of getting a pat on the back for the good work he has done, Ngcuka got a political kick up the butt,' she said.[17]

Sheila Camerer of the DA said he had been 'set up for failure' and had 'finally succumbed to the huge political pressure' put on him by the ANC since taking the decision not to prosecute Zuma. She said that Ngcuka had been 'a tough-minded crime buster who played rough and acted without fear, favour or prejudice when pursuing criminals as required by the constitution'.[18]

'Mission Accomplished' was the *Sunday Times* headline on 1 August, referring to Bulelani's an statement that he needed to move on with his life 'because there isn't anything I am confronted with that I can say I still need to do. My mission here has been accomplished.'[19]

That mission, journalist Phylicia Oppelt pointed out, included setting up the prosecuting authority, bringing together the country's prosecutors under one roof, and setting up the Scorpions investigative unit and the special commercial crimes and asset forfeiture units.

'Sitting across the table from him, I can see why he could be called arrogant,' she wrote. 'In a room full of people, he stands out. He seems almost too comfortable with power and leadership. These are all qualities that would be applauded and rewarded in a boardroom in corporate South Africa. In a civil servant, they are not necessarily appreciated.' Oppelt wondered if Bulelani's successor would 'have the same courage under fire'.[20]

The *Mail & Guardian*'s take was that Bulelani's would be 'big shoes to fill'.[21] 'Skills required: A political player – you will walk a tightrope between trying to run an effective institution and keeping the ruling party happy,' the writer noted. 'You must be a lawyer of standing with the ability to sail close to the wind. In addition to the headline-grabbing work, the job also requires an ability to increase the rate of prosecutions across the criminal justice system, while cracking down on the many criminal syndicates that have taken root in South Africa.'

The writer also noted that 'nerves of steel' would be required for the job. 'The last incumbent had to contend with a judicial commission into allegations that he was an apartheid spy; Congress of South African Trade Union (Cosatu) members baying for his blood at their national conference; and public claims by the African National Congress secretary-general that the investigation of the deputy president was dirty tricks of a special type.'[22]

The person who had been tipped to succeed Bulelani as NDPP was Ngoako Ramatlhodi, a former Limpopo premier and a longstanding ANC member who had worked under the tutelage of Oliver Tambo in exile. Ramatlhodi was, however, unfortunately soon caught up in his own troubles when he found himself under investigation by the Scorpions against a background of allegations of tender-rigging and financial favours. (The case was dropped in 2008 after Ramatlhodi made representations to the NPA.)

Vusi Pikoli, DG of the department of justice, took up the position after Bulelani, in 2005, but his time was short-lived. He found himself facing an inquiry into his fitness to hold office following his decision to charge Zuma with corruption and his authorisation of a raid on Zuma's home in Johannesburg and the presidency offices at the Union Buildings in Pretoria. He was suspended by President Mbeki in September 2007 and finally dismissed by President Mbeki's successor, Kgalema Motlanthe, in February 2009.

While the official reasons for the inquiry into Pikoli's competence were the breakdown in his relationship with Minister Mabandla and concerns about his lack of appreciation for security matters, it was widely believed that, like Bulelani, he was paying the price for pursuing Zuma.

21.

Hoax emails and 'spy tapes'

'It is my considered view that the undisclosed reason for aborting the prosecution on this flimsy basis lies in one thing and one thing alone: that Mpshe abandoned his duty to prosecute without fear or favour.'

Bulelani left the NPA in 2004, but if he thought this was the end of the story, he was mistaken. Ten years later, he was still defending himself against dirty tricks.

Shortly after Zuma was dismissed by President Mbeki in June 2005, following Schabir Shaik's conviction, a series of manufactured emails and groupchats emerged as supposed evidence of a grand conspiracy against Zuma. The emails were sent to journalists in 2005, then, in 2006, 73 pages of emails and chatroom conversations were delivered anonymously in a brown envelope to ANC secretary-general Kgalema Motlanthe.

There were two types of email exchanges in the package. The one group was a rather mixed bag and involved Bulelani; his wife, Phumzile; his close friend, Saki Macozoma; his successor, Vusi Pikoli; DG in the presidency Frank Chikane; government spokesperson Joel Netshitenzhe; and *Mail & Guardian* editor Anton Harber and publisher Matthew Buckland. The central theme here was an alleged conspiracy to destroy Zuma.

In the second set of emails and chatroom conversations, a

HOAX EMAILS AND 'SPY TAPES'

'white man's struggle' is portrayed. These exchanges were purported to be between Tony Leon, the leader of the DA, and a number of Scorpions investigators and prosecutors central to the arms-deal case. These emails were basically racist comments about the ANC government and efforts to reinstate white minority rule – or, as the *Mail & Guardian* put it at the time, what we were expected to believe was that 'a Xhosa cabal, assisted by white reactionaries in the Scorpions, media and opposition', was planning to destroy Zuma and any other powerful figure who stood in the way of its political objectives, most notably Motlanthe himself and NIA DG Billy Masetlha.[1]

When Motlanthe distributed the emails to the ANC's NEC in November 2006, they had already been trashed by Ronnie Kasrils, minister of intelligence, who described them as fraudulent and 'reminiscent of stratcom operations during the apartheid era'.[2]

Once the emails and chats became public, there were many who immediately questioned their authenticity. It's not difficult to see why. In one exchange, for example, 'Ngcuka' informs 'Macozoma', 'We are making sure that Zulu bastard is nailed to the cross,' and 'Macozoma' responds, 'The team will never forget your efforts at getting that Zulu fool out of the way,' and promises that 'Ngcuka' will be 'well compensated'.[3]

'Ngcuka' then asks for help with a R5-million loan in return for his efforts. 'Macozoma' says he will see what he can do but tells 'Ngcuka' not to be 'a cry baby' and that he should have finalised serious deals with 'Vusi' 'as a payback for giving him your position, then he can give you and your boers a lovely security deal'.[4]

In one alleged chatroom discussion between 'Tony Leon' and 'Scorpions investigators' 'Johan du Plooy' and 'Izak du Plooy', 'Johan' wrote, 'These blacks have no intelligence prowess. Their

THE STING IN THE TALE: BULELANI NGCUKA

intelligence officials waste time being drunk in Joburg and Pretoria pubs, while we milk info.'[5]

'We've got the bastard [Zuma] by the balls. He is going straight to jail,' 'Izak' wrote later in the purported discussion, to which 'Leon' replied, 'Great!! In the new Republic you guys need to run the police.'[6]

The emails are alleged to have been exchanged between February and November 2005. This coincided with Zuma's dismissal by President Mbeki in June 2005 and the raid on Zuma's house by the Scorpions in August 2005.

Inspector-general of intelligence Zolile Ngcakani investigated the documents and found them to be false. 'Based on our evaluation of the veracity of the content of the emails, together with our evaluation of the technical feasibility of them being intercepted products, in our opinion the allegedly intercepted emails and chatrooms were in fact mock-ups that sought to resemble the online communication of "targets selected for interception",' he said.[7]

The ANC set up its own commission of inquiry into the emails, under the chairmanship of Hermanus Loots (also known in MK as James Stuart), a senior and highly experienced cadre of the ANC, both militarily and politically. Bulelani spent an entire day with the commission at the ANC headquarters at Luthuli House. Some members of the commission were clearly hostile, he says, but it was a valuable opportunity to provide a briefing on a wide range of issues that had affected his time at the helm of the NPA, including the case against Zuma.

The ANC's NEC, however, rejected the commission's report on technical grounds. One of the problems in the report, according to Ronnie Kasrils, related to its impartiality and how closely Masetlha himself, who was implicated in the saga, had worked with the commission. For example, Kasrils says, the report referred to a technical expert who had advised the commission on how emails could be hacked. When the team was asked in the NEC who the expert was, they admitted that it was Masetlha who had taken them to this expert.[8]

Nevertheless, the report emerged publicly in November 2008 when Masetlha and two others (IT expert Muziwendoda Kunene and former NIA manager for electronic surveillance Funokwakhe Madlala) faced fraud charges and were accused of manufacturing the emails.[9]

Kasrils was also critical of the actions of Motlanthe who, after having received the emails, bypassed Kasrils as the minister of intelligence, and called in both Masetlha and then commissioner of police Jackie Selebi and asked them to investigate the emails. 'This is the root of the problem in South Africa: the ruling party becomes involved in state functionaries. Kgalema spoke to my DG [Masetlha] without my DG informing me what had happened.'[10]

❑

But the hoax emails would still not be the end of the saga. Mokotedi Mpshe was appointed acting NDPP following Pikoli's dismissal, and in 2009 Mpshe withdrew the charges against Jacob Zuma, stating that the head of the Scorpions Leonard McCarthy had abused the legal process.

Mpshe had received tapes from Zuma's lawyers that contained recordings of phone conversations between McCarthy and Bulelani, among others. The conversations between Bulelani and McCarthy relate at times to the Zuma case. Mpshe claimed one discussion that had taken place before the ANC's

Polokwane Conference about the timing of re-charging Zuma had tainted the case. Zuma's lawyers made representations to the NPA that the tapes were evidence that the charges against Zuma were politically inspired, and Mpshe dropped all 783 charges of corruption.

So, what did these 'spy tapes' say? One of the conversations that Mpshe relied on for his decision is one in which McCarthy and Bulelani are talking about whether Zuma will be charged before or after the Polokwane Conference, which started on Sunday 16 December 2007. McCarthy tells Bulelani that 'you guys must just keep your heads open about the "when" factor.'

Bulelani says, 'As long as you don't do it this weekend,' referring to the start of the ANC conference.

'If we hold it back, it will be because the clever people like you and others are saying to us that the country needs cool heads, but I would hate to be seen to be wrong later,' McCarthy says.

'I can't keep an open mind,' Bulelani tells him. 'You can't do it this weekend. Our minds won't change.'

Describing what the conversation was actually about, Bulelani says:

> Brigitte [Mabandla, minister of justice] was away and Zola [Skweyiya] was acting for her. He called me one evening and said he had heard that the Scorpions were about to arrest Zuma. I asked where he had heard this. He said he had just been told that some MK guys had heard this and were assembling in Soweto and were up in arms. It was just before the ANC conference in Polokwane and the situation was bad.
>
> 'I don't know those guys at the NPA, Bul. Please find out what's going on there,' he said.

So I said okay and called Leonard. He told me there was no such thing [no plans to arrest Zuma].

We continued chatting. Now, we like to tease each other. They say that I said to Leonard, 'Don't charge before the conference.' Of course I did. It would have been very stupid to do such a thing. Then they go on to say that that decision would have favoured Mbeki. There's no connection. You're trying to avoid here an issue that would have resulted in chaos in the country. There would have been a bloodbath in the country if that had happened.

The reality is this and Brigitte will back it – she was of the same view. They had received advice and decided as the NPA that they were going to charge Zuma when they were ready. Leonard felt the same way.

Now, the dates become very important here. They had decided before 5 December that they were going to charge Zuma before the conference. Mpshe went to see Brigitte on the 5th to brief her. She told him he was mad [because it would be seen as an attempt to influence the outcome of the conference]. Mpshe came back and told the team and said he had decided not to charge Zuma before the conference.

Leonard was away on leave and heard this from Billy [Downer]. Leonard called Mpshe and sent him an SMS and said that the guys were complaining [about the decision not to charge Zuma before the conference].

Mpshe replied that he had made up his mind [to not charge Zuma before the conference]. The decision was conveyed on 6 December.

Leonard and I spoke a week later. In our conversation, Leonard says to me that I mustn't be surprised if we arrest now. 'We're going to Polokwane and will shoot our way in and arrest him now.'

I said, 'Leonard, please don't.'

He was playing the fool with me. It took me a while to realise it.

It is this conversation that Mpshe relied on to withdraw the charges. I only found out later. He knows he took the decision and why he took the decision, and then tried to blame me.

Bulelani was reluctant to get involved in yet another controversy, and remained silent in the face of the outcry when Mpshe announced his decision in 2009. He only went public five years later, issuing a lengthy statement in 2014 when the DA won a legal battle and gained access to the tapes, and the Supreme Court compelled the NPA to release information relating to the decision to drop the charges against Zuma.[11]

He was still reluctant to weigh in on the matter but, he said, the material that had been released, which included transcripts of the so-called spy tapes, was still being misinterpreted to perpetuate the lie that he had improperly or illegally intervened in a prosecutorial decision. The situation had reached a point where 'there is an understandable interest and expectation for me to say something or be damned'.

The NPA, he said, had interpreted the tapes in a way that suggested he had been involved in 'unlawful interference' with Zuma's case. The truth, however, was that Mpshe had taken the decision to prosecute Zuma on 14 November 2007, long before the recorded conversations in mid-December between Bulelani and McCarthy. On 5 December, Mpshe had decided to delay the launch of the prosecution until after the ANC's conference in Polokwane, and the indictment was finally served in late December.

'Nowhere in his reasons for the decision to stop the prosecution does Mpshe – or any of the individuals who were part of that decision – state when and how any of us influenced him or any member of the prosecution team. Mpshe goes as far as saying the evidence in this matter remains incontrovertible, and yet by some obscure reasoning he decides to stop the prosecution.

'I can still not find the connection between the transcripts of telephone conversations between me and Leonard McCarthy, the ex-head of the now defunct Scorpions, and the decision to withdraw the decision to prosecute.

'Additionally, the transcripts made public are incomplete.

'There are obvious reasons for the NPA's approach in this regard. The intention is, and has always been, to use private conversations between friends, illegally obtained from the National Intelligence Agency interceptions, to divert the public's attention from the real unlawfulness that surrounds these transcripts. Sensational bits of private banter thus had to be what preoccupies the public mind and discourse.'

The statement continued, 'By his own admission, Mpshe's decision to abort the prosecution had relied on the recorded conversations on the timing of the launch of the prosecution. He has gone out of his way to seek to put a strained and opportunistic interpretation [on] the content of the discussion, so as to justify the decision to withdraw the charges and abort the prosecution. In his view, the timing discussion was calculated to benefit one candidate over the other in the political process that was to unfold in Polokwane in December 2007. That interpretation is false. Even if it were true, it would be irrelevant to the question [of] whether aborting the prosecution could be justified.'

In his view, Bulelani said, there was only one reason for aborting the prosecution: 'that Mpshe abandoned his duty to prosecute without fear or favour, and capitulated to the immense political pressure he and the NPA were under'.[12]

Turning to the issue of the timing of the charges and the allegations that Bulelani had influenced McCarthy's decision for political reasons, Bulelani says Mpshe deliberately misled the public. Bulelani refers to a memorandum from Billy Downer, lead prosecutor, to Mpshe on 6 December 2007, in which he says Downer reveals that it was, in fact, Mpshe who had political motivations when it came to the timing of the announcement to charge Zuma.

Downer confirmed this in an affidavit in the High Court in Pretoria in which he states, 'I confirm that on 6 December 2007 Mpshe telephoned me and told me that although he was satisfied with the draft indictment, he had decided to delay the prosecution until the following year because he did not want the NPA to be seen to be responsible for Zuma failing to be elected as ANC president at Polokwane. He said that he had come to this conclusion after seeing a cartoon in which Zuma was depicted running in a race with Mbeki. The cartoon depicted the NPA tripping up Zuma.'[13]

Downer continues, saying that he followed up this conversation with Mpshe by drafting a 'strongly worded memorandum' to Mpshe on 6 December 2007 on behalf of the prosecuting team in which he stated that the team felt that 'any decision to delay the prosecution for reasons unconnected to the prosecution was improper' and that 'the prosecution team felt so strongly about this that we had initially decided to resign from the prosecution in protest, but had reconsidered this in the interests of the NPA.'[14]

In short, Bulelani says, Mpshe's decision to 'stop the prosecution had absolutely nothing to do with the taped conversations but had everything to do with political expediency.'[15]

In addition, Bulelani noted, 'Because of the position I held as the NDPP, and because I have been involved with the case since its inception, the accused [Zuma] has seen fit to drag me into almost all the applications he has brought, compelling me to file affidavits disputing many unfounded allegations made against me. In the result I have been compelled to remain a feature of this matter notwithstanding that I left the NPA ten years ago.

'My continued involvement had nothing to do with any desire to manipulate. The only evidence of the manipulation of the NPA I can find in this matter is that which was carried out by those in the NPA who entertained an unlawful approach to ... listen to illegally obtained recordings. It would seem they had no qualms with the fact that the head of the Scorpions and leader of the prosecuting team's conversations were illegally obtained and ended up in the hands of the accused person's attorney – a conduct that is not only ethically reprehensible but is outright criminality.'[16]

'McCarthy's phone conversations that were part of the so-called spy tapes included chats with family and friends, and conversations with the president and the minister of justice on a range of law-enforcement matters. Conversations with the prosecution team and legal advisors had also been recorded in which prosecution strategy was discussed. These were in the hands of Zuma's defence team and Mpshe apparently saw nothing wrong with this.'

'The circumstances in which the defence team had come into possession of the tapes (which were state material) had never been explained. Not only did the NPA appear to be unconcerned about this but it was also a matter of public knowledge that intelligence officials had acted illegally by providing this information to the attorneys of an accused person – Zuma. The information related to the very case Zuma was charged with. This could mean a prison sentence of 10 years or a fine of R2 million yet the NPA had done nothing about this partisan use of intelligence information. Instead, Mpshe had authorised NPA officials to go to Zuma's attorneys to listen to material of which they were in illegal possession.'

'Why were they so keen to aid and abet a process that was so patently illegal? Why did Mpshe and the NPA engage in this obsequious grovelling to the defence team? Would they have allowed it on any other accused person who was not a high-ranking politician?'[17] [Mpshe in turn said he would not argue with Bulelani 'because that's his opinion and he is entitled to it. He also said Zuma's lawyer had arranged for the tapes to be declassified before sharing them with the NPA.][18]

❏

The saga was still not over, and in 2016, two years after Bulelani released his statement responding to the so-called spy tapes, the High Court in Pretoria declared that Mpshe's decision to drop the charges against Zuma and Thint Holdings must be set aside. Judge Aubrey Ledwaba said that Mpshe should have followed the legal process and allowed the courts to decide whether there had been an abuse of the legal process and whether the charges should be withdrawn. Mpshe, he said, had acted 'alone and impulsively' and his decision was irrational.[19, 20]

An old adversary, Willem Heath, who had advised Zuma in both his corruption and 2005-2006 rape[21] cases, reappeared at this time and jumped into the fray, accusing Bulelani of accepting bribes and allowing himself and the NPA to be 'dictated' to by President Mbeki.[22]

HOAX EMAILS AND 'SPY TAPES'

His attack backfired. Heath, who had run the Special Investigating Unit (SIU) in the late 1990s before being dismissed by then president Thabo Mbeki, had been reappointed in 2016 by President Zuma to replace Willie Hofmeyr as the head of the SIU. Heath made the accusations against Bulelani a few days after his reappointment, but Zuma distanced himself from Heath's broadside, and Heath resigned just two weeks later.

In his response, in an open letter addressed to Heath, Bulelani said it was clear not only that he could not substantiate his wild allegations but that 'your mantra appears to be that such conduct is justified by your objective of vilification and destruction of those you see as your enemies, real or imagined'.[23]

22.
Moving forward

'You learn something under difficult conditions: that people have their own frailties. It's more painful when those close to you hurt you.'

It was only after the Hefer Commission that Bulelani found out just how damaging the spy allegations had been in some quarters.

> Madiba called me and said he wanted to see Phumzile and myself. So Phumzile and I went to see him and had breakfast with him. Graça was also there.
>
> Madiba said, 'That Moerane is a very clever fellow to destroy a chap like Mac. But this allegation must have hurt you. The president [Mbeki] loves you. This commission was a brilliant idea.'
>
> He then told me the whole story, about how Mac had approached him [and convinced him that he, Bulelani, was a spy], and he said he had believed Mac because he had known him longer and had spent time on Robben Island with him. He said he was very close to Mac but now that the whole thing had been exposed, he was sorry for what I'd been put through. He wanted to say it in the presence of my wife and that's why he'd asked Phumzile to come.
>
> I was never very close to Mac but he was still a leader

of the ANC and I respected him. So it was shocking to see that, instead of dealing with his issues, he chose to accuse me of being a spy.

Moe did approach me afterwards and apologised. In fact, during the Hefer Commission itself, he approached Phumzile and said that he wanted an end to it all. We met after the commission and spoke at length. He admitted that he had got it wrong. Their [Shaik and Maharaj's] assumptions had clouded their judgement about how I was doing my work. They were very loyal to Zuma and were prepared to protect him at any costs.

I reminded him that we had been prepared to argue for a non-custodial sentence for Schabir if he had pleaded guilty. Moe said they didn't trust us and thought it was a trap. But we shook hands and I believe we have made our peace.

That's not the case with Maharaj.

❏

The one person who has remained steadfast at Bulelani's side throughout is Phumzile, his wife.

One of the more poignant moments during the Hefer Commission was when Bulelani was handed a letter she had written to him 20 years earlier, when he was in prison. Newspaper headlines at the time read, 'Ngcuka love story unfolds before Hefer'.[1] Bulelani never received the letter during his time in prison – prison authorities had intercepted it. He only finally got it after Dumisani Tabata requisitioned his security files from the national archives while preparing for the Hefer Commission.

He and Phumzile were meant to get married in December

1981 but their plans were interrupted when Bulelani was arrested and subsequently sentenced in 1982. They were finally married 12 days after his release, and after the assassination of Victoria Mxenge, on 15 August 1985.

Phumzile has pursued her own career, and has been an MP, deputy minister and minister, and deputy president. In 2013 she was appointed United Nations undersecretary-general and executive director of UN Women, and in 2021 received the prestigious Nelson Mandela Changemaker Award (an honour awarded to leaders who are continuing Mandela's legacy of peace and social justice) in recognition of the work she's done in that position. Two years previously she'd received the Cannes LionHeart, an honorary award presented to a person or organisation that has harnessed their position to make a significant and positive difference to the world around us, in recognition of her advocacy for women, human rights and social justice.

Phumzile was in cabinet at the time Bulelani held the position of NDPP and this presented its own challenges. She was minister of minerals and energy from 1999 to 2005 and was promoted to deputy president by Mbeki in June 2005 after he dismissed Zuma, a move that made her position even more uncomfortable.

She speaks with her characteristic mix of candour and diplomacy about the difficulties of managing relationships with colleagues and friends. 'It started when I was still a minister. It used to be very tense. We were a divided cabinet and a divided organisation. My approach was that I wasn't going to do anything to make it any worse than it already was. So I made sure that things stayed collegial and did everything that was needed to stay in touch. Even though there were people who could not even stand to look at you, we were still civil towards one another and that helped.

'At all times when we were at meetings we were professional, but it was not the same as it had been before, where we used to socialise and hang out together. There was none of that. You minimised the reason to interact with people and found a way to delegate to other people so that it was never awkward for other people.

'It was a tightrope. I was very clear that my priority was to support Bulelani and stand with my family without being exhibitionist about it but I also wanted to maintain the decorum of being a public representative. I didn't want to create any reason where my behaviour became the story. I didn't want to be the issue. I didn't want my children to be an issue. I stayed under the radar as much as possible and, thank God, nothing horrible happened.

'JZ [Jacob Zuma] himself was always very warm. He used to call me *ntom' khulu* [big girl]. It was inevitable, though, that distance would grow between me and my colleagues in cabinet.

'It was a stressful time for Bulelani but for other people too. It became worse once the Hefer Commission started. I was struck by the number of people for whom this became a burden, by the number of old people who were visibly stressed and hurting. Strangers would come to me and say they were praying for me. This thing had created stress and tension in so many people who had nothing to do with it, who did not deserve it. Even in lifts, people I didn't know would just hold me and say, "I'm part of a prayer group. We are praying for you, and God will reveal the truth and all will end well for your family."'[2]

When it comes to the ill feelings comrades harboured for each other, Phumzile says she found it hard to believe 'how hateful comrades could be towards one another'.

'I thought comrades were prepared to be crueller to one another than they were to the real enemy. And I actually never felt I needed to hate. I was not angry. I was sad.

'The propaganda was so strong. I can't hold a grudge against anyone who believed the worst. I take comfort from the fact that I lost very few of those I regarded as close friends and associates. I lost a lot of friends but the people I regard as my inner crowd, they stuck with us.'[3]

When it comes to processing these difficult feelings, she says, 'You know, Bulelani never wanted to discuss his pain. He was always clear that he didn't want his problems to be the family's problems. We didn't spend much time discussing this or how we were feeling. We would just use our time as a family getting on with the things that we would normally do together.'[4]

And Bulelani wasn't her only worry. 'Of course, I was also worried about our son, Luyolo, who was at boarding school at the time and old enough to follow events. However, he had a very supportive principal and we discussed the need to watch him and see if he wasn't coping. We also made sure we knew his friends and their parents.

'When I look back at that time, one of the most worrying things is that it did take away the space and freedom and youthfulness I would have wished for my child. At the same time, though, he has learned so much from his father and has been inspired by what he achieved at the NPA. It's why he's pursued his studies in peace, security and counter-terrorism.'

Bulelani's insistence on keeping his problems to himself didn't always sit easy with Phumzile. 'There was a time that I wanted us to just sit at the table and talk. I felt he was bottling so much up but there were no outbursts and no anger. Maybe with hindsight it's just as well because I'm not sure how we would have handled it. But I used to worry that this man was going to have a heart attack.'⁵

And it wasn't only her husband's health that worried her – she feared for his life 'all the time'. 'There were so many accusations. And they were made in an atmosphere in which it would have been so easy to incite a lone actor or an organised hit.'

Phumzile is understandably emotional when she thinks back on what she and Bulelani and their family have endured over the years, but says the saving grace through it all has 'always been this thing about being strong in front of the enemy'. 'Throughout it, though, I knew I was not going to give them the satisfaction of knowing how I was feeling. You would hold your head high and remain in control, even if inside you felt like you were dying.'⁶

And she reminds us of what is possible. 'I am so proud, so proud of the work done under Bulelani's leadership, and the demonstration of who we can be, and the fact that we had so many people who did their work, who were beyond reproach in terms of honesty and diligence. I look back and say that even though things have gone terribly wrong, I still hope that we can turn things around.

'I think that it's important that we were able to demonstrate that we can build these institutions and make them work for and with the people. I remember meeting colleagues from the NPA and being struck by their pride and passion and dedication. It was wonderful to see that.

'It's sad that we have lost that but it can't take away the pride that I feel.'⁷

❏

THE STING IN THE TALE: BULELANI NGCUKA

It is difficult to talk about Bulelani without Jacob Zuma's name being mentioned. For many, that is what he is 'famous' for. Bulelani himself is philosophical but remains resolute about the decision he took nearly two decades ago as South Africa's first NDPP.

> I have been criticised extensively, firstly for using the term 'prima facie', then, after Schabir Shaik was convicted, for not charging Zuma in the first place – and subsequently for everything that's happened to the country! 'We would never have ended up with Zuma,' people tell me.
>
> 'That's a political matter,' I say in response. 'You can't solve political matters through the courts.'
>
> I don't regret that I didn't charge Jacob Zuma in 2003. It was the right decision.

After Cyril Ramaphosa was elected president of the ANC at the organisation's 54th national conference in December 2017, the pressure mounted on Zuma to step down. But he dug in his heels, insisting that he be allowed to finish his term of office, something that had been denied his predecessor, Thabo Mbeki, when Zuma took over the ANC top position in 2007.

The ANC's NEC stepped in and decided he had to go. Secretary-general Ace Magashule and deputy secretary-general Jessie Duarte were dispatched to deliver the news to Zuma, who finally announced his resignation on 14 February 2018. Cyril Ramaphosa replaced him as president the following day.

Zuma's legal battles were, however, far from over. In March 2018 the charges against him were reinstated, including 783 incidents of racketeering, corruption, money-laundering and fraud. But Zuma continued to wage war in the courts, and the decision Bulelani took in 2003 continued to be challenged.

The charges against Zuma were amended as the years went on, and by 2021 he faced 16 charges of corruption including nearly 800 charges of fraud, racketeering, money-laundering and tax fraud; he is accused of taking R4 million in bribes from Thales. After 15 years of what has been described as 'Stalingrad' tactics – using methods such as appealing every possible ruling that is unfavourable to the defendant in order to delay or stave off legal proceedings – he finally pleaded not guilty to these charges in May 2021.

His corruption case is not yet finalised but he was sentenced to 15 months' imprisonment in July 2021, in a separate case, for defying a Constitutional Court ruling to appear before the 'Zondo Commission' – the judicial commission of inquiry into allegations of state capture chaired by deputy chief justice Raymond Zondo. The national commissioner of correctional services, Arthur Fraser, decided to grant Zuma medical parole – against the recommendation of the Medical Parole Advisory Board – and Zuma was released in September 2021. This ruling was, however, soon revoked and the former president was ordered back to jail. At the time of writing, a judge had granted Zuma and the department of correctional services leave to appeal the ruling that Fraser's decision to release Zuma on medical parole had been unlawful.

Bulelani has never given up on the ANC and, he notes, things are different under president Ramaphosa's leadership, which is reaching out to people to say, '"Come guys, this is your country, you are welcome to make whatever contribution you are willing to make." I am assisting and I continue to do so because my contribution is appreciated and it's welcome and this is my country too.'[8]

❏

THE STING IN THE TALE: BULELANI NGCUKA

Since the position of National Director of Public Prosecutions (NDPP) was instituted in 1998, not one incumbent has served the full term of ten years. There have been five permanently appointed NDPPs and three acting NDPPs.

Bulelani Ngcuka was in the position for six years, followed by Vusi Pikoli for just more than two and half years, and Mokotedi Mpshe in an acting capacity for nearly three years. Menzi Simelane served from 2009 until 2012, when the Constitutional Court found his appointment irrational. Nomgcobo Jiba then stepped in as acting NDPP, until Mxolisi Nxasana took over in 2013. He exited at just less than two years, after President Zuma established an inquiry to assess his fitness to hold office which never got off the ground, and he later resigned. Shaun Abrahams served from June 2015 to August 2018, and left after the Constitutional Court ruled that his appointment had been irregular. Following Abrahams's departure, Silas Ramaite, a deputy NDPP, was appointed as acting NDPP.[9] In February 2019 President Ramaphosa appointed advocate Shamila Batohi as the first female NDPP.

Bulelani remains the longest-serving NDPP. As South Africa's first NDPP, he built two formidable institutions – the National Prosecuting Authority (NPA) and the Directorate of Special Operations, or Scorpions.

When Bulelani was appointed, one of his closest friends, Saki Macozoma, spoke about his first impressions of Bulelani. He said he found Bulelani 'genuinely warm but he was arrogant, he was pedantic, he was ambitious, he was competitive, he was class conscious.' However, he says, as time went by, he came to know a different person. 'I found over the years an individual who is confident but not cocky, who is intellectually meticulous without yielding to fetishism, who has enough drive to move on in life without sacrificing the accommodation of the aspirations of others, an individual who genuinely cares for people irrespective of their station in life. Above all, I found an extremely generous man, who gives of himself and everything he has.'[10]

Two of the important character strengths that Saki spoke about on that occasion were the fact that Bulelani is slow to anger and his firmness of principle. 'I know of no man who takes as long as Bulelani to get angry,' he said. Saki referred to James Ranisi Jolobe's 1958 novel, *Elundini loThukela*, in which it is written, '*Indoda yingonyama, indoda yingcongolo phezu koThukela*' – 'The right man has the strength of a lion and the flexibility of a reed on the banks of the Thukela river.'

'The reed bends when the flood comes, instead of being broken, and stands upright when the flood is gone,' Saki clarified. 'This is a quality that characterises Bulelani.'

Abbreviations

AFU	Asset Forfeiture Unit
Apla	Azanian People's Liberation Army
Azapo	Azanian People's Organisation
ANC	African National Congress
Codesa	Convention for a Democratic South Africa
Cosatu	Congress of South African Trade Unions
DA	Democratic Alliance
DG	director-general
DPP	Director of Public Prosecutions
DSO	Directorate of Special Operations (Scorpions)
FNB	First National Bank
IDAF	International Defence and Aid Fund
IDOC	Investigating Directorate on Organised Crime
IFP	Inkatha Freedom Party
ILO	International Labour Organization
JACTT	Joint Anti-Corruption Task Team
JSC	Judicial Service Commission
Lagunya	Langa, Gugulethu and Nyanga Taxi Association
MEC	member of the executive council
MK	Umkhonto we Sizwe
MP	member of parliament
Nadel	National Association of Democratic Lawyers
NCOP	national council of provinces

ABBREVIATIONS

NDPP	National Director of Public Prosecutions
NEC	national executive committee
NIA	National Intelligence Agency
NP	National Party
NPA	National Prosecuting Authority
PAC	Pan Africanist Congress
Pagad	People Against Gangsterism and Drugs
PCLU	Priority Crimes Litigation Unit
SADF	South African Defence Force
SAP	South African Police Service
Sars	South African Revenue Service
SASO	South African Students Organisation
Scopa	standing committee on public accounts
SIU	Special Investigating Unit
TRC	Truth and Reconciliation Commission
UDF	United Democratic Front
Unisa	University of South Africa
UWC	University of the Western Cape
Webta	Western Cape Black Taxi Association

References

Africa Criminal Justice Reform. 2018. 'The appointment and dismissal of the NDPP: Instability since 1998'. Dullah Omar Institute, University of the Western Cape. October. https://acjr.org.za/resource-centre/appoint-and-dismiss-of-ndpp-fs-7-fin.pdf

Agliotti, NG. 2007. Statement of Glenn Agliotti taken by Andrew Leask, Chief Special Investigator, Scorpions, 21 January

Ahmed Timol: Truth Prevails. 2019. '43rd Anniversary of Mapetla Mohapi'. 4 August. https://www.ahmedtimol.co.za/2019/08/04/43rd-anniversary-of-mapetla-mohapi

Aluka. 1987. Political Prisoners in South Africa. http://psimg.jstor.org/fsi/img/pdf/t0/10.5555/al.sff.document.nuun1987_15_final.pdf

ANC Today. 2003. 'Letter from the President: Reconciliation and social change must go together'. Vol 4, No. 3. 23-29 January. https://omalley.nelsonmandela.org/omalley/index.php/site/q/03lv03445/04lv04015/05lv04120/06lv04129.htm

Auditor-General. 2000. Special Review of the Selection Process of Strategic Defence Packages for the Acquisition of Armaments at the Department of Defence. Government Printer. http://www.armsdeal-vpo.co.za/special_items/reports/ag_review.pdf

Bain, J. 2002. 'Kebble magnates to answer fraud charges'. *Business Day*. 9 December. https://allafrica.com/stories/200212090768.html

Barrell, H and Soggett, M. 1998. 'Nice guy, but can he do the job?' *Mail&Guardian*. 17 July. https://mg.co.za/article/1998-07-17-nice-guy-but-can-he-do-the-job/

Barron, C. 2014. 'Obituary: David Gleason – columnist who became the paid voice of Brett Kebble'. *Sunday Times*. 16 February.

Bauer, N. 2011. 'Mac Maharaj and controversy: a timeline'. *Mail&Guardian*. 22 November. https://mg.co.za/article/2011-11-22-mac-maharaj-and-controversy-a-timeline/

Berger, G. 2004. Ethics and Excuses: the scapegoating of Vusi Mona. Paper presented to Saccom conference, Port Elizabeth, 1 October. https://guyberger.ru.ac.za/fulltext/hefersaccom1.doc

Biko, S. 1978. *I Write What I Like*. Bowerdean Press

Blaney, J. 2010. 'Building Police Capacity in Post-Conflict Communities'. Paper. Deloitte and Center for Complex Operations. https://africacenter.org/wp-content/uploads/2016/01/Let_Loose_Scorpions.pdf

Boley, J. 2000. 'The Rise and Fall of Billy Rautenbach. How a South African entrepreneur challenged the establishment – and lost .' Automotive News, 1 March. https://www.autonews.com/article/20000301/SUB/3010705/the-rise-and-fall-of-billy-rautenbach

Broughton, T. 2001. '"Drug baron" to pay for fight against crime'. IOL. 8 November. https://www.iol.co.za/news/south-africa/drug-baron-to-pay-for-fight-against-crime-76538

REFERENCES

Brummer, S. 1999. 'Palazzolo: The mobster from Burgersdorp'. *Mail&Guardian*. 19 November. https://mg.co.za/article/1999-11-19-palazzolo-the-mobster-from-burgersdorp/

Bubenzer, O. 2009. *Post-TRC Prosecutions in South Africa: Accountability for political crimes after the Truth and Reconciliation Commission's amnesty process*. Martinus Nijhoff Publishers

Carroll, R. 2004. 'Nuclear charges dropped'. The Guardian. 9 September. https://www.theguardian.com/world/2004/sep/09/southafrica.rorycarroll Accessed 15 March 2022.

Carroll, R. 2003. 'ANC's apartheid-era hero jailed for fraud' *The Guardian*. 20 March. https://www.theguardian.com/world/2003/mar/20/rorycarroll

City Press. 2003. 'Was Ngcuka a spy?' 6 September. https://www.news24.com/citypress/SouthAfrica/News/Was-Ngcuka-a-spy-20100614

CNN. 2003. 'South African white supremacist convicted of bombings'. 12 November. https://edition.cnn.com/2003/WORLD/africa/11/12/safrica.terreblanche.reut/index.html

Cohen, M. 2001. 'Seven escape from S. Africa court' AP News. 4 October. https://apnews.com/article/0e7e7c96138eb7f7eaec9dfc16ae65df

Crime, Law and Social Change. 2001. Part Five: Africa. 36 (241–284). https://doi.org/10.1023/A:1017438522544

Cole, J. 2013. 'The making and re-imagining of Khayelitsha: Report for the Commission of Inquiry into Allegations of Police Inefficiency in Khayelitsha and a Breakdown in Relations between the Community and the Police in Khayelitsha'. January. https://s3-eu-west-1.amazonaws.com/s3.sourceafrica.net/documents/14375/5-b-j-cole-affidavit.pdf

Commey, P. 2014. 'A poisoned chalice: The dilemma of South Africa public prosecutors'. *New African*. 21 July. https://newafricanmagazine.com/6123/

Dennie, G. 1990. 'One King, Two Burials: The Politics of Funerals in South Africa's Transkei'. African Studies Institute seminar paper, University of the Witwatersrand. https://core.ac.uk/download/pdf/39667557.pdf

Dolley, C. 2012. 'How Thai cops arrested Palazzolo'. *Cape Times*. 23 April. https://www.iol.co.za/capetimes/special-reports/how-thai-cops-arrested-palazzolo-1283450

Dugard, J. 2001. From Low Intensity to Mafia War: Taxi Violence in SA (1987-2000). Violence and Transition Series, Centre for the Study of Violence and Reconciliation. May. http://www.csvr.org.za/docs/taxiviolence/fromlowintensity.pdf

Du Pisani, JA, Broodryk, M and Coetzer, PW. 1990. 'Protest Marches in South Africa'. *Journal of Modern African Studies*, Vol 28, No 4

Ellis, E. 2003. 'Mac's astonishing admission'. IOL. 19 November. https://www.iol.co.za/news/politics/macs-astonishing-admission-117460

Ellis, E. 2001. 'Staggie sold R100 000 in drugs a day, judge told'. *Cape Argus*. 19 June

Ellis, E. 2001. 'Pagad cop tells of escaping bloody ambush'. IOL. 14 August. https://www.iol.co.za/news/south-africa/pagad-cop-tells-of-escaping-bloody-ambush-71976

Ellis, E. 2000. 'G-force suspects face over 40 murder charges'. IOL. 11 October. https://www.iol.co.za/news/south-africa/g-force-suspects-face-over-40-murder-charges-50556

Ellis, E and Gordin, J. 2003. 'Former City Press editor branded a "disgrace"'. IOL. 28 November. https://www.iol.co.za/news/politics/former-city-press-editor-branded-a-disgrace-118152

Engineering News. 2002. 'Scorpions in illegal fishing sting'. 31 October. https://www.engineeringnews.co.za/print-version/scorpions-in-illegal-fishing-sting-2002-10-31

Feni, L and Flanagan, L. 2001. 'Two face trial for Bisho massacre', *Daily Dispatch*. 1 June. https://web.archive.org/web/20060701011907/http://www.dispatch.co.za/2001/06/01/easterncape/AAMASACR.HTM

Francis, V. 2001 Prosecution Task Force on Car-Hijacking: Final evaluation report. Bureau of Justice Assistance, USA. November. https://www.ojp.gov/ncjrs/virtual-library/abstracts/prosecution-task-force-car-hijacking-final-evaluation-report

Gould, C and Folb, P. 2002. 'Project Coast: Apartheid's Chemical and Biological Warfare Programme'. United Nations Institute for Disarmament Research Geneva, Switzerland, and Centre for Conflict Resolution, Cape Town, South Africa. https://www.unidir.org/files/publications/pdfs/project-coast-apartheid-s-chemical-and-biological-warfare-programme-296.pdf

Green, P and Randall, E. 1999. 'Anger over asset-grab fiasco'. IOL. 29 August. https://www.iol.co.za/news/south-africa/anger-over-asset-grab-fiasco-10561

Hefer, J. 2004. Commission of Inquiry into Allegations of Spying Against National Director of Public Prosecutions, BT Ngcuka. 19 September 2003 to 7 January 2004. First and Final Report. https://www.justice.gov.za/commissions/comm_hefer/2004%2001%2020_hefer_report.pdf

Henning, M (ed). 2015. *Faith as Politics: Reflections in Commemoration of Beyers Naudé (1915-2004)*. The Nordic Afrika Institute

Herman, P. 2016. 'Decision to drop Zuma corruption charges "irrational", set aside – As it happened'. News24. 29 April. https://www.news24.com/news24/southafrica/news/live-zuma-to-hear-if-spy-tapes-judgment-will-be-set-aside-20160429

Hlongwa, W and Nkosi, S. 1998. 'South Africa: Judge blasts "ANC" Super AG'. allAfrica. 11 December. https://allafrica.com/stories/199812110130.html

Hofmeyr, W. 2007. 'The Role of Specialist Units in the NPA'. Presentation at National Prosecuting Authority Stakeholder Conference, 28-30 March. https://www.npa.gov.za/content/speaker-presentations

Hofmeyr, W. 2002. Seizing Criminal Assets to Fight Crime: National Prosecuting Authority Report to Parliament, AFU. 5 June

REFERENCES

Holden, P and Van Vuuren, H. 2011. *The Devil in the Detail: How the arms deal changed everything*. Jonathan Ball Publishers

Hosken, G. 2004. 'State coffers to get major boost'. IOL. 23 November. https://www.iol.co.za/news/south-africa/state-coffers-to-get-major-boost-227704

Hosken, G. 2002. 'Top dogs nabbed in road fund fraud raid'. IOL. 27 March. https://www.iol.co.za/news/south-africa/top-dogs-nabbed-in-road-fund-fraud-raid-84040

Hunter-Gault, C. 2004. 'Winnie Mandela wins jail appeal'. CNN.com International. 5 July. http://edition.cnn.com/2004/WORLD/africa/07/05/safrica.winnie/

Impact of DSO on Crime in South Africa. 2008. Internal Paper.

IOL. 2003. 'Committed cops put an end to gang's reign'. 28 July. https://www.iol.co.za/news/south-africa/committed-cops-put-an-end-to-gangs-reign-110062

IOL. 2003. 'Ngcuka love story unfolds before Hefer'. 11 December. https://www.iol.co.za/news/politics/ngcuka-love-story-unfolds-before-hefer-119044

IOL. 2001. 'Pagad killer gets 11 life terms for murders'. 29 March. https://www.iol.co.za/news/south-africa/pagad-killer-gets-11-life-terms-for-murders-63154

IOL. 2000. 'Langa's killing "ended in triple murder".' 27 June. https://www.iol.co.za/news/politics/langas-killing-ended-in-triple-murder-41492

Joint Investigation Report into the Strategic Defence Procurement Packages. 2001. November. https://www.gov.za/sites/default/files/gcis_document/201409/jointinvestigationreport0.pdf

Joseph, N. 2003. 'Perlemoen suspect may run racket from prison'. IOL. 12 December. https://www.iol.co.za/news/south-africa/perlemoen-suspect-may-run-racket-from-prison-119061

Justice Budget: Input by National Prosecuting Authority and Specialist Units. 10 June 2003. https://pmg.org.za/committee-meeting/2562/ Accessed 28 December 2003

Khampepe Commission of Inquiry into the Mandate and Location of the Directorate of Special Operations ('The DSO'). Final Report. 2006. Honourable Justice Sisi Khampepe, Commissioner. February

King, EL. 2001. Commission of Inquiry into Cricket Match Fixing and Related Matters Final Report, Judge EL King. June 2001. https://www.gov.za/sites/default/files/gcis_document/201409/kingreport0.pdf

Koch, E. 1996. 'IFP got weapons from the police'. *Mail&Guardian*. 20 September https://mg.co.za/article/1996-09-20-ifp-got-weapons-from-the-police

Kockott, F. 2010. 'Netcare coughs up', *Mail&Guardian*, 12 November. https://mg.co.za/article/2010-11-12-netcare-coughs-up/

Koopman, A. 2003. 'Scorpions boss stung by smear campaign. *Weekend Argus*. 28 July.

Koopman, A. 2003. 'Ngcuka vows to deal with "comrade criminals"'. IOL. 26 July. https://www.iol.co.za/news/politics/ngcuka-vows-to-deal-with-comrade-criminals-110401

Laurence, P. 1999. 'Boesak found guilty of theft and fraud' *Irish Times*, 18 March. https://www.irishtimes.com/news/boesak-foundguilty-of-theft-and-fraud-1.164134

Legalbrief. 2021. 'Dave King, SARS slug it out in high-stakes battle'. 13 December.

Lindow, M. 2003. 'South Africa's abalone plundered / Appetite for valued mollusk fueling social, environmental crisis'. SFGate. 28 November. https://www.sfgate.com/green/article/South-Africa-s-abalone-plundered-Appetite-for-2525863.php

Macozoma, S. 1998. Speech at the celebration of the appointment of Bulelani Ngcuka as the National Director of Public Prosecutions, Kyalami. 9 October. (Author's copy)

Mail&Guardian. 2011. 'ANC: Heath resignation "regrettable"'. 16 December. https://mg.co.za/article/2011-12-16-anc-heath-resignation-regrettable/

Mail&Guardian. 2004. 'Public Protector a liar and a sad case'. 30 May. https://mg.co.za/article/2004-05-30-public-protector-a-liar-and-sad-case/

Mail&Guardian. 2004. 'Big shoes to fill'. 29 July.

Mail&Guardian. 2004. 'Greedy officials grab grants'. 17 December. https://mg.co.za/article/2004-12-17-greedy-officials-grab-grants/

Mail&Guardian. 1998. 'Why are the Eikenhof Three still in jail?' 10 December. https://mg.co.za/article/1998-12-18-why-are-the-eikenhof-three-still-in/

Mail&Guardian. 1998. 'Nkabinde acquitted'. 1 May. https://mg.co.za/article/1998-05-01-nkabinde-acquitted/

Makinana, A, Madisa, K and Khoza, A. 2021. 'Once-spurned Mbeki-ites return to ANC fold'. *Sunday Times*. 24 October. https://www.timeslive.co.za/sunday-times/news/politics/2021-10-24-once-spurned-mbeki-ites-return-to-the-anc-fold/

Malan, R. 2012. *The Lion Sleeps Tonight and Other Stories of Africa*. Grove Press

Mapiloko, J and Sole, S. 2010. 'Kebble's voice from the grave'. *Mail&Guardian*. 4 June. https://mg.co.za/article/2010-06-04-kebbles-voice-from-the-grave/

Marais, J. 2013. 'Why King agreed to R718m for a new start'. *Business Day*. 1 September. https://www.businesslive.co.za/bd/companies/2013-09-01-why-king-agreed-to-r718m-for-a-new-start/

Mavimbela, V. 2018. *Time is Not the Measure*. Real African Publishers

Mbeki, T. 2005. Statement of the President of South Africa, Thabo Mbeki, at the Joint Sitting of Parliament on the Release of Hon Jacob Zuma from his responsibilities as Deputy President: National Assembly, 14 June. http://www.dirco.gov.za/docs/speeches/2005/mbek0614.htm

Mbeki, T. 1999. Address of the President of the Republic of South Africa,

REFERENCES

Thabo Mbeki, at the Opening of Parliament, National Assembly, Cape Town. 25 June

Mbhele, W. 2003. 'Setting the Ngcuka record straight'. *City Press*. 29 November

McCarthy, LF. 2004. Directorate of Special Operations 'Scorpions' Presentation to Parliament. Advocate LF McCarthy. 18 June

McGreal, C. 1999. 'The motiveless murder and Napoleon of Africa.' The Guardian. 16 December. https://www.theguardian.com/world/1999/dec/16/chrismcgreal.

Michaels, J. 2004. 'ANC rebukes trio over spat'. IOL. 2 June. https://www.iol.co.za/news/politics/anc-rebukes-trio-over-spat-213848

Michaels, J. 2004. 'Ngcuka sorry, but says he'll fight Mushwana'. *Cape Times*. 4 June

Mujuzi, JD. 2010. Ten years of the South African Prevention of Organised Crime Act (1999-2009). Criminal Justice Initiative of Open Society Foundation for South Africa

Musgrave, A and Malefane, M. 2003. 'NDPP found me guilty with no evidence: Zuma', IOL. 24 August. https://www.iol.co.za/news/politics/ndpp-found-me-guilty-with-no-evidence-zuma-111554

National Prosecuting Authority Annual Report 2005-2006

National Prosecuting Authority Annual Report 2001-2002

National Prosecuting Authority Annual Report 1999-2000

National Prosecuting Authority; Asset Forfeiture Unit, Special Investigating Unit, Directorate of Special Operations: Budget Hearings, 5 June 2002. https://pmg.org.za/committee-meeting/1540/

National Prosecuting Authority Parliamentary Report 2002/2003

Newman, L. 2004. 'Scorpions make R1bn Mandrax bust'. IOL. 16 August. https://www.iol.co.za/news/south-africa/scorpions-make-r1bn-mandrax-bust-219651

News24. 2015. 'ANC obsession with conspiracies is dangerous'. 16 March. https://www.news24.com/News24/ANC-obsession-with-conspiracies-is-dangerous-20150430

News24. 2014. 'De Lille built career on arms deal – critic'. 9 October. https://www.news24.com/News24/De-Lille-built-career-on-arms-deal-critic-20141009

News24. 2006. 'Got the bastard by the balls'. 24 March. https://www.news24.com/news24/got-the-bastard-by-the-balls-20060324

News24. 2004. 'Ngcuka: Hefer united us'. 11 February. https://www.news24.com/News24/Ngcuka-Hefer-united-us-20040211

News24. 2004. 'It's open war'. 30 May. https://www.news24.com/news24/its-open-war-20040530

News24. 2004. 'NPA won't prosecute ANC 37'. 2 June. https://www.news24.com/news24/npa-wont-prosecute-anc-37-20040602

News24. 2004. 'Ngcuka, Mbeki showdown looms'. 6 June. https://www.news24.com/news24/ngcuka-mbeki-showdown-looms-20040606

News24. 2004. 'Ngcuka was pushed – DA'. 26 July. https://www.news24.com/news24/ngcuka-was-pushed-da-20040726

News24. 2004. 'Shaik: French fax surfaces'. 19 October. https://www.news24.com/News24/Shaik-French-fax-surfaces-20041019

News24. 2002. 'Fishing king fined R250 000'. 4 November. https://www.news24.com/News24/Fishing-king-fined-R250-000-20021104

News24. 2001. 'Scopa to compile new arms deal report'. 28 February. https://www.news24.com/News24/Scopa-to-compile-new-arms-deal-report-20010228

News24. 2001. 'Baqwa threatens Noseweek'. 12 April. https://www.news24.com/News24/Baqwa-threatens-Noseweek-20010412

Ngcuka, B. 2014. 'How Mpshe manipulated the spy tapes'. *TimesLive Lifestyle*. 5 October. https://www.timeslive.co.za/sunday-times/lifestyle/2014-10-05-how-mpshe-manipulated-the-spy-tapes/

Ngcuka, B. 2011. 'An Open Letter to Advocate Willem Heath'. *TimesLive*. 11 December

Ngcuka, BT. 2004. National Prosecuting Authority Briefing to Parliament, BT Ngcuka, 17-18 June

Ngcuka, B. 2003. Submission prepared for Hefer Commission. (Author's copy)

Ngcuka, B. 2003. 'Asoze ndijike – I will not turn back'. IOL. 11 December. https://www.iol.co.za/news/politics/asoze-ndijike-i-will-not-turn-back-119048

Nhlapo, T and SAPA-AP. 2003. 'Mega Mandrax bust breaks SA record'. IOL. 4 July. https://www.iol.co.za/news/south-africa/mega-mandrax-bust-breaks-sa-record-109163

Nicholson, Z. 2011. 'End of the road for LeisureNet fraudsters'. *Cape Times*. 27 March.

Parks, M. 1985. 'Black police caught in web of S African strife: Soldier stoned to death by mourners after rites for lawyer'. *Los Angeles Times*, 12 August. https://www.latimes.com/archives/la-xpm-1985-08-12-mn-3941-story.html

Parliament of the Republic of South Africa. 2001. Procedural Developments in the National Assembly: Third Session – Second Parliament, January to December. https://www.parliament.gov.za/storage/app/media/NA-Procedural-Devs/4.pdf

Pikoli, V and Wiener, M. 2013. *My Second Initiation: The memoir of Vusi Pikoli*, Picador Africa.

Polity. 2003. 'Cosatu members support Zuma at congress'. 17 September. https://www.polity.org.za/article/cosatu-members-support-zuma-at-congress-2003-09-17

Polity. 2019. '"I was not sure NPA's prospects of success were strong enough for a winnable case against Zuma," Ngcuka says in court papers'. News24Wire, 13 March. https://www.polity.org.za/article/i-was-not-sure-npas-prospects-of-success-were-strong-enough-for-a-winnable-case-

REFERENCES

against-zuma-ngcuka-says-in-court-papers-2019-03-13

Potgieter, D. 2013. 'Eugene De Kock's explosive 64-tonne question'. *Daily Maverick*. 27 March. https://www.dailymaverick.co.za/article/2013-03-27-eugene-de-kocks-explosive-64-tonne-question/

Pressly, D. 2004. 'National assembly mildly rebukes Ngcuka'. *Mail&Guardian*. 25 June

Pretoria News, 1992. 'Why Was SADF in Phola Park?' 10 April 1992. http://www.historicalpapers.wits.ac.za/inventories/inv_pdfo/AK2702/AK2702-I-001-jpeg.pdf

Prevention of Organised Crime Amendment Act, No 24, 1999

Prevention of Organised Crime Act, No 121, 1998. https://www.justice.gov.za/legislation/acts/1998-121.pdf

Ragavaloo, A. 2008. *Richmond: Living in the shadow of death*. STE Publishers. Kindle edition

Redpath, J. 2004. 'Monograph 96: The Scorpions: Analysing the Directorate of Special Operations'. https://www.files.ethz.ch/isn/118337/96%20FULL.pdf

Report in Terms of Section 35(2)(b) of the National Prosecuting Authority Act, Act No 32 of 1998 [as amended], pertaining to the arms deal investigation into allegations of corruption involving Mr Jacob Zuma, in particular insofar as it relates to his relations with Schabir Shaik, the Nkobi group of companies and the Thomson/Thales group of companies, 23 August 2003

Report on the work of the IMT, Eastern Cape. NCOP. 11 September 2003

Richards, R. 2000. Address at the 2000 annual national conference of the Security Association of South Africa, Midrand. 12 October

Roberts, B. 1999. '"Convoluted Act" sees Basson' assets returned'. *Mail&Guardian*. 26 August. https://mg.co.za/article/1999-08-26-convoluted-act-sees-bassons-assets-returned/

SABC. 2000. Application of Phila Martin Dolo. 24 July. Truth Commission Special Report. https://sabctrc.saha.org.za/originals/amntrans/2000/200724jh.htm

SABC. n.d. TRC Final Report, Volume 2, Chapter 3. Sub Section 26. https://sabctrc.saha.org.za/reports/volume 2/chapter3/subsection26.html

SABC. n.d. TRC Final Report. Vol 3, Ch 3. Truth Commission Special Report. https://sabctrc.saha.org.za/reports/volume3/chapter3/subsection30.htm

SABC. n.d. Amnesty Hearings: Proceedings held at Durban, 5 November 1996. Truth Commission Special Report. https://sabctrc.saha.org.za/documents/amntrans/durban/54689.htm

SABC. n.d. Transcripts for Section 7 of Episode 4. Truth Commission Special Report https://sabctrc.saha.org.za/tvseries/episode4/section7.htm

SAPA. 2004. 'Ngcuka forced to quit, says PAC'. IOL. 25 July. https://www.iol.co.za/news/politics/ngcuka-forced-to-quit-says-pac-217996

SAPA. 2003. 'Zuma questions Scorpions' motives'. Polity. 23 July. https://www.polity.org.za/print-version/zuma-questions-scorpionsx2019-motives-2003-07-28

SAPA. 2003. 'Maharaj resigns from FirstRand'. IOL. 14 August. https://www.iol.co.za/news/politics/maharaj-resigns-from-firstrand-110944

SAPA. 2003. 'Shaik "has file with 880 spy suspects"'. IOL. 21 November. https://www.iol.co.za/news/politics/shaik-has-file-with-880-spy-suspects-117281

SAPA. 2003. 'Mo hands over secret database of 888 "spies".' IOL, 24 November. https://www.iol.co.za/news/politics/mo-hands-over-secret-database-of-888-spies-117754

SAPA. 2003. 'City Press makes front page apology to Ngcuka'. IOL. 30 November. https://www.iol.co.za/news/politics/city-press-makes-front-page-apology-to-ngcuka-117571

SAPA. 2001. 'Seized assets' money to go back to victims'. News24. 18 March. https://www.news24.com/news24/seized-assets-money-to-go-back-to-victims-20010318

SAPA. 2001. 'Stolen cellphone won't keep Boesak in jail'. IOL. 17 May. https://www.iol.co.za/news/south-africa/stolen-cellphone-wont-keep-boesak-in-jail-65010

SAPA. 2000. 'Alleged kidnappers' assets can be seized'. IOL. 7 January. https://www.iol.co.za/news/south-africa/alleged-kidnappers-assets-can-be-seized-25103

SAPA. 2000. 'Biggest Mandrax bust in SA history'. IOL. 15 August. https://www.iol.co.za/news/south-africa/biggest-mandrax-bust-in-sa-history-47309

SAPA. 2000. 'Constitutional Court upholds Rautenbach raid.' IOL, 25 August. https://www.iol.co.za/news/south-africa/constitutional-court-upholdsrautenbach-raid-48155

SAPA. 2000. 'They can't scare us off – Ngcuka'. News24. 8 September. https://www.news24.com/news24/they-cant-scare-us-off-ngcuka-20000908

SAPA. 2000. '"Drug kingpin" rearrested at Swazi border'. IOL. 16 September. https://www.iol.co.za/news/africa/drug-kingpin-rearrested-at-swazi-border-43456

SAPA. 2000. 'Rautenbach's assets seized'. News24. 19 September. https://www.news24.com/news24/rautenbachs-assets-seized-20000919-2

SAPA. 2000. 'Pension fraudsters get 8 years'. News24. 28 November. https://www.news24.com/News24/Pension-fraudsters-get-8-years-20001128

SAPA. 1999. 'Ngcuka not sure if TRC cases worth cost'. IOL. 26 August. https://www.iol.co.za/news/south-africa/ngcuka-not-sure-if-trc-cases-worth-cost-10666

Schapiro, M. 2008. 'South Africa's nuclear underground'. RevealNews. 10 April. https://revealnews.org/article/south-africas-nuclear-underground/

Schönteich, M. 2003. 'NPA in the dock. Thumbs up for prosecution service'. *South African Crime Quarterly*. 2003, No 3

REFERENCES

Schönteich, M. 2001. 'Lawyers for the People: The South African Prosecution Service', Monograph

Schönteich, M and Louw, A. 2001. 'Crime in South Africa: A country and cities profile'. Institute for Security Studies. Occasional Paper No 49-2001. https://issafrica.s3.amazonaws.com/site/uploads/paper49.pdf

Scorpions Closure public hearings. 2008. Day 7 & response to public submissions. 10 September. https://pmg.org.za/committee-meeting/9611/

Scorpions Closure public hearings. 2008. Day 6 & response to public submissions. 9 September. https://pmg.org.za/committee-meeting/9602/

Scorpions' Report to Parliament, 2003. (Author's copy.)

Scorpions. 1999. Briefing. 16 November. https://pmg.org.za/committee-meeting/4714/

Seepe, J and Mkhabela, M. 2003. 'Ngcuka "Turns to God"'. *City Press*. 21 September

Sergeant, B. 2006. *Brett Kebble: The Inside Story*. Zebra Press

Shaik, M. 2020. *The ANC Spy Bible: Surviving across enemy lines*. Tafelberg

Shaik, M. 2003. Submission in the Hefer Commission of Enquiry. O'Malley archives. https://omalley.nelsonmandela.org/omalley/index.php/site/q/03lv03445/04lv04015/05lv04120/06lv04123.htm

Smith, A. 2003. 'Band of brothers in the thick of things'. 22 November. IOL. https://www.iol.co.za/news/politics/band-of-brothers-in-the-thick-of-things-117369

Sole, S. 2012. 'Zuma tapes: A timeline'. *Mail&Guardian*. 2 November. https://mg.co.za/article/2012-11-02-00-zuma-tapes-a-timeline/

Sole, S. 2012. 'Scorpions probe Jacob Zuma'. Mail&Guardian. 29 November. https://mg.co.za/article/2012-11-29-scorpions-probe-jacob-zuma

Sole, S. 2003. 'Ngcuka: "If you shoot at the king, don't miss."' *Mail&Guardian*. 12 September https://mg.co.za/article/2003-09-12-00-ngcuka-if-you-shoot-at-the-king-dont-miss/

Sole, S and Dawes, N. 2005. 'Spy-war emails: What they really say'. *Mail&Guardian*. 15 December. https://mg.co.za/article/2005-12-15-spywar-emails-what-they-really-say/

South African History Online. n.d. Message to the Soweto Rally to Welcome Released Leaders by OR Tambo, 29 October 1989. https://sahistory.org.za/archive/message-soweto-rally-welcome-released-leaders-o-r-tambo-29-october-1989

South Africa Travel Online. n.d. History of Trade Unions in South Africa. https://www.southafrica.to/history/TradeUnions/TradeUnionHistory.php

Special Report on an Investigation by the Public Protector of a Complaint by Deputy President J Zuma against the National Director of Public Prosecutions and the National Prosecuting Authority in Connection with a Criminal Investigation Conducted Against Him. 28 May 2004. https://static.pmg.org.za/docs/040529pprotect.htm

Squires, Judge H. 2005. Judgement in the Case of Schabir Shaik: Judge Squires In the High Court of South Africa (Durban and Coastal Local Division) CASE NO:

CC27/04 Stone, C, America C and India Baird, M. 2003. 'Prosecutors in the Front Line: Increasing the effectiveness of criminal justice in South Africa'. Paper. Bureau of Justice Assistance and the Vera Institute of Justice

Sunday Times. 2014. 'Watchdog backs Sunday Times against Munusamy'. 14 September. https://www.timeslive.co.za/sunday-times/lifestyle/2014-09-14-watchdog-backs-sunday-times-against-munusamy/

Sunday Times Lifestyle. 2004. 'Mission Accomplished'. 1 August. https://www.timeslive.co.za/sunday-times/lifestyle/2004-08-01-mission-accomplished/

Swart, M. 2008. 'The Wouter Basson prosecution: The closest South Africa came to Nuremberg?' Max-Planck-Institut für ausländisches öffentliches Recht und Völkerrecht Mia Swart. https://www.zaoerv.de/68_2008/68_2008_1_b_209_226.pdf

Taylor, R. 2002. 'Justice Denied: Political violence in KwaZulu-Natal after 1994'. *African Affairs*, 101 (405). October

The African Communist. 1983. 'Who is committing treason?' No 92, First Quarter. Inkululeko Publications, London. http://psimg.jstor.org/fsi/img/pdf/t0/10.5555/al.sff.document.0001.9976.000.092.1982.pdf

Thuthuzela Care Centres brochure. 2009. National Prosecuting Authority, Pretoria. August

Truth and Reconciliation Commission. 1997. Legal Hearing, 27–29 October. https://www.justice.gov.za/trc/special/legal/legal.htm

Tsedu, M. 2003. 'Why we did not run the Ngcuka spy story'. *Sunday Times*. 21 September

Van Kessel, I. 2000. *'Beyond Our Wildest Dreams': The United Democratic Front and the Transformation of South Africa*. University of Virginia Press

Van Rheede, J. 2002. 'Tombstone taken as pyramid schemers pay up'. IOL. 18 September. https://www.iol.co.za/news/south-africa/tombstone-taken-as-pyramid-schemers-pay-up-94749

Vapi, X, Msomi, S, Boyle, B and Mbhele, W. 2004. 'Ngcuka quits'. *Sunday Times*. 25 July

Vapi, X. 1999. 'Asset Unit raids drug lord's home'. IOL. 15 October. https://www.iol.co.za/news/south-africa/asset-unit-raids-druglords-home-16271

Wa Afrika, M. 2014. *Nothing left to Steal: Jailed for telling the truth*. Penguin Books

Wa Afrika, M. 2014. 'Zuma revealed as hidden hand in spy scandal'. *Sunday Times*. 7 August

Wa Afrika, M, Bezuidenhout, J and Jurgens, A. 2002. 'Arms-deal suspect defends Zuma'. *Sunday Times*. 15 December

Wa Afrika, M, Hofstatter, S and Rampedi, P. 2014. 'NPA boss lied about spy tapes: Ngcuka lashes out at Mpshe and Zuma'. *TimesLive*. 5 October.

REFERENCES

https://www.timeslive.co.za/politics/2014-10-05-npa-boss-lied-about-spy-tapes-ngcuka-lashes-out-at-mpshe-and-zuma Wheels24. 2009. 'R40m fine for ex-Hyundai boss'. News24. 23 September. https://www.news24.com/wheels/r40m-fine-for-ex-hyundai-sa-boss-20090923

Williams, M. 2004. 'US charges SA man over nukes' IOL. 13 January. https://www.iol.co.za/news/south-africa/us-charges-sa-man-over-nukes-120545

Wines, M. 205. 'Mark Thatcher pleads guilty in plot'. *The New York Times*. 14 January. https://www.nytimes.com/2005/01/14/world/europe/mark-thatcher-pleads-guilty-in-plot.html

Work in Progress No. 7 March 1979 (http://www.aluka.org/

Wotshela, L. 2020. 'Unfulfilled potential: Confined destiny of historical studies at University of Fort Hare, 1960–2015'. *Southern Journal for Contemporary History*, 45(2): 1-32.

Yekela, D. 1988. 'The Life and Times of Kama Chungwa'. MA thesis, Rhodes University.

Yeld, J. 2004. 'Secret agent sank "perlemoen godmother"'. IOL. 8 June. https://www.iol.co.za/news/south-africa/secret-agent-sank-perlemoen-godmother-213979

Zapiro. 1999. Cartoon in *Mail&Guardian*. 26 August

Zavis, A. 1996. 'Mob burns Cape Town gang leader to death'. AP News. 5 August. https://apnews.com/article/7c95a7e39cfcfd360c89bad40c7ffb12

Court documents

2018. High Court of South Africa (Gauteng Division, Pretoria). Supporting Affidavit on Behalf of First Respondent, Raymond Christopher Macadam Case No. 76755/18. 1 November

2015. High Court of South Africa (Gauteng Division, Pretoria). Confirmatory Affidavit: WJ Downer. Case No 19577/2009. 2 June

2013. US District Court Southern District of New York. Plaintiff against AM Bengis et al. Case No 1:03-cr-00308-LAK Document 249. Filed 14 June 2013

2010. South Gauteng High Court. Johannesburg. The State v JS Selebi. Case No 25/09. Judgment. 5 July

2005. High Court of South Africa (Transvaal Provincial Division). Yengeni vs State (A1079/03) [2005] ZAGPHC 117. Judgment. 11 November

2005. High Court of South Africa (Natal Provincial Division). Affidavit of Mr Ngcuka in State vs Zuma, Thint Holdings (Southern Africa) and Thint Pty Ltd. Case number CC 358/2005

2005. High Court (Durban and Coast Local Division). Answering Affidavit: The Accused's Counter-Applications for a Permanent Stay of Prosecution. Leonard Frank McCarthy. Case No CC358/2005

2004. Constitutional Court of South Africa. The State versus Wouter Basson. Case CCT30/03. Judgment

2003. Regional Court. (Regional Division of Northern Transvaal.) The State vs TS Yengeni and MJ Woerfel. Case No 14/09193/01. Accused No 1's Plea of Guilty

2003. Western Cape High Court, Cape Town. National Director of Public Prosecutions v Prophet (5926/01) [2003] ZAWCHC 16. Judgment. 22 May

2002. Constitutional Court of South Africa. National Director of Public Prosecutions and Another v Mohamed NO and Others. Case CCT 13/02. Judgement. 12 June

1999. Supreme Court of Appeal. Judgment. S v Ndweni and Others (376/94, 390/94, 639/98) [1999] ZASCA 51; [1999] 4 All SA 377 (A). 31 August

1999. Supreme Court of Appeal of South Africa. National Director of Public Prosecutions vs GG Carolus and others. Case No 162/99. Judgment. 1 December

Interviews by author

Bulelani Ngcuka, 2015 to 2021

Ronnie Kasrils, 20 January 2022

Madeleine Fullard, 28 August 2021

Phumzile Mlambo-Ngcuka, 10 January 2017

Dumisani Tabata, 10 February 2017

Lungisa Dyosi, 29 November 2016

Press statements and addresses by Bulelani Ngcuka

2014. Statement by Bulelani Ngcuka, former NDPP, on the release of transcripts of proceedings of intercepted communications between him and Mr LF McCarthy as well as internal NPA memoranda relating to the decision to terminate the prosecution in the matter of S v Zuma and Thint Holdings. (Author's copy)

2009. Statement by Bulelani Ngcuka, 5 October

2004. Address by Head of the NPA, Mr Bulelani Ngcuka, to the Johannesburg Press Club. 22 January

2004. Address by Bulelani Ngcuka at the 1st Dullah Omar Memorial Lecture, University of Western Cape, 22 November

2004. Address by the National Director of Public Prosecutions, BT Ngcuka, at the Annual General Meeting of the Institute of Directors, Cape Town, 3 June

2003. Press statement by Bulelani Thandabantu Ngcuka, National Director of Public Prosecutions, on the decision on whether to prosecute after the completion of the investigation against Deputy President, Mr Jacob Zuma, Schabir Shaik and others. 23 August

2000. Speech to National Prosecuting Authority Senior Management Conference by National Director of Public Prosecutions BT Ngcuka

Acknowledgements

I would like to thank Bulelani Ngcuka first, for all his patience and time over a number of years. I would also like to thank Phumzile Mlambo-Ngcuka, Lungisa Dyosi, Sipho Ngwema, Madeleine Fullard, Bulelwa Conco Makeke and Saki Macozoma. My thanks also to Nkanyezi Tshabalala of Jonathan Ball Publishers, and editor Tracey Hawthorne.

Notes

Preface

1   The World Council of Churches' Programme to Combat Racism was launched in 1969, and played an important role in international solidarity and humanitarian support for the liberation movement.
2   The South African Students' Organisation (SASO) was formed in 1968 after some members of the University of Natal's Black Campus Student Representative Council broke away from the largely white National Union of South African Students.
3   Both Cecil Somyalo and Dumile Kondile became judges of the High Court in the post-1994 new dispensation.
4   Place names are rendered as they were at the time of the narrative.
5   Biko, S (1978). *I Write What I Like*. Bowerdean Press.
6   An agency of the United Nations whose mandate is to advance social and economic justice through setting international labour standards.
7   The senate was the upper house of the parliament of South Africa from 1910 to 1981, and again from 1994 to 1997. In its second iteration, it was indirectly elected by members of each of the nine provincial legislatures, with each province having ten senators. In 1997 it was replaced with the national council of provinces.
8   Henning, M (ed). 2015. *Faith as Politics: Reflections in Commemoration of Beyers Naudé (1915-2004)*. The Nordic Afrika Institute.

Author's note

1   'Prima facie', Latin for 'at first sight', describes a case in law in which there is sufficient evidence to justify a verdict, unless disproved or rebutted.

Chapter 1

1   All chapter-opener quotations are Bulelani Ngcuka's.
2   Press statement by Bulelani Thandabantu Ngcuka, National Director of Public Prosecutions, on the decision on whether to prosecute after

the completion of the investigation against Deputy President, Mr Jacob Zuma, Schabir Shaik and others, 23 August 2003. http://www.armsdeal-vpo.co.za/special_items/statements/ngcuka_statemnt.htm Accessed 1 December 2021.
3. Ibid.
4. All blocked quotations are Bulelani Ngcuka's from interviews with the author from 2015 to 2021.
5. High Court of South Africa (Natal Provincial Division). Affidavit of Mr Ngcuka in State vs Zuma, Thint Holdings (Southern Africa) and Thint Pty Ltd. Case number CC 358/2005. https://omalley.nelsonmandela.org/omalley/cis/omalley/OMalleyWeb/dat/AffidavitNgcuka.pdf Accessed 3 December 2021.
6. Holden, P and Van Vuuren, H. 2011. *The Devil in the Detail: How the arms deal changed everything*. Jonathan Ball Publishers.
7. High Court of South Africa (Natal Provincial Division). Affidavit of Mr Ngcuka in State vs Zuma, Thint Holdings (Southern Africa) and Thint Pty Ltd. Case number CC 358/2005. https://omalley.nelsonmandela.org/omalley/cis/omalley/OMalleyWeb/dat/AffidavitNgcuka.pdf Accessed 3 December 2021.
8. Press statement by Bulelani Thandabantu Ngcuka, National Director of Public Prosecutions on the decision on whether to prosecute after the completion of the investigation against Deputy President, Mr Jacob Zuma, Schabir Shaik and others, 23 August 2003. http://www.armsdeal-vpo.co.za/special_items/statements/ngcuka_statemnt.htm Accessed 1 December 2021.
9. Polity. 2019. '"I was not sure NPA's prospects of success were strong enough for a winnable case against Zuma," Ngcuka says in court papers'. News24Wire, 13 March. https://www.polity.org.za/article/i-was-not-sure-npas-prospects-of-success-were-strong-enough-for-a-winnable-case-against-zuma-ngcuka-says-in-court-papers-2019-03-13 Accessed 12 June 2021.
10. Sole, S. 2003. 'Ngcuka: "If you shoot at the king, don't miss."' *Mail & Guardian*, 12 September https://mg.co.za/article/2003-09-12-00-ngcuka-if-you-shoot-at-the-king-dont-miss/ Accessed 23 December 2021.
11. Musgrave, A and Malefane, M. 2003. 'NDPP found me guilty with no evidence: Zuma', IOL News. 24 August. https://www.iol.co.za/news/politics/ndpp-found-me-guilty-with-no-evidence-zuma-111554 Accessed 1 December 2021.
12. Ibid.
13. In 2003 this was a brand-new party, formed by De Lille, previously a member of the Pan Africanist Congress (PAC) from 1987 to 2003. The Independent Democrats disbanded in 2014.
14. Musgrave, A and Malefane, M. 2003. 'NDPP found me guilty with no evidence: Zuma', IOL News. 24 August. https://www.iol.co.za/news/politics/ndpp-found-me-guilty-with-no-evidence-zuma-111554 Accessed 1 December 2021.

15. Ibid.
16. Polity. 2003. 'Cosatu members support Zuma at congress' 17 September. https://www.polity.org.za/article/cosatu-members-support-zuma-at-congress-2003-09-17 Accessed 1 December 2021.
17. Musgrave, A and Malefane, M. 2003. 'NDPP found me guilty with no evidence: Zuma', IOL News. 24 August. https://www.iol.co.za/news/politics/ndpp-found-me-guilty-with-no-evidence-zuma-111554 Accessed 1 December 2021.
18. Ibid.
19. Ironically though, as Bulelani recalls, when Zuma was challenged at a later date in parliament by Tony Leon, leader of the opposition, and asked why he hadn't resigned after the announcement in September 2003, he responded by saying that the problem with Leon was that he didn't trust the NDPP whereas he, Zuma, did - and the NDPP had said there was no case against him.
20. Press statement by Bulelani Thandabantu Ngcuka, National Director of Public Prosecutions, on the decision whether to prosecute after the completion of the investigation into Deputy President Jacob Zuma, Schabir Shaik and others, 23 August 2003. http://www.armsdeal-vpo.co.za/special_items/statements/ngcuka_statemnt.htm Accessed 1 December 2021.

Chapter 2

1. The title of a poem by John Clare (1793-1864).
2. News24. 2014. 'De Lille built career on arms deal – critic'. 9 October. https://www.news24.com/News24/De-Lille-built-career-on-arms-deal-critic-20n009 Accessed 2 December 2021.
3. Auditor-General. 2000. Special Review of the Selection Process of Strategic Defence Packages for the Acquisition of Armaments at the Department of Defence. Government Printer, p10. http://www.armsdeal-vpo.co.za/special_items/reports/ag_review.pdf Accessed 1 December 2021.
4. Parliament of the Republic of South Africa. 2001. Procedural Developments in the National Assembly: Third Session – Second Parliament, January to December, p5 https://www.parliament.gov.za/storage/app/media/NA-Procedural-Devs/4.pdf Accessed 23 December 2021.
5. News24, 2011. The 'Heath' is on. News24, 10 December. https://www.news24.com/News24/The-Heath-is-on-20150429 Accessed 16 March 2011.
6. Legalbrief, 2011. 'Heath blames Mbeki for Zuma rape, corruption charges'. 5 December https://legalbrief.co.za/story/heath-blames-mbeki-for-zuma-rape-corruption-charges/ Accessed 18 March 2022
7. News24. 2001. 'Baqwa threatens Noseweek'. 12 April. https://www.news24.com/News24/Baqwa-threatens-Noseweek-20010412 Accessed 2 December 2021.

NOTES

8   Joint Investigation Report into the Strategic Defence Procurement Packages. 2001. November. https://www.gov.za/sites/default/files/gcis_document/201409/jointinvestigationreport0.pdf Accessed 2 December 2021.
9   News24. 2001. 'Scopa to compile new arms deal report'. 28 February. https://www.news24.com/News24/Scopa-to-compile-new-arms-deal-report-20010228 Accessed 23 December 2021.
10 Joint Investigation Report into the Strategic Defence Procurement Packages. 2001. November. https://www.gov.za/sites/default/files/gcis_document/201409/jointinvestigationreport0.pdf Accessed 2 December 2021.
11 Ibid.

Chapter 3

1   Now Makhanda.
2   High Court (Durban and Coast Local Division). Answering Affidavit: The Accused's Counter-Applications for a Permanent Stay of Prosecution. Leonard Frank McCarthy, Case No CC358/2005. http://www.armsdeal-vpo.co.za/special_items/jacob_zuma_trial/answ-affidavit_mccarty.html Accessed 2 December 2021.
3   In 1998 Tony Yengeni, at the time the chair of the joint standing committee on defence, had received a sizeable discount on a Mercedes Benz 4x4 bought from DaimlerChrysler, but he denied having received it and he did not disclose this information to parliament.
4   High Court (Durban and Coast Local Division). Answering Affidavit: The Accused's Counter-Applications for a Permanent Stay of Prosecution. Leonard Frank McCarthy, Case No CC358/2005. http://www.armsdeal-vpo.co.za/special_items/jacob_zuma_trial/answ-affidavit_mccarty.html Accessed 2 December 2021.
5   Report in Terms of Section 35(2)(b) of the National Prosecuting Authority Act, Act No 32 of 1998 [as amended], pertaining to the arms deal investigation into allegations of corruption involving Mr Jacob Zuma, in particular insofar as it relates to his relations with Schabir Shaik, the Nkobi group of companies and the Thomson/Thales group of companies, 23 August 2003.
6   High Court (Durban and Coast Local Division). Answering Affidavit: The Accused's Counter-Applications for a Permanent Stay of Prosecution. Leonard Frank McCarthy, Case No CC358/2005. http://www.armsdeal-vpo.co.za/special_items/jacob_zuma_trial/answ-affidavit_mccarty.html Accessed 2 December 2021.
7   Schabir Shaik was a director of African Defence Systems, a subsidiary of Thomson-CSF (also known as Thales and Thint).
8   News24. 2004. 'Shaik: French fax surfaces'. 19 October. https://www.news24.com/News24/Shaik-French-fax-surfaces-20041019. Accessed 2 December 2021.
9   Judgement: Judge Hillary Squires Judge Squires In the High Court of

South Africa (Durban and Coastal Local Division) CASE NO: CC27/04 https://omalley.nelsonmandela.org/omalley/index.php/site/q/03lv03445/04lv04015/05lv04148/06lv04149.htm Accessed 16 March 2022

10   A mutual legal assistance treaty is an agreement between two or more countries to gather and exchange information with the aim of enforcing the law.

11   High Court (Durban and Coast Local Division). Answering Affidavit: The Accused's Counter-Applications for a Permanent Stay of Prosecution. Leonard Frank McCarthy, Case No CC358/2005. http://www.armsdeal-vpo.co.za/special_items/jacob_zuma_trial/answ-affidavit_mccarty.html Accessed 2 December 2021.

12   Sole, S. 2012. 'Scorpions probe Jacob Zuma'. *Mail & Guardian*, 29 November. https://mg.co.za/article/2012-11-29-scorpions-probe-jacob-zuma/ Accessed 2 December 2021.

13   Nkobi Investments was Schabir Shaik's company. In September 1999, this company acquired a 25 percent shareholding in Thint (named Thomson-CSF up to August 2003). The idea was that Nkobi would enter into a joint venture with Thomson in the arms deal business. The company and several of its subsidiaries were eventually found guilty of corruption, along with Shaik, and fined a total of R3.6 million.

14   High Court (Durban and Coast Local Division). Answering Affidavit: The Accused's Counter-Applications for a Permanent Stay of Prosecution. Leonard Frank McCarthy, Case No CC358/2005. http://www.armsdeal-vpo.co.za/special_items/jacob_zuma_trial/answ-affidavit_mccarty.html Accessed 3 December 2021.

15   The executive council of a province is the cabinet of the provincial government; it consists of the premier of the province and five to ten other members.

16   *Sunday Times*. 2014. 'Watchdog backs Sunday Times against Munusamy'. 14 September. https://www.timeslive.co.za/sunday-times/lifestyle/2014-09-14-watchdog-backs-sunday-times-against-munusamy/ Accessed 23 December 2021.

17   Wa Afrika, M. 2014. *Nothing Left to Steal: Jailed for telling the truth*. Penguin Books.

18   Ibid.

19   Wa Afrika, M. 2014. 'Zuma revealed as hidden hand in spy scandal'. *Sunday Times*. 7 August. https://www.timeslive.co.za/politics/2014-08-07-zuma-revealed-as-hidden-hand-in-spy-scandal/ Accessed 4 September 2020.

20   Ibid.

21   Wa Afrika, M. 2014. *Nothing Left to Steal: Jailed for telling the truth*. Penguin Books.

22   Ibid.

23   In the course of their work, they also consulted senior counsel Marumo Moerane for an independent view on the case. (He finally concurred

NOTES

with the view that there was not sufficient evidence for a winnable case.)
24   Author interview with Lungisa Dyosi, 29 November 2016.
25   Ibid.
26   Department of International Relations and Cooperation. 2005. Statement of the President of South Africa, Thabo Mbeki, at the Joint Sitting of Parliament on the Release of Hon Jacob Zuma from his responsibilities as Deputy President: National Assembly, 14 June. http://www.dirco.gov.za/docs/speeches/2005/mbek0614.htm Accessed 3 December 2021.

Chapter 4

1   Yekela, D. 1988. 'The Life and Times of Kama Chungwa'. MA thesis, Rhodes University.
2   Author interview with Dumisani Tabata, 10 February 2017.
3   Transkei was one of ten 'bantustans' (or 'homelands') set aside for black inhabitants of South Africa as part of the policy of apartheid. The others were Lebowa, Bophuthatswana, Ciskei, Venda, Gazankulu, KaNgwane, KwaNdebele, KwaZulu and QwaQwa.
4   Boniswa was an ardent feminist and trade union organiser. She was detained in 1980 for her underground work in the PAC and left the country in 1983 but continued to work inside and outside South Africa as a member of the PAC and its armed wing, the Azanian People's Liberation Army (Apla). She died in March 1985 when she and five other Apla members were ambushed while crossing the border from Lesotho into South Africa. Her remains were brought home by the NPA's Missing Persons Unit in 2011.
5   Wotshela, L. 2020. 'Unfulfilled potential: Confined destiny of historical studies at University of Fort Hare, 1960-2015'. *Southern Journal for Contemporary History*, 45(2): 1-32.
6   A series of demonstrations and protests led by black schoolchildren that began in Soweto on the morning of 16 June 1976.

Chapter 5

1   Personal communication with author.
2   This nickname was given to him by a colleague, JKK Mthiyane, who had offices in the same building as GM in the 1970s and early 1980s. Mthiyane (who died in 2021) went on to become the deputy president of the Supreme Court of Appeal and a judge in the Constitutional Court.
3   To gain practical experience during his studies, Bulelani had started working at the Magistrate's Court during his university holidays, as a complaints clerk, a clerk for the civil court, a clerk for the criminal court and an interpreter.
4   A few days after Bulelani's arrival, the police came looking for Sizinzo. Bulelani found out later that Sizinzo had in fact left the country with

another activist, Mduduzi Guma, to join the ANC in exile. Both he and Mduduzi were killed in the Matola Massacre in Mozambique in 1981, in which 12 members of Umkhonto we Sizwe, the armed wing of the ANC, died in an SADF cross-border raid. Bulelani and Griffiths assisted Sizinzo's family to attend his funeral in Mozambique.

5   Now Gqeberha.
6   Ahmed Timol: Truth Prevails. 2019. '43rd Anniversary of Mapetla Mohapi'. 4 August. https://www.ahmedtimol.co.za/2019/08/04/43rd-anniversary-of-mapetla-mohapi. Accessed 8 September 2020.
7   Thenjiwe went on to become a senior MK commander, and she and Bulelani became close friends. She held many senior positions in pre- and post-democratic South Africa, including deputy secretary-general of the ANC, chairperson of the commission on gender equality and a number of ambassadorial posts.
8   Ahmed Timol: Truth Prevails. 2019. '43rd Anniversary of Mapetla Mohapi'. 4 August. https://www.ahmedtimol.co.za/2019/08/04/43rd-anniversary-of-mapetla-mohapi. Accessed 8 September 2020.
9   Author interview with Phumzile Mlambo-Ngcuka, 10 January 2017.
10   Work in Progress No. 7 March 1979 (http://www.aluka.org/)
11   Dennie, G. 1990. 'One King, Two Burials: The Politics of Funerals in South Africa's Transkei'. African Studies Institute seminar paper, University of the Witwatersrand. https://core.ac.uk/download/pdf/39667557.pdf Accessed 6 December 2021.
12   SABC. n.d. Transcripts for Section 7 of Episode 4. Truth Commission Special Report. https://sabctrc.saha.org.za/tvseries/episode4/section7.htm Accessed 23 December 2021; SABC. n.d. Amnesty Hearings: Proceedings held at Durban, 5 November 1996. Truth Commission Special Report. https://sabctrc.saha.org.za/documents/amntrans/durban/54689.htm Accessed 23 December 2021.
13   Ibid.
14   Ibid.

Chapter 6

1   Rev Xundu, a lifelong anti-apartheid activist and member of the UDF and Release Mandela Committee, died in January 2015 and was afforded a special provincial state funeral.
2   Bulelani did not know it at the time, but Taylor was also one of those responsible for Griffiths' murder. (TRC Final Report, Volume 2, Chapter 3. Sub Section 26. https://sabctrc.saha.org.za/reports/volume2/chapter3/subsection26.html Accessed 13 February 2022.) He was charged, along with Johannes van der Hoven, in 1997 but was acquitted on the basis of insufficient evidence.
3   *The African Communist*. 1983. 'Who is committing treason?' No 92, First Quarter. Inkululeko Publications, London. http://psimg.jstor.org/fsi/img/pdf/t0/10.5555/al.sff.document.0001.9976.000.092.1982.pdf Accessed 6 December 2021.
4   Tom Charlemagne was one of the Robben Island prisoners released

in 1973, only to be rearrested in 1977. He played an important role in ANC underground structures.
5   Bulelani completed his LLB in 1985 with a dissertation on labour law, and immediately registered for a BA in international relations.
6   SABC. n.d. TRC Final Report. Vol 3, Ch 3. Truth Commission Special Report. https://sabctrc.saha.org.za/reports/volume3/chapter3/subsection30.htm Accessed 6 December 2021.
7   Parks, M. 1985. 'Black police caught in web of S African strife: Soldier stoned to death by mourners after rites for lawyer'. *Los Angeles Times*. 12 August. https://www.latimes.com/archives/la-xpm-1985-08-12-mn-3941-story.html Accessed 6 December 2021.

Chapter 7

1   Author interview with Phumzile Mlambo-Ngcuka, 10 January 2017.
2   In 1991, with the unbanning of liberation movements in South Africa, the IDAF reviewed its position, and Horst and Bulelani interviewed candidates to head up the South African Legal Defence Fund. One of those they appointed was Ntobeko Patrick Maqubela.
3   Baldwin Sjollema was awarded the Order of the Companions of OR Tambo in 2004 by the South African government for his contribution to the anti-apartheid struggle.

Chapter 8

1   Van Kessel, I. 2000. *'Beyond Our Wildest Dreams'*: *The United Democratic Front and the Transformation of South Africa*. University of Virginia Press. p38.
2   Cole, J. 2013. 'The making and re-imagining of Khayelitsha: Report for the Commission of Inquiry into Allegations of Police Inefficiency in Khayelitsha and a Breakdown in Relations between the Community and the Police in Khayelitsha'. January. p32. https://s3-eu-west-1.amazonaws.com/s3.sourceafrica.net/documents/14375/5-b-j-cole-affidavit.pdf Accessed 7 December 2021.
3   IOL. 2000. 'Langa's killing "ended in triple murder".' 27 June. https://www.iol.co.za/news/politics/langas-killing-ended-in-triple-murder-41492 Accessed 7 December 2021.
4   Balfour was held for five months after his detention in 1989 and left for Australia soon after his release.
5   Du Pisani, JA, Broodryk, M and Coetzer, PW. 1990. 'Protest Marches in South Africa'. *Journal of Modern African Studies*, Vol 28, No 4. pp589-590.
6   South African History Online. n.d. Message to the Soweto Rally to Welcome Released Leaders by OR Tambo, 29 October 1989. https://sahistory.org.za/archive/message-soweto-rally-welcome-released-leaders-o-r-tambo-29-october-1989 Accessed 13 February 2022.

Chapter 9

1. Mandela was, however, soon back in a Mercedez-Benz. A few days after his release, Moss Mayekiso, the general secretary of the National Union of Metal Workers of South Africa, approached the Mandela Reception Committee and told them that workers wanted to build a car for Mandela. Because it was 'a gift from the workers themselves', the committee agreed, and that's how Madiba got his famous red Mercedez-Benz.

2. Winnie had planned to return immediately to Johannesburg with Mandela and had not brought a change of clothes. She therefore appeared for Mandela's press interview the following day wearing a dress she had borrowed from Bulelani's wife, Phumzile.

3. Diminutive form of Nomzamo; Winnie's full birth name was Nomzamo Winifred Zanyiwe Madikizela.

4. The government prohibited the publication of photos of Mandela during his many years in prison, and few people knew what he looked like at the time of his release.

5. Mandela would later meet Bush in December 1991 on his first visit to the USA.

6. Aluka. 1987. Political Prisoners in South Africa. http://psimg.jstor.org/fsi/img/pdf/t0/10.5555/al.sff.document.nuun1987_15_final.pdf Accessed 24 December 2021.

7. Arthur was appointed the first president of the Constitutional Court in 1994.

8. Dugard, J. 2001. *From Low Intensity to Mafia War: Taxi Violence in SA (1987-2000)*. Violence and Transition Series, Centre for the Study of Violence and Reconciliation. May. http://www.csvr.org.za/docs/taxiviolence/fromlowintensity.pdf Accessed 7 December 2021.

9. South Africa Travel Online. n.d. History of Trade Unions in South Africa. https://www.southafrica.to/history/TradeUnions/TradeUnionHistory.php Accessed 29 September 2020.

10. Both Waluś and Derby-Lewis were convicted of Hani's killing and sentenced to death in October 1993; their sentences were later commuted to life. Derby-Lewis was released in 2015 after serving 22 years and died the following year. Waluś has applied for and been denied parole on four different occasions. At the time of writing, the Constitutional Court was reviewing his case.

Chapter 10

1. The Admission of Legal Practitioners Amendment Act, 1995, came into effect on 1 July 1995, doing away with the requirement of Afrikaans for admission to practise as an advocate in the Supreme Court.

Chapter 11

1. Commey, P. 2014. 'A poisoned chalice: The dilemma of South Africa

public prosecutors'. *New African*. 21 July. https://newafricanmagazine.com/6123/ Accessed 23 August 2021.
2. Barrell, H and Soggett, M. 1998. 'Nice guy, but can he do the job?' *Mail & Guardian*. 17 July. https://mg.co.za/article/1998-07-17-nice-guy-but-can-he-do-the-job/ Accessed 28 January 2021.
3. Ibid.
4. Ibid.
5. Ibid.
6. Bulelani credits De Vries for agreeing to second a number of his experienced deputies to assist in setting up the NPA head office.
7. Address by Bulelani Ngcuka at the 1st Dullah Omar Memorial Lecture, University of Western Cape, 22 November 2004.
8. Roussouw was one of a group of former attorneys-general who appeared before the TRC and was the only one who appeared to offer a wholehearted apology for the part he'd played in upholding the apartheid system. While his colleagues (including Jan d'Oliveira, Tim McNally, Christo Nel and Klaus von Lieres) attempted to explain away their actions, Roussouw acknowledged his contribution to the division and oppression of the South African people and asked for their forgiveness. (Truth and Reconciliation Commission. 1997. Legal Hearing, 27–29 October. https://www.justice.gov.za/trc/special/legal/legal.htm Accessed 14 February 2022.)
9. Speech by Saki Macozoma at the celebration of the appointment of Bulelani Ngcuka as the National Director of Public Prosecutions, Kyalami, 9 October 1998. (Author's copy)

Chapter 12

1. National Prosecuting Authority Annual Report 1999-2000.
2. Address by Bulelani Ngcuka at the 1st Dullah Omar Memorial Lecture, University of Western Cape, 22 November 2004.
3. Bulelani says that prosecutors had been 'sucking from the hind teat' for too long: not only was their professional status not given full recognition, but they were often starved of the necessary resources. Efforts to amend the NPA Act to ensure the NPA assumed full financial responsibility for prosecutors remained unresolved at the time of Bulelani's resignation in 2004.
4. Address by Bulelani Ngcuka at the 1st Dullah Omar Memorial Lecture, University of Western Cape, 22 November 2004.
5. Speech to National Prosecuting Authority Senior Management Conference by National Director of Public Prosecutions BT Ngcuka, 2000.
6. National Prosecuting Authority Annual Report 2001-2002, p15.
7. Ibid, p16.
8. National Prosecuting Authority Briefing to Parliament, BT Ngcuka, 17–18 June 2004.

9   Author interview with Lungisa Dyosi, 29 November 2016.
10 Schönteich, M. 2001. 'Lawyers for the People: The South African Prosecution Service'. Monograph. Ch. 7.
11 Address by BT Ngcuka at the 1st Dullah Omar Memorial Lecture, University of Western Cape, November 22, 2004.
12 Ibid.
13 Stone, C, America C and India Baird, M. 2003. 'Prosecutors in the Front Line: Increasing the effectiveness of criminal justice in South Africa'. Paper. Bureau of Justice Assistance and the Vera Institute of Justice.
14 Thoko Majokweni was one of the first female black prosecutors promoted by Bulelani, and in 1999 was the first female special DPP appointed in the Office of the NDPP. She retired in 2018 and went on to represent South Africa in the diplomatic corps.
15 Thuthuzela Care Centres brochure. 2009. National Prosecuting Authority, Pretoria. August.
16 Briefing to Parliament by National Director of Public Prosecutions, BT Ngcuka, 17-18 June 2004.
17 Hofmeyr, W. 2007. 'The Role of Specialist Units in the NPA'. Presentation at National Prosecuting Authority Stakeholder Conference, 28-30 March. https://www.npa.gov.za/content/speaker-presentations Accessed 9 December 2021.
18 National Prosecuting Authority Parliamentary Report 2002/2003, p20.
19 National Prosecuting Authority Briefing to Parliament, BT Ngcuka, 17-18 June 2004.
20 Kockott, F. 2010. 'Netcare coughs up', *Mail & Guardian*, 12 November. https://mg.co.za/article/2010-11-12-netcare-coughs-up/ Accessed 9 December 2021.
21 Pretoria News, 1992. 'Why Was SADF in Phola Park?' 10 April 1992. http://www.historicalpapers.wits.ac.za/inventories/inv_pdfo/AK2702/AK2702-I-001-jpeg.pdfAccessed 16 March 2022
22 Wines, M. 205. 'Mark Thatcher pleads guilty in plot'. *The New York Times*, 14 January. https://www.nytimes.com/2005/01/14/world/europe/mark-thatcher-pleads-guilty-in-plot.html Accessed 14 February 2022.
23 Williams, M. 2004. 'US charges SA man over nukes' IOL. 13 January. https://www.iol.co.za/news/south-africa/us-charges-sa-man-over-nukes-120545 Accessed 28 December 2021.
24 Schapiro, M. 2008. 'South Africa's nuclear underground'. *RevealNews*. 10 April. https://revealnews.org/article/south-africas-nuclear-underground/ Accessed 9 December 2021.
25 Carroll, R. 2004. 'Nuclear charges dropped'. The Guardian. 9 September. https://www.theguardian.com/world/2004/sep/09/southafrica.rorycarroll Accessed 15 March 2022.
26 Swart, M. 2008. 'The Wouter Basson prosecution: The closest South

Africa came to Nuremberg?' Max-Planck-Institut für ausländisches öffentliches Recht und Völkerrecht Mia Swart. https://www.zaoerv.de/68_2008/68_2008_1_b_209_226.pdf Accessed 9 December 2021.

27   Gould, C and Folb, P. 2002. 'Project Coast: Apartheid's Chemical and Biological Warfare Programme'. United Nations Institute for Disarmament Research Geneva, Switzerland, and Centre for Conflict Resolution, Cape Town, South Africa. p240 https://www.unidir.org/files/publications/pdfs/project-coast-apartheid-s-chemical-and-biological-warfare-programme-296.pdf Accessed 9 December 2021.

28   Constitutional Court of South Africa. 2004. The State versus Wouter Basson. Case CCT30/03. Judgment.

29   National Prosecuting Authority Annual Report 2005-2006. p53.

30   Report on the work of the IMT, Eastern Cape. NCOP. 11 September 2003; and Briefing to Parliament by National Director of Public Prosecutions, BT Ngcuka, 17-18 June 2004.

31   *Mail & Guardian*. 2004. 'Greedy officials grab grants'. 17 December. https://mg.co.za/article/2004-12-17-greedy-officials-grab-grants/ Accessed 9 December 2021.

32   In 2005 the legality of the Scorpions' mandate was called into question and problems were raised about the apparently strained relationship between the Scorpions and the SAPS. President Mbeki appointed Judge Sisi Khampepe to inquire into and make recommendations regarding the mandate and location of the Scorpions.

33   Impact of DSO on Crime in South Africa. 2008. Internal Paper.

34   Ibid.

35   Author interview with Lungisa Dyosi, 29 November 2016.

36   SAPA. 1999. 'Ngcuka not sure if TRC cases worth cost'. IOL. 26 August. https://www.iol.co.za/news/south-africa/ngcuka-not-sure-if-trc-cases-worth-cost-10666 Accessed 15 March 2021.

37   Bubenzer, O. 2009. *Post-TRC Prosecutions in South Africa: Accountability for political crimes after the Truth and Reconciliation Commission's amnesty process*. Martinus Nijhoff Publishers. p29.

38   CNN. 2003. 'South African white supremacist convicted of bombings'. 12 November. https://edition.cnn.com/2003/WORLD/africa/11/12/safrica.terreblanche.reut/index.html Accessed 9 December 2021; and Bubenzer, O. 2009. *Post-TRC Prosecutions in South Africa: Accountability for political crimes after the Truth and Reconciliation Commission's amnesty process*. Martinus Nijhoff Publishers. p64.

39   The charges against Koole and Van Zyl were later provisionally withdrawn, the Amnesty Committee was never convened, and the charges were never reinstated.

40   News24. 2004. 'NPA won't prosecute ANC 37'. 2 June. https://www.news24.com/news24/npa-wont-prosecute-anc-37-20040602 Accessed 15 March 2021.

41   Feni, L and Flanagan, L. 2001. 'Two face trial for Bisho massacre',

Daily Dispatch. 1 June. https://web.archive.org/web/20060701011907/http://www.dispatch.co.za/2001/06/01/easterncape/AAMASACR.HTM Accessed 15 March 2021.

42   Bubenzer, O. 2009. *Post-TRC Prosecutions in South Africa: Accountability for political crimes after the Truth and Reconciliation Commission's amnesty process.* Martinus Nijhoff Publishers. p55.

43   High Court of South Africa (Gauteng Division, Pretoria). 2018. Supporting Affidavit on Behalf of First Respondent, Raymond Christopher Macadam Case No. 76755/18. 1 November.

44   Ibid.

Chapter 13

1   Supreme Court of Appeal. 1999. Judgment. S v Ndweni and Others (376/94, 390/94, 639/98) [1999] ZASCA 51; [1999] 4 All SA 377 (A) (31 August 1999). p4.

2   *Mail & Guardian*. 1998. 'Why are the Eikenhof Three still in jail?' 10 December. https://mg.co.za/article/1998-12-18-why-are-the-eikenhof-three-still-in/ Accessed 10 December 2021.

3   SABC. 2000. Application of Phila Martin Dolo. 24 July. Truth Commission Special Report https://sabctrc.saha.org.za/originals/amntrans/2000/200724jh.htm Accessed 25 January 2022.

4   Supreme Court of Appeal. 1999. Judgment. S v Ndweni and Others (376/94, 390/94, 639/98) [1999] ZASCA 51; [1999] 4 All SA 377 (A) (31 August 1999). pp10-11.

5   Hlongwa, W and Nkosi, S. 1998. 'South Africa: Judge blasts "ANC" Super AG'. *Mail & Guardian*. 11 December. https://allafrica.com/stories/199812110130.html Accessed 28 December 2021.

6   DaimlerChrysler was a 'sister company' of the European Aeronautic Defence and Space Company (EADS), one of the potential suppliers of weapons in the arms deal. The car purchase was facilitated by Michael Woerfel, CEO of EADS, and had taken place while the government was in the process of identifying preferred tenders during the arms deal. When EADS later become a beneficiary of the arms deal, this raised suspicions that the discount Yengeni had received was an act of corruption between Yengeni and Woerfel.

7   Carroll, R. 2003. 'ANC's apartheid-era hero jailed for fraud' *The Guardian*. 20 March. https://www.theguardian.com/world/2003/mar/20/rorycarroll Accessed 8 October 2020.

8   Ibid.

9   Regional Court. (Regional Division of Northern Transvaal.) 2003. The State vs TS Yengeni and MJ Woerfel. Case No 14/09193/01. Accused No 1's Plea of Guilty. p5.

10   Ibid. pp6-7.

11   This issue came up again in 2008 during the hearings at parliament on the Scorpions' closure, when the unit was accused of being 'infiltrated'

by the old order. Willie Hofmeyr explained that nine of approximately 300 investigators in the Scorpions had worked for the former apartheid security police. (Scorpions Closure public hearings. 2008. Day 6 & response to public submissions. 9 September. https://pmg.org.za/committee-meeting/9602/ Accessed 25 January 2022.)

12   In 2004, the theft charge was overturned on appeal by Judge Eberhard Bertelsmann and the fraud sentence converted to a suspended sentence. Explaining his decision, Judge Bertelsmann said Madikizela-Mandela's actions had not been committed for personal gain but added that 'dishonesty in high places cannot be tolerated either'. He later said Madikizela-Mandela had 'engaged in a Robin Hood-like scheme to help poor persons to obtain funds from a banking institution'. (Hunter-Gault, C. 2004. 'Winnie Mandela wins jail appeal'. CNN.com International. 5 July. http://edition.cnn.com/2004/WORLD/africa/07/05/safrica.winnie/ Accessed 10 December 2021; and High Court of South Africa (Transvaal Provincial Division). Yengeni vs State (A1079/03) [2005] ZAGPHC 117 (11 November 2005). Judgment. para 68.)

13   In 1998, Bophuthatswana's ex-president, Lucas Mangope, was found guilty on 102 counts of theft and fraud. He received a two-year suspended sentence and was ordered to repay his victims.

14   Laurence, P. 1999. Boesak found guilty of theft and fraud' *Irish Times*, 18 March. https://www.irishtimes.com/news/boesak-found-guilty-of-theft-and-fraud-1.164134 Accessed 18 March 2022.

15   SAPA. 2001. 'Stolen cellphone won't keep Boesak in jail'. IOL. 17 May. https://www.iol.co.za/news/south-africa/stolen-cellphone-wont-keep-boesak-in-jail-65010 Accessed 10 December 2021.

16   India refused to make the evidence (tapes) available to the King Commission. While this impeded the work of the commission, Judge King conceded that the Indian authorities may have had good reason to keep the tapes under wraps. (Commission of Inquiry into Cricket Match Fixing and Related Matters Final Report, Judge EL King. June 2001. p8. https://www.gov.za/sites/default/files/gcis_document/201409/kingreport0.pdf Accessed 10 December 2021.)

17   Commission of Inquiry into Cricket Match Fixing and Related Matters Final Report, Judge EL King. June 2001. para 65. https://www.gov.za/sites/default/files/gcis_document/201409/kingreport0.pdf Accessed 10 December 2021.

18   Boley, J. 2000. 'The Rise and Fall of Billy Rautenbach. How a South African entrepreneur challenged the establishment - and lost.' *Automotive News*, 1 March. https://www.autonews.com/article/20000301/SUB/3010705/the-rise-and-fall-of-billy-rautenbach Accessed 16 March 2022

19   McGreal, C. 1999. 'The motiveless murder and Napoleon of Africa.' *The Guardian*. 16 December. https://www.theguardian.com/world/1999/dec/16/chrismcgreal. Accessed 24 March 2022.

20   SAPA. 2000. 'Constitutional Court upholds Rautenbach raid.' IOL, 25 August. https://www.iol.co.za/news/south-africa/constitutional-court-upholds-rautenbach-raid-48155 Accessed 16 March 2022

21 SAPA. 2000. 'Rautenbach's assets seized'. News24. 19 September. https://www.news24.com/news24/rautenbachs-assets-seized-20000919-2 Accessed 10 December 2021.
22 Ibid.
23 Wheels24. 2009. 'R40m fine for ex-Hyundai boss'. News24. 23 September. https://www.news24.com/wheels/r40m-fine-for-ex-hyundai-sa-boss-20090923 Accessed 10 December 2021.
24 South Gauteng High Court. Johannesburg. The State v JS Selebi. Case No 25/09. 5 July 2010. Judgment. para 70.
25 Agliotti had given $30 000 (about R240 000) of this amount to Selebi. (Ibid. para 103.)
26 Ibid. para 101.
27 Ibid. para 105.
28 The letter included questions about Rautenbach's business dealings in Africa and asked about his dealings, if any, with intelligence officials and whether he was aware of accounts being used to launder money in South Africa. (Ibid.)
29 Ibid. para 406.
30 Statement by Bulelani Ngcuka, 5 October 2009.

Chapter 14

1 Ellis, E. 2001. 'Pagad cop tells of escaping bloody ambush'. IOL. 14 August. https://www.iol.co.za/news/south-africa/pagad-cop-tells-of-escaping-bloody-ambush-71976 Accessed 9 December 2021.
2 Ellis, E. 2001. 'Staggie sold R100 000 in drugs a day, judge told'. *Cape Argus*. 19 June.
3 Zavis, A. 1996. 'Mob burns Cape Town gang leader to death'. AP News. 5 August. https://apnews.com/article/7c95a7e39cfcfd360c89bad40c7ffb12 Accessed 20 March 2021.
4 Ellis, E. 2000. 'G-force suspects face over 40 murder charges'. IOL. 11 October. https://www.iol.co.za/news/south-africa/g-force-suspects-face-over-40-murder-charges-50556 Accessed 9 December 2021.
5 SAPA. 2000. 'They can't scare us off – Ngcuka'. News24. 8 September. https://www.news24.com/news24/they-cant-scare-us-off-ngcuka-20000908 Accessed 9 December 2021.
6 Cohen, M. 2001. 'Seven escape from S. Africa court' AP News. 4 October. https://apnews.com article/0e7e7c96138eb7f7eaec9dfc16ae65df Accessed 9 December 2021.
7 IOL. 2001. 'Pagad killer gets 11 life terms for murders'. 29 March. https://www.iol.co.za/news/south-africa/pagad-killer-gets-11-life-terms-for-murders-63154 Accessed 9 December 2021.
8 Francis, V. 2001. Prosecution Task Force on Car-Hijacking: Final evaluation report. Bureau of Justice Assistance, USA. November. p2 https://www.ojp.gov/ncjrs/virtual-library/abstracts/prosecution-task-

NOTES

force-car-hijacking-final-evaluation-report Accessed 10 December 2021.
9 Ibid. pii.
10 Ibid.
11 Ibid.
12 Speech to National Prosecuting Authority Senior Management Conference by BT Ngcuka, National Director of Public Prosecutions, 2000.
13 Francis, V. 2001. Prosecution Task Force on Car-Hijacking: Final evaluation report. Bureau of Justice Assistance, USA. November. p9 https://www.ojp.gov/ncjrs/virtual-library/abstracts/prosecution-task-force-car-hijacking-final-evaluation-report Accessed 10 December 2021.
14 Koch, E. 1996. 'IFP got weapons from the police'. *Mail & Guardian*. 20 September. https://mg.co.za/article/1996-09-20-ifp-got-weapons-from-the-police Accessed 8 October 2020.
15 Potgieter, D. 2013. 'Eugene De Kock's explosive 64-tonne question'. *Daily Maverick*. 27 March. https://www.dailymaverick.co.za/article/2013-03-27-eugene-de-kocks-explosive-64-tonne-question/ Accessed 10 December 2021.
16 Ibid.
17 Taylor, R. 2002. 'Justice Denied: Political violence in KwaZulu-Natal after 1994'. *African Affairs*, 101 (405). October.
18 *Mail & Guardian*. 1998. 'Nkabinde acquitted'. 1 May. https://mg.co.za/article/1998-05-01-nkabinde-acquitted/ Accessed 10 December 2021.
19 Ragavaloo, A. 2008. *Richmond: Living in the shadow of death*. STE Publishers. Kindle edition. p242.
20 Ibid. p288.
21 Impact of DSO on Crime in South Africa. 2008. Internal paper.

Chapter 15

1 National Prosecuting Authority; Asset Forfeiture Unit, Special Investigating Unit, Directorate of Special Operations: Budget Hearings, 5 June 2002. https://pmg.org.za/committee-meeting/1540/ Accessed 28 December 2021.
2 The preamble to the Prevention of Organised Crime Act, No 121 of 1998, made it clear that extraordinary measures were going to be taken, and that it was going to be very tough on crime. And the penalties were severe – the maximum penalty for racketeering was R1 billion or life, the highest on the statute book. Money-laundering and being in possession of the proceeds of crime could mean a fine of R100 million or 30 years' imprisonment.
3 Mujuzi, JD. 2010. *Ten years of the South African Prevention of Organised Crime Act (1999-2009)*. Criminal Justice Initiative of Open Society Foundation for South Africa. p2.
4 In April 2001, Willie Hofmeyr was promoted to the position of deputy NDPP. He still headed up the unit but Ouma Rabaji was appointed as special director in the unit.

5   Prevention of Organised Crime Act 121 of 1998. https://www.justice.gov.za/legislation/acts/1998-121.pdf
6   Western Cape High Court, Cape Town. 2003. National Director of Public Prosecutions v Prophet (5926/01) [2003] ZAWCHC 16 (22 May 2003). Judgment.
7   Constitutional Court of South Africa. 2002. National Director of Public Prosecutions and Another v Mohamed NO and Others. Case CCT 13/02. Judgment. 12 June. para 17. http://www.saflii.org/za/cases/ZACC/2002/9.html Accessed 28 December 2021.
8   National Prosecuting Authority Parliamentary Report 2002/2003. p7.
9   Ibid.
10 Address by the National Director of Public Prosecutions, BT Ngcuka, at the Annual General Meeting of the Institute of Directors, Cape Town, 3 June 2004.
11 Author interview with Lungisa Dyosi, 29 November 2016.
12 Supreme Court of Appeal of South Africa. 1999. National Director of Public Prosecutions vs GG Carolus and others. Case No 162/99. Judgment. http://www.saflii.org/za/cases/ZASCA/1999/101.pdf Accessed 17 February 2022.
13 Roberts, B. 1999. '"Convoluted Act" sees Basson' assets returned'. *Mail & Guardian*. 26 August. https://mg.co.za/article/1999-08-26-convoluted-act-sees-bassons-assets-returned/ Accessed 15 February 2022.
14 Zapiro. 1999. Cartoon in *Mail & Guardian*. 26 August.
15 Green, P and Randall, E. 1999. 'Anger over asset-grab fiasco'. IOL. 29 August. https://www.iol.co.za/news/south-africa/anger-over-asset-grab-fiasco-10561 Accessed 13 December 2021.
16 Prevention of Organised Crime Amendment Act, No 24, 1999.
17 National Prosecuting Authority Annual Report 2001-2002. p29.
18 Western Cape High Court, Cape Town. 2003. National Director of Public Prosecutions v Prophet (5926/01) [2003] ZAWCHC 16 (22 May 2003). Judgment. para 28.
19 Ibid. para 58.
20 National Prosecuting Authority Annual Report 1999-2000.
21 National Prosecuting Authority Annual Report 2001-2002. p34.
22 National Prosecuting Authority; Asset Forfeiture Unit, Special Investigating Unit, Directorate of Special Operations: Budget Hearings, 5 June 2002. https://pmg.org.za/committee-meeting/1540/ Accessed 17 February 2022.
23 Hofmeyr. W. 2002. Seizing Criminal Assets to Fight Crime: National Prosecuting Authority Report to Parliament, AFU. 5 June.
24 Author interview with Lungisa Dyosi, 29 November 2016.
25 SAPA. 2000. 'Pension fraudsters get 8 years'. News24. 28 November. https://www.news24.com/News24/Pension-fraudsters-get-8-

years-20001128 Accessed 13 December 2021.

26   Author interview with Lungisa Dyosi, 29 November 2016
27   SAPA. 2000. 'Alleged kidnappers' assets can be seized'. IOL. 7 January. https://www.iol.co.za/news/south-africa/alleged-kidnappers-assets-can-be-seized-25103 Accessed 25 January 2022.
28   SAPA. 2001. 'Seized assets' money to go back to victims'. News24. 18 March. https://www.news24.com/news24/seized-assets-money-to-go-back-to-victims-20010318 Accessed 13 December 2021.
29   *Crime, Law and Social Change*. 2001. Part Five: Africa. 36 (241–284). p260. https://doi.org/10.1023/A:1017438522544.
30   Vapi, X. 1999. 'Asset Unit raids drug lord's home'. IOL. 15 October. https://www.iol.co.za/news/south-africa/asset-unit-raids-druglords-home-16271 Accessed 14 December 2021.
31   SAPA. 2000. '"Drug kingpin" rearrested at Swazi border'. IOL. 16 September. https://www.iol.co.za/news/africa/drug-kingpin-rearrested-at-swazi-border-43456 Accessed 14 December 2021.
32   Broughton, T. 2001. '"Drug baron" to pay for fight against crime'. IOL. 8 November. https://www.iol.co.za/news/south-africa/drug-baron-to-pay-for-fight-against-crime-76538 Accessed 14 December 2021.
33   Van Rheede, J. 2002. 'Tombstone taken as pyramid schemers pay up'. IOL. 18 September. https://www.iol.co.za/news/south-africa/tombstone-taken-as-pyramid-schemers-pay-up-94749 Accessed 14 December 2021.

Chapter 16

1   Schönteich, M and Louw, A. 2001. 'Crime in South Africa: A country and cities profile'. Institute for Security Studies. Occasional Paper No 49-2001. https://issafrica.s3.amazonaws.com/site/uploads/paper49.pdf Accessed 9 October 2020.
2   Blaney, J. 2010. 'Building Police Capacity in Post-Conflict Communities'. Paper. Deloitte and Center for Complex Operations. pp12-13. https://africacenter.org/wp-content/uploads/2016/01/Let_Loose_Scorpions.pdf Accessed 1 October 2020.
3   Address of the President of the Republic of South Africa, Thabo Mbeki, at the Opening of Parliament, National Assembly, Cape Town, 25 June 1999.
4   Mbeki had given his ministers just two weeks to finalise everything. It would, in fact, take 18 months from Mbeki's announcement for the Scorpions' legislation to be passed by parliament.
5   In terms of the NPA Act, No 32 of 1998, Section 7 https://www.gov.za/sites/default/files/gcis_document/201409/a32-98.pdf Accessed 15 February 2022
6   Schönteich, M. 2001. 'Lawyers for the People: The South African Prosecution Service', Monograph. p43.

7   Richards, R. 2000. Address at the 2000 annual national conference of the Security Association of South Africa, Midrand. 12 October.
8   Schönteich, M. 2001. 'Lawyers for the People: The South African Prosecution Service', Monograph. p43.
9   Directorate of Special Operations 'Scorpions' Presentation to Parliament. Advocate LF McCarthy. 18 June 2004.
10   Author interview with Lungisa Dyosi, 29 November 2016.
11   Khampepe Commission of Inquiry into the Mandate and Location of the Directorate of Special Operations ('The DSO'). Final Report. 2006. Honourable Justice Sisi Khampepe, Commissioner. February. pp108-110.
12   Author interview with Lungisa Dyosi, 29 November 2016.
13   Parliamentary Monitoring Group. 2008. Scorpions Closure public hearings: Day 7 & response to public submissions. 10 September. https://pmg.org.za/committee-meeting/9611/ Accessed 13 December 2021.
14   Redpath, J. 2004. 'Monograph 96: The Scorpions: Analysing the Directorate of Special Operations'. p21. https://www.files.ethz.ch/isn/118337/96%20FULL.pdf Accessed 13 December 2021.
15   Ibid. p24.
16   Parliamentary Monitoring Group. 1999. Scorpions: briefing. 16 November. https://pmg.org.za/committee-meeting/4714/ Accessed 9 October 2020.
17   Roughly translated, '*guanxi*' means 'relationship' and refers to the Chinese system of building mutually beneficial networks that can be used for business and personal purposes. These relationships are generally much deeper than the normal business relationships in the West.
18   Since opening up to the outside world in 1994, South Africa had become part of the international drug trafficking network. Mandrax, a street name for a drug containing the sedative methaqualone, was the second most commonly used illicit drug at the time.
19   SAPA. 2000. 'Biggest Mandrax bust in SA history'. IOL. 15 August. https://www.iol.co.za/news/south-africa/biggest-mandrax-bust-in-sa-history-47309 Accessed 13 December 2021.
20   Scorpions' Report to Parliament, 2003. (Author's copy.)
21   Nhlapo, T and SAPA-AP. 2003. 'Mega Mandrax bust breaks SA record'. IOL. 4 July. https://www.iol.co.za/news/south-africa/mega-mandrax-bust-breaks-sa-record-109163 Accessed 13 December 2021.
22   Newman, L. 2004. 'Scorpions make R1bn Mandrax bust'. IOL. 16 August. https://www.iol.co.za/news/south-africa/scorpions-make-r1bn-mandrax-bust-219651 Accessed 13 December 2021.
23   Lindow, M. 2003. 'South Africa's abalone plundered / Appetite for valued mollusk fueling social, environmental crisis'. SFGate. 28 November. https://www.sfgate.com/green/article/South-Africa-s-abalone-plundered-Appetite-for-2525863.php Accessed 3 October 2020.

NOTES

24 Yeld, J. 2004. 'Secret agent sank "perlemoen godmother"'. IOL. 8 June. https://www.iol.co.za/news/south-africa/secret-agent-sank-perlemoen-godmother-213979 Accessed 13 December 2021.

25 Joseph, N. 2003. 'Perlemoen suspect may run racket from prison'. IOL. 12 December. https://www.iol.co.za/news/south-africa/perlemoen-suspect-may-run-racket-from-prison-119061 Accessed 13 December 2021.

26 US District Court Southern District of New York. Plaintiff against AM Bengis et al. Case No 1:03-cr-00308-LAK Document 249. Filed 14 June 2013.

27 *Engineering News*. 2002. 'Scorpions in illegal fishing sting'. 31 October. https://www.engineeringnews.co.za/print-version/scorpions-in-illegal-fishing-sting-2002-10-31 Accessed 2 September 2021.

28 News24. 2002. 'Fishing king fined R250 000'. 4 November. https://www.news24.com/News24/Fishing-king-fined-R250-000-20021104 Accessed 2 September 2021.

29 Impact of DSO on Crime South Africa. 2008. Internal paper.

30 Marais, J. 2013. 'Why King agreed to R718m for a new start'. *Business Day*. 1 September. https://www.businesslive.co.za/bd/companies/2013-09-01-why-king-agreed-to-r718m-for-a-new-start/ Accessed 13 December 2021.

31 Legalbrief. 2021. 'Dave King, SARS slug it out in high-stakes battle'. 13 December.

32 Hosken, G. 2004. 'State coffers to get major boost'. IOL. 23 November. https://www.iol.co.za/news/south-africa/state-coffers-to-get-major-boost-227704 Accessed 13 December 2021.

33 Nicholson, Z. 2011. 'End of the road for LeisureNet fraudsters'. *Cape Times*. 27 March.

34 Ibid.

35 Ibid.

36 Impact of DSO on Crime South Africa. 2008. Internal paper.

37 National Prosecuting Authority Parliamentary Report 2002/2003. p17.

38 IOL. 2003. 'Committed cops put an end to gang's reign'. 28 July. https://www.iol.co.za/news/south-africa/committed-cops-put-an-end-to-gangs-reign-110062 Accessed 13 December 2021.

39 Prevention of Organised Crime Act, No 121, 1998. Schedule 1. https://www.justice.gov.za/legislation/acts/1998-121.pdf

40 National Prosecuting Authority Parliamentary Report 2002/2003. p16.

41 Ibid.

42 National Prosecuting Authority Annual Report 2005-2006. p39.

43 Brummer, S. 199. 'Palazzolo: The mobster from Burgersdorp'. *Mail & Guardian*. 19 November. https://mg.co.za/article/1999-11-19-palazzolo-the-mobster-from-burgersdorp/ Accessed 25 January 2022.

44 *Crime, Law and Social Change*. 2001. Part Five: Africa. 36 (241–284). p260. https://doi.org/10.1023/A:1017438522544.

45	Dolley, C. 2012. 'How Thai cops arrested Palazzolo'. *Cape Times.* 23 April. https://www.iol.co.za/capetimes/special-reports/how-thai-cops-arrested-palazzolo-1283450 Accessed 13 December 2021.
46	Pikoli, V and Wiener, M. 2013. *My Second Initiation: The memoir of Vusi Pikoli.* Picador Africa. p185.
47	Redpath, J. 2004. 'Monograph 96: The Scorpions: Analysing the Directorate of Special Operations'. pp34-35. https://www.files.ethz.ch/isn/118337/96%20FULL.pdf Accessed 13 December 2021.
48	Hosken, G. 2002. 'Top dogs nabbed in road fund fraud raid'. IOL. 27 March. https://www.iol.co.za/news/south-africa/top-dogs-nabbed-in-road-fund-fraud-raid-84040 Accessed 13 December 2021.
49	Redpath, J. 2004. 'Monograph 96: The Scorpions: Analysing the Directorate of Special Operations'. p54. https://www.files.ethz.ch/isn/118337/96%20FULL.pdf Accessed 13 December 2021.
50	National Prosecuting Authority Parliamentary Report 2002/2003. p14.
51	National Prosecuting Authority Annual Report 2005-2006. p34.
52	Redpath, J. 2004. 'Monograph 96: The Scorpions: Analysing the Directorate of Special Operations'. p52 https://www.files.ethz.ch/isn/118337/96%20FULL.pdf Accessed 13 December 2021.
53	Justice Budget: Input by National Prosecuting Authority and Specialist Units. 10 June 2003. https://pmg.org.za/committee-meeting/2562/ Accessed 28 December 2003.
54	Schönteich, M. 2003. 'NPA in the dock. Thumbs up for prosecution service'. South African Crime Quarterly. 2003, No 3.
55	Blaney, J. 2010. 'Building Police Capacity in Post-Conflict Communities'. Paper. Deloitte and Center for Complex Operations. p13. https://africacenter.org/wp-content/uploads/2016/01/Let_Loose_Scorpions.pdf Accessed 13 December 2021.

Chapter 17

1	Mapiloko, J and Sole, S. 2010. 'Kebble's voice from the grave'. *Mail & Guardian.* 4 June. https://mg.co.za/article/2010-06-04-kebbles-voice-from-the-grave/ Accessed 25 January 2022.
2	Wa Afrika, M, Bezuidenhout, J and Jurgens, A. 2002. 'Arms-deal suspect defends Zuma'. *Sunday Times.* 15 December.
3	Koopman, A. 2003. 'Scorpions boss stung by smear campaign. *Weekend Argus.* 28 June.
4	Koopman, A. 2003. 'Ngcuka vows to deal with "comrade criminals"'. IOL. 26 July 2003. https://www.iol.co.za/news/politics/ngcuka-vows-to-deal-with-comrade-criminals-110401 Accessed 14 December 2021.
5	Bain, J. 2002. 'Kebble magnates to answer fraud charges'. *Business Day.* 9 December. https://allafrica.com/stories/200212090768.html Accessed 28 December 2002.
6	Malan, R. 2012. *The Lion Sleeps Tonight and Other Stories of Africa.* Grove Press. p262.

NOTES

7 Statement of Norbett Glenn Agliotti, taken by Andrew Leask, Chief Special Investigator, Directorate of Special Operations, National Prosecuting Authority. Johannesburg, 21 November 2007. paras 47-49.

8 The Shaik brothers are Chippy, the former head of the government's arms procurement committee; Schabir, whose company got a slice of the R66-billion arms deal; Moe, a former ANC intelligence operative; and Yunis, who was part of the legal team representing Moe at the Hefer Commission. A fifth brother, Faizel, is not involved in politics. (Smith, A. 2003. 'Band of brothers in the thick of things'. 22 November. IOL. https://www.iol.co.za/news/politics/band-of-brothers-in-the-thick-of-things-117369 Accessed 15 December 2021.)

9 Statement of Norbett Glenn Agliotti, taken by Andrew Leask, Chief Special Investigator, Directorate of Special Operations, National Prosecuting Authority. Johannesburg, 21 November 2007. paras 47-49.

10 After Kebble's death, Gleason was exposed as having received payments from Kebble when the estate sued him for 22 payments of R50 000 and upwards between 2003 and 2005. (Barron, C. 2014. 'Obituary: David Gleason – columnist who became the paid voice of Brett Kebble'. *Sunday Times*. 16 February.)

11 Sergeant, B. 2006. *Brett Kebble: The Inside Story*. Zebra Press.

12 Ngcuka, B. 2003. Submission prepared for Hefer Commission. (Author's copy)

13 SAPA. 2003. 'Zuma questions Scorpions' motives'. Polity. 23 July. https://www.polity.org.za/print-version/zuma-questions-scorpionsx2019-motives-2003-07-28 Accessed 15 December 2021.

14 Ngcuka, B. 2003. Submission prepared for Hefer Commission. (Author's copy)

15 Ibid.

16 Ibid.

Chapter 18

1 *City Press*. 2003. 'Was Ngcuka a spy?' 6 September. https://www.news24.com/citypress/SouthAfrica/News/Was-Ngcuka-a-spy-20100614 Accessed 15 December 2021.

2 The National Intelligence Service was replaced on 1 January 1995 by the South African Secret Service and the National Intelligence Agency (NIA).

3 *City Press*. 2003. 'Was Ngcuka a spy?' 6 September. https://www.news24.com/citypress/SouthAfrica/News/Was-Ngcuka-a-spy-20100614 Accessed 15 December 2021.

4 SAPA. 2003. 'Shaik "has file with 880 spy suspects"'. IOL. 21 November. https://www.iol.co.za/news/politics/shaik-has-file-with-880-spy-suspects-117281 Accessed 16 December 2021.

5 Bauer, N. 2011. 'Mac Maharaj and controversy: a timeline'. *Mail & Guardian*. 22 November. https://mg.co.za/article/2011-11-22-

mac-maharaj-and-controversy-a-timeline/ Accessed 26 January 2022.
6   SAPA. 2003. 'Maharaj resigns from FirstRand'. IOL. 14 August. https://www.iol.co.za/news/politics/maharaj-resigns-from-firstrand-110944 Accessed 15 December 2021.
7   Berger, G. 2004. Ethics and Excuses: the scapegoating of Vusi Mona. Paper presented to Saccom conference, Port Elizabeth, 1 October. https://guyberger.ru.ac.za/fulltext/hefersaccom1.doc Accessed 28 December 2021.
8   Ibid.
9   Author interview with Dumisani Tabata, 10 February 2017.
10 Ibid.
11 Seepe, J and Mkhabela, M. 2003. 'Ngcuka "Turns to God"'. *City Press*. 21 September.
12 Tsedu, M. 2003. 'Why we did not run the Ngcuka spy story'. *Sunday Times*. 21 September.
13 Author interview with Madeleine Fullard, 28 August 2021.
14 In 1989 Gideon Nieuwoudt, along with two other white security police, planted a bomb in a car in Port Elizabeth, killing four black police officers. Nieuwoudt, who claimed he killed his colleagues because they'd joined the ANC, was sentenced to 20 years.
15 Author interview with Madeleine Fullard, 28 August 2021.
16 Ibid.
17 In the late 1990s Siphiwe Nyanda, then deputy head of the South African National Defence Force, and others (including Winnie Mandela) were accused by General Georg Meiring, head of the defence force, of being involved in a plan to unseat President Mandela. Mandela appointed a commission of inquiry headed by Ismail Mahomed, Pius Langa and Richard Goldstone, which dismissed the claims and described Meiring's accusations as a fantasy. Meiring resigned in disgrace. (News24. 2015. 'ANC obsession with conspiracies is dangerous'. 16 March. https://www.news24.com/News24/ANC-obsession-with-conspiracies-is-dangerous-20150430 Accessed 28 December 2021.)
18 Author interview with Dumisani Tabata, 10 February 2017.
19 A reference to amaGqunukhwebe, the tribe Bulelani belongs to.
20 Author interview with Dumisani Tabata, 10 February 2017.

Chapter 19

1   Commission of Inquiry into Allegations of Spying Against National Director of Public Prosecutions, BT Ngcuka. 19 September 2003 to 7 January 2004. First and Final Report. p6. https://www.justice.gov.za/commissions/comm_hefer/2004%2001%2020_hefer_report.pdf Accessed 16 December 2021.
2   Ibid.
3   Address by the Head of the National Prosecuting Authority, Mr Bulelani

NOTES

       Ngcuka, to the Johannesburg Press Club. 22 January 2004.

4   Ngcuka, B. 2003. Submission prepared for Hefer Commission. (Author's copy)

5   Commission of Inquiry into Allegations of Spying Against National Director of Public Prosecutions, BT Ngcuka. 19 September 2003 to 7 January 2004. First and Final Report. p56. https://www.justice.gov.za/commissions/comm_hefer/2004%2001%2020_hefer_report.pdf Accessed 16 December 2021.

6   Ibid. p42.

7   Ellis, E. 2003. 'Mac's astonishing admission'. IOL. 19 November. https://www.iol.co.za/news/politics/macs-astonishing-admission-117460 Accessed 28 December 2021.

8   Moe Shaik Submission in the Hefer Commission of Enquiry. O'Malley archives. https://omalley.nelsonmandela.org/omalley/index.php/site/q/03lv03445/04lv04015/05lv04120/06lv04123.htm Accessed 16 December 2021.

9   However, under cross-examination he told the commission that he had handed his 'secret' database – consisting of ten CDs – to the legal advisor of intelligence minister Lindiwe Sisulu and that he was no longer in possession of the database. (SAPA. 2003. 'Mo hands over secret database of 888 "spies".' IOL, 24 November. https://www.iol.co.za/news/politics/mo-hands-over-secret-database-of-888-spies-117754 Accessed 18 February 2022.)

10   SAPA. 2003. 'Shaik "has file with 880 spy suspects"'. IOL. 21 November. https://www.iol.co.za/news/politics/shaik-has-file-with-880-spy-suspects-117281 Accessed 16 December 2021.

11   Author interview with Dumisani Tabata, 10 February 2017.

12   Commission of Inquiry into Allegations of Spying Against National Director of Public Prosecutions, BT Ngcuka. 19 September 2003 to 7 January 2004. First and Final Report. pp43-44. https://www.justice.gov.za/commissions/comm_hefer/2004%2001%2020_hefer_report.pdf Accessed 16 December 2021.

13   Ibid. p21.

14   Ibid.

15   Mavimbela, V. 2018. *Time is Not the Measure*. Real African Publishers. p340.

16   Commission of Inquiry into Allegations of Spying Against National Director of Public Prosecutions, BT Ngcuka. 19 September 2003 to 7 January 2004. First and Final Report. p45. https://www.justice.gov.za/commissions/comm_hefer/2004%2001%2020_hefer_report.pdf Accessed 16 December 2021.

17   Ibid. p46.

18   Ibid. pp39-40.

19   Ibid. p5.

20 Berger, G. 2004. Ethics and Excuses: the scapegoating of Vusi Mona. Paper presented to Saccom conference, Port Elizabeth, 1 October. https://guyberger.ru.ac.za/fulltext/hefersaccom1.doc Accessed 28 December 2021.

21 Ellis, E and Gordin, J. 2003. 'Former City Press editor branded a "disgrace"'. IOL. 28 November. https://www.iol.co.za/news/politics/former-city-press-editor-branded-a-disgrace-118152 Accessed 16 December 2021.

22 Hefer said that he had been asked to refer Mona to the NPA for possible perjury charges but 'I would rather not do so because his employer has relieved him from his duties and, although his dismissal arose from other causes, I am satisfied that he has discredited himself to such a degree in the newspaper community that he will not find it easy to procure employment in that field again'. (Commission of Inquiry into Allegations of Spying Against National Director of Public Prosecutions, BT Ngcuka. 19 September 2003 to 7 January 2004. First and Final Report. p60-63. https://www.justice.gov.za/commissions/comm_hefer/2004%2001%2020_hefer_report.pdf Accessed 16 December 2021.)

23 Mbhele, W. 2003. 'Setting the Ngcuka record straight'. *City Press*, 29 November.

24 SAPA. 2003. 'City Press makes front page apology to Ngcuka'. IOL. 30 November. https://www.iol.co.za/news/politics/city-press-makes-front-page-apology-to-ngcuka-117571 Accessed 16 December 2021.

25 Commission of Inquiry into Allegations of Spying Against National Director of Public Prosecutions, BT Ngcuka. 19 September 2003 to 7 January 2004. First and Final Report. p51. https://www.justice.gov.za/commissions/comm_hefer/2004%2001%2020_hefer_report.pdf Accessed 16 December 2021.

26 Ibid.

27 Author interview with Dumisani Tabata, 10 February 2017

28 Ibid.

29 Ngcuka, B. 2003. Submission prepared for Hefer Commission (author's copy); and Ngcuka, B. 2003. 'Asoze ndijike – I will not turn back'. IOL. 11 December. https://www.iol.co.za/news/politics/asoze-ndijike-i-will-not-turn-back-119048 Accessed 16 December 2021.

30 Ibid.

31 *ANC Today*. 2003. 'Letter from the President: Reconciliation and social change must go together'. Vol 4, No. 3. 23-29 January. https://omalley.nelsonmandela.org/omalley/index.php/site/q/03lv03445/04lv04015/05lv04120/06lv04129.htm Accessed 16 December 2021.

32 Ibid.

33 Ibid.

34 Moe Shaik Submission in the Hefer Commission of Enquiry. O'Malley archives. https://omalley.nelsonmandela.org/omalley/index.php/

site/q/03lv03445/04lv04015/05lv04120/06lv04123.htm Accessed 16 December 2021.

35 Having defended Jacob Zuma so resolutely, Moe Shaik found himself on the opposite side in 2011 when he, along with two other top intelligence officials, was forced to resign as head of the South African Secret Service, apparently for authorising an investigation of the Gupta family. Ironically, it was now Shaik himself who was labelled a spy, and who found himself having to state that 'at no time was I an agent for the apartheid intelligence services or for any foreign intelligence services'. (Shaik, M. 2020. *The ANC Spy Bible: Surviving across enemy lines.* Tafelberg.)

Chapter 20

1 Address by Head of the NPA, Mr Bulelani Ngcuka, to the Johannesburg Press Club, 22 January 2004. https://www.polity.org.za/article/ngcuka-johannesburg-press-club-22012004-2004-01-22 Accessed 17 December 2021.

2 Ibid.

3 Ibid.

4 Ibid.

5 News24. 2004. 'Ngcuka: Hefer united us'. 11 February. https://www.news24.com/News24/Ngcuka-Hefer-united-us-20040211 Accessed 17 December 2021.

6 Special Report on an Investigation by the Public Protector of a Complaint by Deputy President J Zuma against the National Director of Public Prosecutions and the National Prosecuting Authority in Connection with a Criminal Investigation Conducted Against Him. 28 May 2004. https://static.pmg.org.za/docs/040529pprotect.htm Accessed 17 December 2021.

7 Ibid.

8 *Mail & Guardian.* 2004. 'Public Protector a liar and a sad case'. 30 May. https://mg.co.za/article/2004-05-30-public-protector-a-liar-and-sad-case/ Accessed 17 December 2021.

9 Ibid.

10 News24. 2004. 'It's open war'. 30 May. https://www.news24.com/news24/its-open-war-20040530 Accessed 17 December 2021.

11 Michaels, J. 2004. 'ANC rebukes trio over spat'. IOL. 2 June. https://www.iol.co.za/news/politics/anc-rebukes-trio-over-spat-213848 Accessed 17 December 2021.

12 Michaels, J. 2004. 'Ngcuka sorry, but says he'll fight Mushwana'. *Cape Times.* 4 June.

13 Ibid.

14 News24. 2004. 'Ngcuka, Mbeki showdown looms'. 6 June. https://www.news24.com/news24/ngcuka-mbeki-showdown-looms-20040606 Accessed 28 December 2021.

15 Pressly, D. 2004. 'National assembly mildly rebukes Ngcuka'. *Mail & Guardian*. 25 June.
16 Vapi, X, Msomi, S, Boyle, B and Mbhele, W. 2004. 'Ngcuka quits'. *Sunday Times*. 25 July.
17 SAPA. 2004. 'Ngcuka forced to quit, says PAC'. IOL. 25 July. https://www.iol.co.za/news/politics/ngcuka-forced-to-quit-says-pac-217996 Accessed 17 December 2021.
18 News24. 2004. 'Ngcuka was pushed – DA'. 26 July. https://www.news24.com/news24/ngcuka-was-pushed-da-20040726 Accessed 28 December 2021.
19 Oppelt, P. 2004. 'Mission accomplished: Outgoing NPA head Bulelani Ngcuka is no "headless chicken,"' *Sunday Times*. 1 August.
20 Ibid.
21 *Mail & Guardian*. 2004. 'Big shoes to fill'. 29 July.
22 Ibid.

Chapter 21

1 Sole, S and Dawes, N. 2005. 'Spy-war emails: What they really say'. *Mail & Guardian*. 15 December. https://mg.co.za/article/2005-12-15-spywar-emails-what-they-really-say/ Accessed 20 December 2021.
2 Stratcom, or 'strategic communications', was a police unit set up during apartheid to create and spread false narratives against political enemies of the National Party government. (Ibid.)
3 Ibid.
4 Ibid.
5 News24. 2006. 'Got the bastard by the balls'. 24 March. https://www.news24.com/news24/got-the-bastard-by-the-balls-20060324 Accessed 20 December 2021.
6 Ibid.
7 Ibid.
8 Author interview with Ronnie Kasrils, 20 January 2022.
9 Masetlha, Kunene and Madlala were acquitted in 2009, three years after the emails had surfaced.
10 Author interview with Ronnie Kasrils, 20 January 2022.
11 Statement by Bulelani Ngcuka, former NDPP, on the release of transcripts of proceedings of intercepted communications between him and Mr LF McCarthy as well as internal NPA memoranda relating to the decision to terminate the prosecution in the matter of S v Zuma and Thint Holdings. (Author's copy)
12 Ngcuka, B. 2014. 'How Mpshe manipulated the spy tapes'. *Sunday Times*. 5 October.
13 High Court of South Africa (Gauteng Division, Pretoria). Confirmatory Affidavit: WJ Downer. Case No 19577/2009. 2 June 2015. para 51.

14. Ibid. paras 62-63.
15. Ngcuka, B. 2014. 'How Mpshe manipulated the spy tapes'. *TimesLive Lifestyle*. 5 October. https://www.timeslive.co.za/sunday-times/lifestyle/2014-10-05-how-mpshe-manipulated-the-spy-tapes/ Accessed 26 January 2022.
16. Ibid.
17. Ibid.
18. Wa Afrika, M, Hofstatter, S and Rampedi, P. 2014. 'NPA boss lied about spy tapes: Ngcuka lashes out at Mpshe and Zuma'. *TimesLive*. 5 October. https://www.timeslive.co.za/politics/2014-10-05-npa-boss-lied-about-spy-tapes-ngcuka-lashes-out-at-mpshe-and-zuma/ Accessed 18 March 2022.
19. Herman, P. 2016. 'Decision to drop Zuma corruption charges "irrational", set aside - As it happened'. News24. 29 April. https://www.news24.com/news24/southafrica/news/live-zuma-to-hear-if-spy-tapes-judgment-will-be-set-aside-20160429 Accessed 30 December 2021.
20. This meant the NPA was now legally obliged to charge Zuma unless it appealed the decision. It did indeed appeal but lost the appeal in 2017 when the Supreme Court of Appeal upheld the 2016 ruling. The NPA reinstated the charges against Zuma in 2018.
21. In November 2005, an investigation began into charges that Jacob Zuma had raped a 31-year-old family friend at his home in Johannesburg. The alleged victim, Fezekile Ntsukela Kuzwayo, a member of a prominent ANC family and an HIV-positive Aids activist, used the alias 'Khwezi' to protect her identity. Rape charges were filed against Zuma in December 2005. On 8 May 2006, the court dismissed the charges on the grounds that the sexual act in question had been consensual.
22. *Mail & Guardian*. 2011. 'ANC: Heath resignation "regrettable"'. 16 December. https://mg.co.za/article/2011-12-16-anc-heath-resignation-regrettable/ Accessed 21 December 2021.
23. Ngcuka, B. 2011. 'An Open Letter to Advocate Willem Heath'. *TimesLive*. 11 December.

Chapter 22

1. IOL. 2003. 'Ngcuka love story unfolds before Hefer'. 11 December. https://www.iol.co.za/news/politics/ngcuka-love-story-unfolds-before-hefer-119044 Accessed 21 December 2021.
2. Author interview with Phumzile Mlambo-Ngcuka, 10 January 2017.
3. Ibid.
4. Ibid.
5. Ibid.
6. Ibid.
7. Ibid.

8 Makinana, A, Madisa, K and Khoza, A. 2021. 'Once-spurned Mbeki-ites return to ANC fold'. *Sunday Times*. 24 October. https://www.timeslive.co.za/sunday-times/news/politics/2021-10-24-once-spurned-mbeki-ites-return-to-the-anc-fold/ Accessed 22 December 2021.

9 Africa Criminal Justice Reform. 2018. 'The appointment and dismissal of the NDPP: Instability since 1998'. Dullah Omar Institute, University of the Western Cape. October. https://acjr.org.za/resource-centre/appoint-and-dismiss-of-ndpp-fs-7-fin.pdf Accessed 22 December 2021.

10 Speech by Saki Macozoma at the celebration of the appointment of Bulelani Ngcuka as the National Director of Public Prosecutions, Kyalami, 9 October 1998. (Author's copy)

Index

Ackerman, Anton *see* advocates
Ackermann, Laurie 160 *see also* Supreme Court
activist(s) 38, 40, 94–5, 106, 110, 187
   ANC 61–2, 76, 82
   anti-apartheid 77, 97
   Black Consciousness 51
   Jabavu, David 38
   Ngcukana, Boniswa 40
   Pebco Three 94, 187
   political 97, 114
   UDF 130
   veteran 83
Acts
   Arms and Ammunition 256
   Companies 181
   Criminal Procedure 203
   electoral 150
   Human Tissue 181
   Income Tax 181
   Non-Proliferation of Weapons of Mass Destruction 183
   NPA 173, 206
   Nuclear Energy 183
   Prevention of Organised Crime 33, 181, 185, 231, 232, 234, 256
   Public Finance Management 180
   Stock Exchange Control 181
   Suppression of Communism 55
   Terrorism 60, 63, 74
Adam, Dawood 180, 217
Admission of Advocates Amendment Bill 157
Advocate Devil *see* de Ville, Rosier *under* advocates
advocates 161, 162, 176, 177, 255
   Ackerman, Anton 181, 183, 184, 186, 187, 193

Batohi, Shamila 203–4, 336
Davids, Lynette 32, 278
de Ville, Rosier 157, 167
Dyosi, Lungisa 5, 32, 171, 176, 184–5, 233, 237, 246, 248, 278
Heath, Willem 8–10, 268, 326–27
Jordaan, Chris 180
Macadam, Chris 219, 223, 225
Majokweni, Thoko 178
Mapoma, Siyabulela 'Saks' 32, 186
Mastenbroek, Rudolph 32
Moerane, Boyce Marumo 80, 161, 290, 305, 328
Mzinyathi, Sibongile 32, 186
Nel, Gerrie 4–5, 206, 219
Nthai, Seth 307–8
Pretorius, Torie 183
affirmative action 141–42
AFU *see* Asset Forfeiture Unit (AFU)
agenda 30, 48, 102, 168, 275
Agent RS452 282-83, 293, *see also* Brereton, Vanessa
Aggett, Neil 77, 117
Agliotti, Glenn 207, 209, 268, 272
Agusta, Ricardo 257 *see also* Malatsigate
amnesty 70, 181, 186–88, 191, 192, 223, 235
ANC Women's League 198
ANC Youth League 6, 266
anti-apartheid 77, 90, 97, 104, 105, 125, 199
   movement 87, 92, 105, 121
   sports boycott 115
   struggle 44, 199
   support 102
apartheid police 51, 94, 104, 114, 227, 287

Apla *see* Azanian People's Liberation Army
apology/ies 10, 31, 295, 301, 306
Appeal Court 193, 236
arms deal 1–33, 265 *see also* Shaik, Chippy; Zuma, Jacob; Thales
arms cache(s) 138, 211, 222
Asmal, Kader 105, 139, 141
Aspirant Prosecutors' Programme 176
assassination(s) 149, 224, 275–76
Asset Forfeiture Unit (AFU) 10, 184–85, 205, 208
Atkinson, Phyllis 177
attorney(s)-general 164, 168–69, 172–73, 190
Ayob, Ismail 155
Azanian People's Liberation Army (Apla) 191–92, 237
Azanian People's Organisation (Azapo) 84–5, 102

Balfour, Ngconde 112, 114–15, 202–3, , 361
banning order 52, 53, 66, 118
Baqwa, Lillian 56
Baqwa, Selby 10, 13, 89, 163
Barritt, David 267–68
Basson, Wouter 183, 234
Batohi, Shamila 203, 336
Bengu, Sibusiso 99, 112
Bennet, Sue 181
Bhabha, Mohammed 152, 308
Biko, Steve 44, 50–1, 58–9, 77
Bisho Massacre 148, 188
Bizos, George *see* lawyers
Black Sash 54, 117
blackmail 1, 210, 298
Bloch, Graeme 145
Boesak, Allan 119, 120, 127, 199–201

383

Boipatong massacre 147
bombing 94, 186, 211–13, 215, 282
Botha, PW 89–90
Brereton, Vanessa *see* lawyers *and* Agent RS452
bribe agreement 2, 15
Buthelezi, Mangosuthu 5, 102, 221

Camerer, Sheila 313
campaign 107, 116, 194, 244, 268, 270, 284–85, 305 *see also* Defiance Campaign
dirty tricks 265, 314, 316
smear 267, 269, 290 *see also* Kebble, Brett
urban-terror 211–18
Cannes LionHeart 330
car bomb 94, 187, 212
Carolus, Cheryl 121, 128
Carolus, Gavin 233–34
cases
arms deal *see* arms deal
Bethal 58
Billy Rautenbach 204, 207, 209
Bisho Massacre 148, 188
carjacking 219
civil 50, 233
corruption 2, 3, 5, 180, 184, 236, 303, 309, 335
criminal 233, 238
drug 236
Eikenhof Three 190–93
fraud and corruption 15, 185, 205
GEMS 254
Hansie Cronje 201–4
Indigo 256
international nuclear proliferation 182
Ismail Edwards 218
Joseph Mdluli 50–1, 74
Kidneygate 181
King Sabata Dalindyebo 66
Ladysmith Mafia 256
Madoda Daki 137–38
Malatsigate 257

Mansoer Leggett 218
motor-vehicle accident 67
Muntu Timothy Nxumalo 63
Penuell Maduna 61–2 *see also* Maduna, Penuell
Peter Jones 104
Simon Prophet 235–36
Thembisa Mbilini 64
TRC 186, 187, 188
Zeph Mothopeng 49
Charlemagne, 'Oom Tom' 85, 86, 360
Chaskalson, Arthur *see* judges
chief whip 10, 150–4, 160, 194, 195, 307
Chikane, Frank 119, 292, 316
Chiwayo, Lassie 152
Christie, Renfrew 140
Ciskei 92, 148, 173, 188, 257
City Press 273, 275–77, 279, 281–82, 294–95, 297
code of conduct 172
Coetsee, Kobie 134, 151, 154, 159, 165
Coetzee, Dirk 69–70
commissioner of prisoners *see* Willemse, Willie
communication 15, 76, 101, 148, 219, 318
Community Courts project 179
Congress of South African Trade Unions (Cosatu) 6, 109, 148, 314
conspiracy 26, 30, 183–84, 237, 239, 316
constitution 9, 141, 161, 165, 190, 245, 288, 297, 313
interim 150
new 121, 139, 147, 163–64, 178
constitutional committee 139, 140, 147, 164
Convention for a Democratic Future 121

Convention for a Democratic South Africa (Codesa) 147
conviction rate 179, 180, 219, 259 *see also* cases
Corder, Hugh 140
Council of Churches 101, 112
coup 147, 182, 284
court
Appeal 193, 236
Constitutional 9, 57, 115, 140, 160–61, 183–84, 193, 206, 236, 335–36
criminal 232
high 173, 209, 324, 326
homeland 66
International Criminal 181
Magistrate's 47, 48, 173
Regional 61
sexual offences 179
specialist 179
Supreme 60, 160, 193, 254, 322
traditional 163
criminal prosecutions 2, 9, 268
Cronje, Hansie *see* cases
Cronje, Hermione 171, 237–38
Cwele, Siyabonga 152

D'Oliveira, Jan 168, 173, 190–92, 227
Daily Dispatch 51, 65,
DaimlerChrysler 194, 366
Daki, Madoda 137–38
Davids, Faiek 217
Davis, Angela 105–6
Davis, Dennis 140
De Beers 265, 266, 269
De Klerk, FW 115, 119, 120, 126–28, 133, 136, 147–48, 163
De Kock, Eugene 221–22, 223, 227
De Lange, Johnny 128, 145, 151, 235, 260
De Lille, Patricia 5, 8, 13, 312–13
De Ville, Rosier *see* advocates
De Vries, Andre 168, 173

INDEX

death penalty 64, 1154
Defiance Campaign 85, 110, 118
democracy 2, 5, 6, 7, 83, 131, 161, 242
  constitutional 140–41, 143
departments
  correctional services 335
  defence 8, 12
  environmental affairs 250
  information 257
  justice 171, 180, 220, 244, 245, 314
  public works 38
  social development 184
  social services 237
  trade and industry 250
  transport 274
Derby-Lewis, Clive 149, 362
detention 44, 50, 55, 64, 74–81, 110, 113, 117
  without trial 288
Diba, Vincent 134, 146
Didcott, John *see* judges
Director of Public Prosecutions (DPP) 4, 10, 20, 173, 204, 222, 223
Direko, Winkie 152, 161, 280
Dlali, David 138
Dlamini, Chris 126, 138
docket(s) 175–76, 216, 220, 225, 253
Dolo, Phila 191–92 *see also* Apla
Downer, Billy *see* prosecutors
DPP *see* Director of Public Prosecutions (DPP)
Dr Death *see* Basson, Wouter
Drug Enforcement Agency 238, 250, 251
Du Plessis, Charl 173
Du Toit, Nick 182 *see also* SADF
Dugmore, Cameron 145
Dyosi, Lungisa *see* advocates
Ebrahim, Abdus Salaam 213–15, 218

Edwards, Ismail 218
Edwards, Karl 273
elections 105, 119, 143, 148, 149, 225, 241
  1994 142, 151, 186, 222
  1999 242
  2004 31
Erasmus, Connie 217, 236
Ernstzen, John 161
execution(s) 106, 114, 115, 121

Fernandez, Lovell 140, 169
Ferreira, Gerda *see* prosecutors
Figland, Sheila 171
First National Bank (FNB) 115, 116, 117, 132
Fivaz, George 217, 224, 280
Foxcroft, John *see* judges
Freedom Charter 104
Freedom Front 157, 158
Fullard, Madeleine 282
funerals 94, 304
  Chris Hani 71
  Cradock Four 91
  Griffiths Mxenge 72–4
  Victoria Mxenge 92, 95

Gaba, Mpumelelo 81
Gabela, Nkosinati 256
Gasa, David Sponono 65 *see also* Umlazi Residents' Association
Gatting, Mike 115 *see also* First National Bank (FNB)
Geneva. 98–103
Gerwel, Jakes 140, 155
Gibson, Douglas 167
Gigaba, Malusi 6
Ginwala, Frene 19, 160
Goldstone, Richard 161
Goldstone Commission 221, 227, 376
Gool, Bennie 214
Gordhan, Pravin 76, 78
government departments 13, 185, 233
Gqozo, Oupa 148, 257
Griebenouw, Brigadier 128, 130, 133

Groenewald, Tienie 157
Groenewald, Roelie 167
Gumede, Archie 106–7 *see also* UDF

Hani, Chris 42, 67, 71, 97, 112, 148–9
Harare Declaration 120–21
Hartzenberg, Willie *see* judges
Haysom, Fink 139
Hefer Judicial Commission of Inquiry 284–85, 286–301, 300, 302–4, 329
Hefer, Joos *see* judges
Henning, Jan *see* prosecutors
hijacking(s) 179, 219, 220, 250, 255
hit list 146, 149
Hofmeyr, Willie 128, 231–32, 235–36, 282, 304, 307, 327
  head of AFU 10, 205, 208–9, 231–32
  senior UDF leader 116
Hongo, Mbulelo 72, 81
Huddleston, Trevor 105
Huna, Lumko 112
hunger strike(s) 77, 84, 85, 117, 133, 135, 136, 137

IDOC *see* Investigating Directorate on Organised Crime
Inkatha Freedom Party (IFP) 5, 14, 102, 147, 152, 167, 221
International Defence and Aid Fund (IDAF) *see* Kleinschmidt, Horst
International Labour Organization (ILO) 98, 101
Investigating Directorate on Organised Crime (IDOC) 170, 179. 212, 219, 220, 225
Irish Anti-apartheid Movement *see* Asmal, Kader
Issel, Johnny 145

385

Jackson, Jesse 127
Jana, Priscilla 89
Janson, Punt 55 *see* minister of Bantu administration
Jele, Josiah 112, 113
Jeneker, Ebrahim 218
Joint Anti-Corruption Task Team 184, 185, 186
Jolobe, Litha 77, 81, 276
Jonker, Casper 225
Joseph, Helen 93
judges
    Chaskalson, Arthur 133, 139, 143, 159, 160, 162, 193, 285
    Didcott, John 63, 161, 162
    Erasmus, Connie 217, 236
    Foxcroft, John 218
    Hartzenberg, Willie 183–84
    Heath, Willem 8–10, 268, 326–27
    Hefer, Joos 269, 274, 285–86, 289, 291–95, 299
    Khampepe, Sisi 247–48, 260, 365
    King, Edwin 202–4
    Langa, Pius *see* Langa, Pius
    Ledwaba, Aubrey 326
    Leon, Ramon 60, 89
    Saldanha, Vincent 186
    Skweyiya, Lewis 57, 60, 139, 162
    Southwood, Brian 206
    Squires, Hilary 15, 33
    Van der Walt, Piet 191–93
    Wilson, Andrew 57
Judicial Service Commission (JSC) 161
judiciary 5, 9, 142–43, 271

Kahn, Frank 10, 168, 173, 177, 200, 201, 204
Karni, Asher 182
Kasrils, Ronnie 148, 317, 318, 319
Kathrada, Ahmed 120

Kebble, Brett 266–68, 270–72
Kennedy, Edward 102
Kentridge, Sydney 60, 89
Keys, Derek 153
Kgositsile, Baleka 160
Khampepe Commission 184–85, 247, 365
King, Edwin *see* judges
Kinnock, Glenys 105
Kinnock, Neil 105
Kleinschmidt, Horst 97
Koeberg nuclear power station 94
Koole, Johannes 187, 365
Kriegler, Johann 161–62
Krisch 182 *see* Wisser, Gerard
Kwezi, Frank Kutumba 239 *see also* AFU

Langa, Pius 84, 99, 114, 125, 134, 139, 376
    constitutional court 161
lawyers
    Bizos, George 60, 134, 139, 161, 287, 292
    Brereton, Vanessa 283, 293
    Burhali, Cynthia 142
    Cachalia, Azhar 125
    Gumbi, Mojanku 142, 305
    human-rights 283, 287
    Langa, Pius *see* Langa, Pius
    Mahlati, Cawe 142
    Moroka, Kgomotso 142
    Motsepe, Patrice 142, 161
    Ngoepe, Bernard 99
    Rabaji, Ouma 142
    Sandi, Bonile 118
    Seriti, Willie 134
    Tabata, Dumisani 38, 99, 104, 277, 291, 296, 329
    Tlakula, Pansy 142
    Zama, Linda 99, 125
Leggett, Mansoer 218
Lekota, Mosiuoa 'Terror' 12, 165
Lengisi, Amos 144, 146
Leon, Ramon *see* judges

Leon, Tony 317
life sentence(s) 187, 218, 225, 227, 237, 256
Luhabe, Wendy 216
Luthuli, Albert 71, 318

Mabandla, Brigitte 139, 142, 307, 315, 320
Macadam, Chris 219, 223, 225
Macozoma, Saki 16, 127, 166, 170, 216, 265, 267, 316–17, 336
Madala, Tholie 160 *see also* Supreme Court
Madubela, Stormont *see* murder
Maduna, Penuell 25, 31, 138, 196, 244, 267–68 *see also* Penuell Maduna *under* cases
Maharaj, Mac 273–75, 278, 283–84, 286–87, 289–90, 292, 296, 329
Mahlati, Lungi 173 *see also* du Plessis, Charl
Mahomed, Ismail 160 *see also* Supreme Court
Mail & Guardian 26, 304, 313, 316, 317
Makana, Simon 152
Makathini, Johnny 102
Makgothi, Henry 'Squire' 152
Malan, Rian 267
Mamasela, Joe 69, 70
Manana, Naphthali 82
Mandela/De Klerk Record of Understanding 148
Mandela. Makgatho 119
Mandela, Nelson *see also* Rivonia trialists 25, 66, 119, 125, 163, 165, 153–57, 194, 205, 328, 362, 366, 376
    70th birthday 113
    Grand Parade speech 131–32
    release from prison 127–133

INDEX

Mandela Reception Committee 127–133
Mandela, Winnie 66, 128–31, 198–99, 367
Manley, Michael 104
Mann, Simon 181
Manuel, Trevor 12, 117, 127, 144, 255
Mapoma, Siyabulela 'Saks' 32, 186
Maqetuka, Jeff 208
Maqhutyana, Richard 81
Maqubela, Ntobeko Patrick 50, 60, 72, 76, 79–82, 125, 276, 295
Masemola, Jafta 120
Mashamba, George 152
Masincedane Committee 111
mass action 148
Mass Democratic Movement 110
massacres 94, 147, 148, 188, 224
Matanzima, Kaizer 66
match-fixing 201–2
Mavimbela, Vusi 292–93
Mazwai, Thami 82
Mbeki, Thabo 9, 12, 26, 31, 33, 107, 154–55, 167, 200, 235, 241–42, 245, 267, 277, 284–85, 299, 312, 365
Mbeki, Govan (Oom Gov) 42, 129, 151, 154
McCarthy, Leonard 319-27.
Mchunu, Ernest 152, 157
McNally, Tim 168–69, 224–25
Meiring, Georg 153, 376
mercenaries 181–82
Metele, Alfred 126
Meyer, Piet 234
Meyer, Roelf 148
Mfenyana, Sindiso 151
Mhlaba, Raymond 120, 126
ministers of
  Bantu administration 55
  defence 8, 12, 20, 65

education 99
finance 153, 255
intelligence 221, 317, 319
justice 55, 180, 202, 325
  Kobie Coetsee 134
  Mabandla, Brigitte 320
  Maduna, Penuell 18, 194, 305, 307
  Omar, Dullah 157, 299
labour 167
minerals and energy 11, 153, 265, 330
police 53, 65, 74, 192, 194, 214, 216
public enterprises 12
social development 31,160
sport 202
the bantustan of Transkei 147
transport 225, 273, 274, 287
Minty, Abdul 105
MK see Umkhonto we Sizwe
Mkhatshwa, Smangaliso 93
Mkosana, Vakele 188
Mkwayi, Wilton 84, 120, 152
Mlambo-Ngcuka, Phumzile ix, 11, 18, 60, 73–4, 76, 78, 83–4, 90, 95, 96, 99–100, 103, 107, 131, 167, 265, 267, 277, 296, 305, 316, 328–33, 362
Mlangeni, Andrew 120
Moerane, Boyce Marumo see advocates
Mohapi, Mapetla 51
Mohapi, Mapetla Nohle 50, 51
Mokgoro, Yvonne 161, 162
Molefe, Phil 215
Molefe, Popo 127
Mona, Vusi 275, 294, 376, 378
Moorcroft, Errol 152
Moosa, Essa 139
Moosa, Mohseen 152
Moosa, Valli 127, 150

Mopp, Adrian 217
Moroka, Kgomotso 142
Moseneke, Dikgang 134, 285
Motherwell Four see bombing
Motlanthe, Kgalema 32, 301, 307, 314, 316, 317, 319
Motsoaledi, Elias 120
Motsuenyane, Sam 152
Mowzer, Saleem 130
Moyses, Bill 195
Mpahlwa, Luyanda 74, 81
Mpetha, Oscar 120
Mpshe, Mokotedi 222–23, 316, 319–27, 336
Msimang, Khosi 247
Msimang, Mendi 154
Msoki, Mzwandile 112
Mtintso, Thenjiwe 51, 308, 360
Mufamadi, Sydney 126, 192, 216, 241
Munusamy, Ranjeni 30, 274, 282, 295, 296
murder 70, 179, 183, 187–88, 190, 217, 234, 239, 256, 272
  Biko, Steve 44
  government employee 237
  Hani, Chris 149
  Langa, Ben 114
  Lategan, Ben 218
  Madubela, Stormont 111
  Maqubela, Ntobeko see Maqubela, Ntobeko Patrick
  Mdluli, Joseph 50–1, 74
  Mxenge, Griffiths see Mxenge, Mlungisi Griffiths
  Mxenge, Victoria see Mxenge, Victoria
  Pebco Three 94, 187
  Staggie, Rashaad 213
  third force 227
  Thompson, Percy 224
Mureinik, Ettiene 161
Murray, Christina 140
Mvelase, Dipuo 180, 310
Mxenge, Mlungisi Griffiths 46–8, 62, 68–70, 72, 104

387

Mxenge, Victoria 49, 54, 68, 72, 84, 90, 92, 95, 330
Myakayaka-Manzini, Mavivi 160
Mzamile, Gonya 188
Mzinyathi, Sibongile 32, 186

Nadel *see* National Association of Democratic Lawyers
Nair, Billy 83
National African Federation Chamber 152
National Association of Democratic Lawyers (Nadel) 114, 125, 163, 289
National council of provinces (NCOP) 152, 165
National Intelligence Agency (NIA) 185, 238, 323
National Intelligence Service 273
Ncube, Sister Bernard 92
Ndabazitha massacre 224 *see also* massacre
Ndabeni, Thabo 82
Ndamase, Gabula 80
negotiation(s) 87, 106, 121, 125, 133–34, 139, 147, 149, 248
Nel, Gerrie *see* advocates
Nelson Mandela Changemaker Award 330
Netshitenzhe, Joel 154, 316
Ngcakani, Zolile 318
Ngcuka Affair 300–1
Ngcuka, Bulelani
 apartheid spy *see* spy allegations
 appointment as NDPP 170
 brother Vuyani 38, 47, 48, 84, 104, 109, 112, 115
 chief whip 151
 engagement 84
 Master's degree 168
 sisters 38, 103
 son Luyolo 103, 332
 wedding 91, 95–6, 99
Ngoasheng, Moss 106

Ngobeni, Solomon *see* execution(s)
Ngobese, Sabelo 62
Ngqulunga, Brian 69, 70
Ngwema, Sipho 171, 226, 268, 281, 353
Nhlanhla, Joe 217, 221
Nieuwoudt, Gideon 187
Nkabinde, Sifiso 224
Nofomela, Almond 69, 70
Nqakula, Charles 65
Ntombela, Seketsheketshe 62
Ntsaluba, Mzwandile 173 *see also* Roberts, Les
Nzo, Alfred 97, 98

O'Regan, Kate 161–62
Oliver, Gordon 119
Omar, Dullah 117, 125–27, 131, 144–46, 166–68, 170, 217, 299
 chair of the UDF 110, 112
 lawyer 133–36, 139–40
 minister of justice 157–59
 minister of transport 225
 not opposing bail 191–92
 on Griffiths Mxenge, 72–3
Omar, Farieda 119
Operation Vula 273, 289
Organisation of African Unity 121

Pagad 212–15, 217, 218
Pahad, Aziz, 97
Palazzolo, Vito 257–58
Palme, Lisbet 105
Palme, Olaf 105
Pan Africanist Congress (PAC) 5, 8, 19, 40, 49, 85, 133
parole 197, 200, 210, 335
Payi, Clement 114
Pebco Three *see* murder
People Against Gangsterism and Drugs (Pagad) *see* Pagad
perlemoen 179, 236, 250, 251

Peter, Petrus 237 *see also* Yanta, Nolundi
Pikoli, Vusi 33, 188, 258, 313, 316
Pitsiladis, John 238
Pitsiladis, Rena 238
Pitso, Dorcas 239
Pityana, Barney 155, 163
poaching 179, 251, 252
police corruption 242, 252
police station(s) 57–8, 211, 214, 219
 CR Swart 69, 74, 77
 Diepkloof 191
 Fish Hoek 117
 John Vorster Square 77
 Newlands 117
 Richmond 224
political prisoners 81, 85, 87, 89, 137
 release of 106, 121, 133–35, 148
Porritt, Gary 180–81
Port Elizabeth 58, 129, 180, 197, 233, 280, 282, 283
 Black Civic Organisation 94
Powell, Phillip 221
press conference 11, 12, 13, 132, 156
Prime Evil *see* de Kock, Eugene
Priority Crimes Litigation Unit (PCLU) 181
Programme to Combat Racism 101
propaganda 105, 284, 285, 332
Prophet, Simon *see* Simon Prophet *under* cases
prosecutors
 as human-rights activists 178
 Downer, Billy 4, 11, 177, 321, 324
 Ferreira, Gerda 4, 11, 15, 177, 194
 Henning, Jan 169, 174, 175, 194, 281
public protector 9, 10, 11, 163, 171, 303–9

INDEX

Radue, Ray 152, 161
Ragavaloo, Andrew 224–25
Ramaite, Silas 32, 46, 173, 188, 304, 336
Ramaphosa, Cyril 126, 129, 132, 148, 265, 334
Ramatlhodi, Ngoako 314
Ratteree, Bill 101
Rautenbach, Billy *see* cases
reconnaissance work *see* Renfrew Christie
Reserve Bank 153, 253, 255
Richer, Pete 208, 247
Richmond 223–25
Rivonia trialists 119, 133, 137
Roberts, Les 168, 173
Roussouw, Neil 169, 171
rugby 39, 44, 76, 115, 156
rumours 105–6, 120, 125–26, 265–6, 269, 275
Rwelamira, Merdard 140

SABC 214–15, 226, 280, 304, 305
Sachs, Albie 139, 140, 141, 161, 162
SADF 94, 182, 221
Saldanha, Vincent 186
Scorpions
 City Deep bust 250
 corporate-identity hijacking 255
 fraudulent transactions 259
 gang warfare 255
 GEMS case *see* cases
 heist, biggest 248
 Hollywood style of arrests 227
 investigators 16, 19, 28, 238, 251, 317
King, Dave 253
Ladysmith Mafia *see* cases
Marx, Elizabeth 251 *see also* perlemoen
Msimang, Khosi 247
Ngwema, Sipho 268
Operation Guanxi 250
Palazzolo, Vito 257

Project Yield 252
Quantico 245
Richards, Ruben 243
Rolls-Royces 260
Scotland Yard 245
Serious Fraud Office 254
South Africa's FBI 246
tender fraud 253
Travelgate matter 258
troika methodology 247
website-spoofing 255
Sefako, Marvin 91 *see also* murder
Selebi, Jackie 204, 209–10, 217, 267, 276, 319
Selfe, James 152
senate 151–52, 354
Seriti, Willie *see* lawyers
Sexual Offences and Community Affairs Unit 178 *see also* Majokweni, Toko *under* advocates
Sexwale, Tokyo 134
Shaik, Chippy 20, 287, 375
Shaik, Riaz 'Moe' 273-74, 281, 283, 286, 290–92, 296, 301, 379
Shaik, Schabir 26, 28, 33, 265, 268, 274, 287, 316, 334, 358
Sigcau, Stella 147
Sisulu, Albertina 72–3, 120
Sisulu, Walter 119, 125
Sjollema, Baldwin 98, 101, 361
Skweyiya, Lewis 60, 139,162
Skweyiya, Zola 98–9, 105, 107, 113, , 139, 167, 217
 acting minister of justice 320
 see also minister of social development *under* ministers of
Slovo, Joe 97, 149
Smith, Ronny Johnny 238
Sonn, Percy 170, 190, 202, 212, 214, 217, 219
South African Defence Force *see* SADF
South African Municipal

Workers' Union 72, 254
South African police 69, 118, 147, 180, 182, 197, 221, 249
South African Revenue Service (Sars) 250, 253, 254
Southwood, Brian *see* judges
Special Investigating Unit (SIU) 8, 9, 184, 185, 327
Specialised Commercial Crimes Unit 180, 260
spy allegations 275, 276, 281, 285, 328
Staggie, Rashaad 213–14, 218, 257
Stals, Chris 153
Stofile, Arnold 154, 156, 160
Strategic Defence Package *see* arms deal
Stratton, John 268 *see also* Kebble, Brett
Strijdom JG 156
suicide 51, 77, 272
Sunday Times 29, 30, 77, 205, 215, 265, 274, 281–82, 312, 313
Sunday World 266, 269
Supreme Court 60, 160–61, 193, 254, 322
syndicates 219–20, 227, 233, 250–51, 255, 259, 314

Tabata, Dumisani 38, 99, 104, 277, 291, 296, 329
Taho, Mpilo 81
Tambo, Oliver 26, 42, 92, 102, 104, 105–7, 112, 120, 133, 314
Taylor, Andy 74–5, 80, 360
Terre'Blanche, Eugene 186–87
terrorism 74, 80, 134, 181, 186
Thales 2–3, 15, 22–3, 28, 33, 335
Thatcher, Mark 182
Theron, Pieter 218

389

Thétard, Alain 2, 15, 17, 22–4, 278 see also Thales
Thomson, Percy 224
Tinto, Christmas 144–45
Tlhabi, Redi 280
transcripts 59, 201, 322, 323
transformation 143, 162, 166, 172, 176, 217
Transkei 40, 66, 75–6, 106, 147, 173
TRC see Truth and Reconciliation Commission
treason 57, 77, 80, 81, 84, 110, 134
Trengove, Wim 161
Truth and Reconciliation Commission (TRC) 69–70, 91, 114, 116, 181, 186–89, 191–92, 282
Tsedu, Mathatha. 30, 281
Tshikalanga, David 'Spyker' 69, 70 see also Mxenge, Griffiths
Tshwete, Steve 84, 92, 93, 165, 198, 212, 214, 243
Tsiki, Naledi 134
Tutu, Desmond 72, 73, 102, 112, 118–19, 129–31
Tyobeka, Vuyiswa 152

UDF see United Democratic Front
Uitenhage Massacre 94
Umkhonto we Sizwe (MK) 112–13, 188, 277, 318
cadre(s) 51, 115

Umlazi Residents' Association 65 see also Gasa, David Sponono
unbanning 90, 121, 143
Unisa see University of South Africa (Unisa)
United Democratic Front (UDF) 76, 90 92, 94, 109, 115, 119, 128, 138, 199, 232
activist 130 see also Mowzer, Saleem
leader(ship) 110, 116, 117, 126, 131
president 106 see also Gumede, Archie
Western Cape 110, 113, 121
United Nations 105, 106, 121, 330
University
of Cape Town (UCT) 115, 140
of Fort Hare 38, 41, 42, 43–4, 176
of South Africa (Unisa) 43, 55, 87
of the Western Cape (UWC) 119, 139–140, 144
of the Witwatersrand 121
of Zululand 152
urban terror 198, 211–18,

Van Breda, Alex 150, 152, 153, 156
Van den Heever, Randall 144
Van der Byl, Rodney 224 see also Richmond
Van der Hoven, Johannes 69 see also Mxenge, Griffiths
Van der Merwe, Koos 167
Van der Walt, Piet see judges
Van Niekerk, Kraai 152
Van Zyl, David 74 see also Mdluli, Joseph
Van Zyl, Johannes 187, 365
Venda 102, 158, 173
vigilante group 111

Viljoen, Willie 217
Visagie, Schalk 212 see also bombing
Vlakplaas 69, 187, 221, 227 see also Coetzee, Dirk
Voortrekkerhoogte, 94

wa Afrika, Mzilikazi 29–30
Waluś, Janusz 149, 362 see also Hani, Chris
warder(s) 82, 84, 88, 91
Western Cape Taxi War 145
Willemse, Willie 127–128, 136
Wisser, Gerard 182–83 see also Krisch
witdoeke see vigilante group
World Alliance of Reformed Churches 199 see also Boesak, Allan

Xulu, Lucky 114
Xundu, Mcebisi 71

Yacoob, Zac 93, 162
Yanta, Nolundi 237 see also Peter, Petrus
Yekiso, James 109
Yengeni, Tony 10, 18, 194–97 see also Ferreira, Gerda and Jenning, Jan under prosecutors
Young Women's Christian Association 96, 99
Youth League 6, 266 see also Gigaba, Malusi

Zapiro 235
Zikalala, Snuki 215 see also MK
Zondi, Musa 152
Zuma, Jacob 2–7, 17, 22–33, 26, 265, 307, 312, 319, 331, 334–35, 381
Accused No.1 2–3

www.ingramcontent.com/pod-product-compliance
Lightning Source LLC
Chambersburg PA
CBHW070835160426
43192CB00012B/2192